MAN-O-WAR CAY
BAHAMA ISLANDS

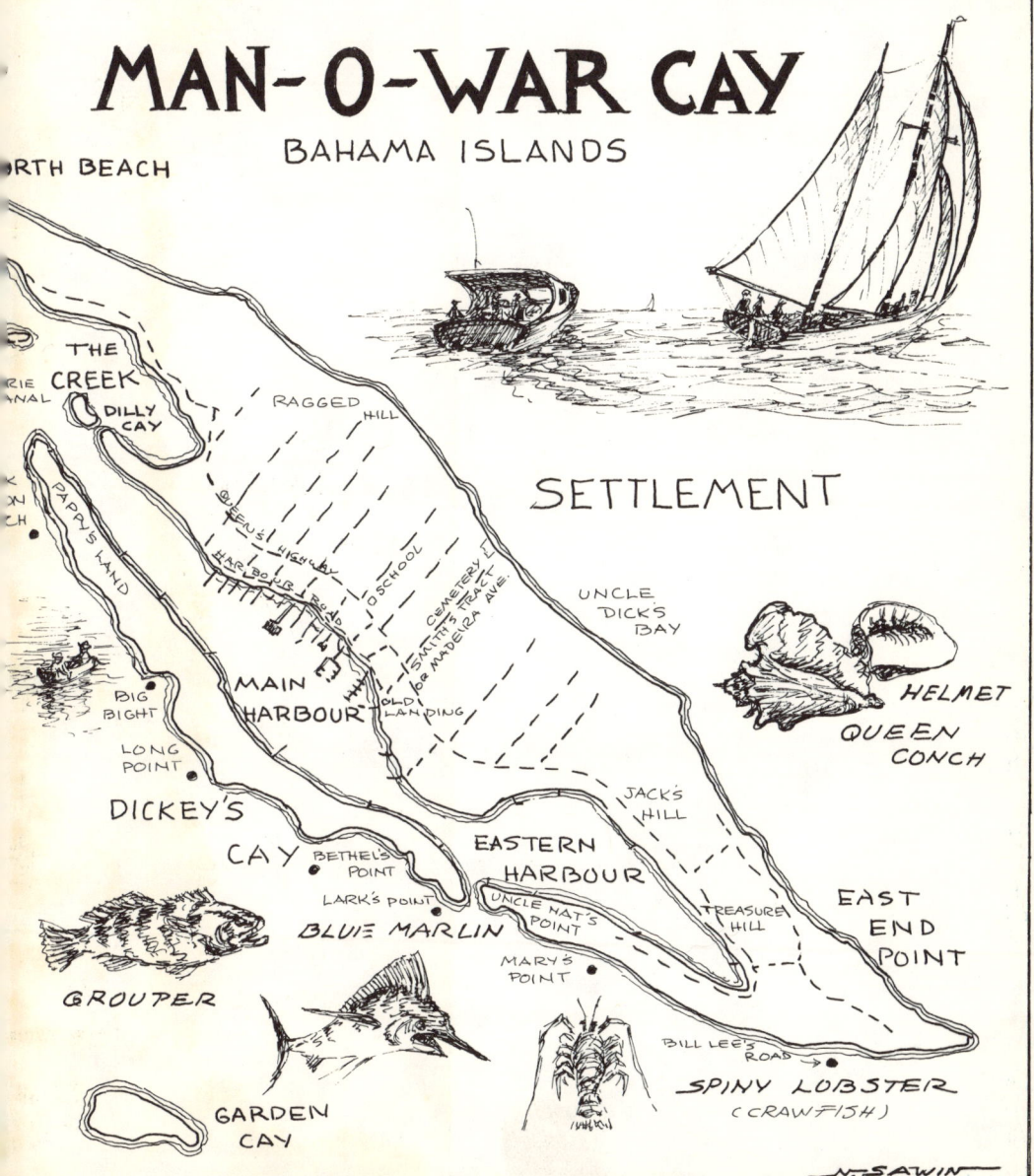

N. SAWIN

MAN-O-WAR
My Island Home
A History of an Outer Abaco Island

BY HAZIEL L. ALBURY

Drawings by Nancy Sawin
Holly Press

Library of Congress Catalog Card Number: 77-87225
Copyright © 1977 by The Holly Press, Hockessin, Delaware

All Rights Reserved

Printed in the United States of America
by
Cowan Printing Incorporated
Bridgeton, New Jersey

Contents

Foreword
Chapter
I.	Island Life	1
II.	The Wild Life of Our Island	25
III.	The Government of Our Island and Our Country	31
IV.	A Religious People	35
V.	Training Children for an Abundant Life	41
VI.	Island Industries	53
VII.	The Health of Our People	77
VIII.	Transportation and Communication: Then and Now	89
IX.	Firsts: The Coming of New Fangled Gadgets	95
X.	Sports and Recreation	99
XI.	The Coming of the Americans	107
XII.	Some Personal Experiences	117
XIII.	Stories and Anecdotes	135
XIV.	In Conclusion	145

Appendix
A	Genealogy	149
B	Colorful Expressions	157
C	Customs New to Americans	159
D	Island Recipes	161
	Index	165

List of Illustrations and Photos

	Page
Our Harbour	2, 3
Our Homes	6, 7, 8, 9
Inside Our Homes	12, 13
The Wild Life of Our Island	28, 29
A Religious People	36, 37
Training Children for an Abundant Life	46, 47
Island Industries	58, 59, 60, 61, 74, 75
Photographs	84, 85, 86, 87

*Dedicated to
my beloved Mary, without
whose help this book
would not have been.*

Acknowledgments

Many people have helped me in all of the tasks which must be done to write and publish a book. The idea and the encouragement to put pen to paper came from Elva and Marie Richardson. Kit DeLanoy listened to many tape recordings from my interviews and typed them for me. Alice Lee Pearce helped pull together the colorful expressions which are listed in the appendix.

Malvern and Pat Morse worked many hours putting names on the family tree. Evidence of this is a ten-foot chart across the Morse's kitchen wall in Sunset Cottage.

Dottie and Phil Sawin gave continuous support, provided a place for Nancy Sawin, Phil's sister, to stay while on the island working, and Dottie carefully read and gave suggestions to the first draft. Nancy acted as editor working with me to complete the book and to get the manuscript ready for the printer.

My deep appreciation goes to Mary for her support, her help with gathering material and information and her smile no matter what my problem. My sincere thanks to my island family in general and to Mamma and Uncle Norman in particular.

I extend a grateful heart to my daughters Minerva, Denise, Winnie, and Martha who not only helped me in the present task but who through the years have allowed me the time to carry some of the responsibilities which have fallen to me as a member of our Settlement, time which might have been theirs.

The author and the artist apologize for any errors which may exist in the book. If there are any omissions, it has been entirely unintentional.

H.L.A.

Preface

A chapter of this book is devoted to "firsts" — the first gramophone to come to the island, and the first electricity plant. But a very important "first" is the book itself, which the author has modestly omitted from the list. For here we have the first comprehensive description and history of Man-O-War Cay, Abaco, Bahamas. It not only fills an immediate need but it will be here to entertain and inform future generations into the farthest reaches of our history.

Mr. Haziel Albury has every reason to be proud of his accomplishment which to him, no doubt, has been a labour of love. Of his dear "Island Home" he writes with relish, sincerity and affectionate understanding. In short, it is written as only Mr. Albury could write it.

In the denouement of his subject he covers a wide range of topics, from fishes and birds, to mailboats and hurricanes. But, essentially, it is a story of people and, specifically, those people who, in one way or another, have contributed to the welfare, progress and lore of Man-O-War Cay.

The lifestyle of the inhabitants is quite different now to what it was even a generation or two ago. The past, however, will not be forgotten because of the interest that Mr. Albury has taken in it. He describes the old habits, customs and occupations in remarkable detail.

There is an air of modernity and prosperity about Man-O-War today but he makes it plain that the inhabitants have not lost their traditional characteristics. They remain law-abiding, good neighbours to each other, kind to visitors, honest, industrious and God-fearing.

As President of The Bahamas Historical Society, it gives me great pleasure to welcome this new addition to the written record of our country, and to compliment Mr. Haziel Albury for writing it. I do hope that this book will meet with the success it deserves.

Dr. E. Paul Albury,
President,
The Bahamas Historical Society

Chapter I. Island Life

How did it get its name? This question is often asked by the many visitors who come to the tiny island called Man-O-War Cay. In the Bahamas, a cay (pronounced key) is a common term for the smaller islands lying close to the major islands of the Bahama Chain. Man-O-War Cay lies off the Northeastern shore of Great Abaco Island. It is approximately two hundred miles east of Miami, Florida.

There are two theories offered as to the source of Man-O-War's name. Some think it comes from the British Man-O-War or Frigate ships which were wrecked on our reefs. This theory carries even more weight if you study the outlines of the island approaching from the ocean, for it looks like a Frigate ship. Furthermore, the proportions of the ship are roughly similar to those of our island. Others think the island was named for the Man-O-War or Frigate bird. This island was at one time a breeding ground for these birds. Whatever the origin of the name, Man-O-War Cay is a charming little isle, very attractive and now quite well known to many who seek a quiet peaceful spot. It lies at latitude 26° 35" N. and longitude 27° W., just five miles northwest of Elbow Cay light and eight miles northeast by north of the Marsh Harbour International Airport. It is about two and a half miles long and approximately a quarter of a mile at its widest part. There are three harbours, the main one, protected by Dickey's Cay to the Southwest; the Eastern Harbour; and the Creek. In the main harbour, which is the largest, there are now a marina, two public docks, two dry docks, several private docks and moorings. In the Eastern Harbour and the Creek there are private docks and moorings. These harbours are some of the safest hurricane harbours in the Bahamas.

Like most of the good anchorage harbours in our Commonwealth, the entrances were naturally shallow. In those early days, especially during the sponging industry, the schooners and sloops had to be taken out of the harbour with high tide.

When I was a boy, money was granted several times by our Government to deepen or improve the depth of the entrance of our main harbour. There were no dredgers in this area at that time, so the dredging was done by shovels with the men usually working at low tide. The mud was put into dinghies and emptied outside the harbour. The wages were six-pence or seven cents an hour.

In 1949 Captain Leslie Albury of Man-O-War Cay was employed by Uncle Will and two of our first American residents, Ted Zickes and Bill Lee, to improve the entrance to our main harbour and eastern harbour. Dynamite, a homemade drag,

Man-O-War: My Island Home

Island Life

and boats' propellers were used in this operation. The deeper channel enabled boats to maneuver with less difficulty.

Later, as the number of yachts coming to our fair island increased, my people petitioned our Government for money to open up a good channel to accommodate visitors as well as ourselves. One day Uncle Will received a letter from our good friend and Representative in the House of Assembly, Mr. Harold Johnson, with the welcome news that we would be able to get money to do the dredging at Man-O-War Cay. The dredge, a LCT barge with a crane, skippered by Captain Willie Albury of Harbour Island, arrived on a Sunday morning. Mr. David Morrison, Harbour Engineer and Acting Harbour Master in Nassau, was in charge of this project. Mr. Morrison, Captain Willie and his chief engineer, Lloyd Roberts, with others worked hard at this job. Unfortunately, they were unable to complete the channel that trip. However, after several more periods of dredging, further improvements were made. This has proved to be a great asset to our community.

Some of the Americans living in the Creek area hired Sea Breezes dredge from Marsh Harbour to open an entrance and clear a channel between the main harbour and the creek. This opening is known as the Erie Canal.

There are white sandy beaches on both sides of the island. The beaches on the northeast side are protected from the great Atlantic Ocean by the barrier reef, so there are many excellent swimming spots.

Two natural channels lead from the ocean, one around each end of our island, to the sheltered waters of the Abaco Sea. These channels are known as Man-O-War Cay Channels. The Abaco Sea, the body of water between the main island of Abaco and the Cays, is excellent for cruising and sailing. The average depth of water is about fifteen feet.

Some of the property of Man-O-War is still called by the original names: Jack's Hill, Skinner's Hill, Rugged Hill, Mary's Point, Uncle Nat's Point, and Pappy's Land. The original name of the cemetery road or Madeira Avenue is "Smith's Tract." How did it get this name? The Sawyers owned the land to the southeast, and Mammy Nellie owned the land adjoining and running to the northwest. There was often a contention about the boundary line, though they never came to blows. Pappy Ben had a brain-wave. He said that his cousin, Smith, was the Surveyor General of the Bahamas, so he told Dick Sawyer that the boundary line would not be settled until they got higher powers. It was mutually agreed that Pappy's cousin would come over from Nassau and settle the dispute once and for all! He came and found some extra land, more than the Grant stated. In those early days they were not particular about measuring the land to the even foot. Sometimes, they used special trees as markers. Anyhow, when Surveyor Smith found the extra land, he gave it to Mammy Nellie and Dick Sawyer, making them both happy.

The Surveyor's fee was twenty pounds, about one hundred and ten dollars. This was considered a great deal of money. That's the reason he gave the extra land to Mammy Nellie and Dick Sawyer. The tract through the bushes was cut as ordered by Mr. Smith thus establishing the boundary line. It was then called and has been often referred to as "Smith's Tract." Many years later it was paved.

As mentioned, when Mammy Nellie and later her children divided their land among their relatives, trees were used as markers; so most of the original documents on Man-O-War property there is the phrase "more or less." If the land was rocky, especially on a hilltop, this was not considered good for farming, so a larger portion or more footage was given. Today these rocky hilltops are the most valuable for building vacation homes for our visitors. These visitors are not like the early settlers who were Loyalists in the 1780's fleeing the United States. Today the Americans are getting away from the fast pace of life in their country, and they have been well received by my people.

I love people, and this is the story of my people and their island. It began with Benjamin Archer, lovingly known as Pappy Archer, and his wife, known as Mammy Archer, Loyalists from New England by way of the Carolinas. They settled in Marsh Harbour on the Island of Abaco after the American War of Independence. Their home was near Noggy's Point where the main public dock is now located. Pappy Archer and Mammy Archer had three children: Benjamin, Jr., Eleanor, and Rebecca. Pappy Archer bought sixty acres of land on Man-O-War Cay from the Crown. Lord Dunmore was Governor of the Bahamas at that time (1787-1797).

As a young man young Benjamin did not see much future for him in the Bahamas, so he left Marsh Harbour and went to Key West, Florida. There he invented a steel drill used for building lighthouses. Rebecca stayed with her parents and later married Mr. J.W. Collins, great grandfather of Harry Collins, one of the boat-builders of Marsh Harbour. Harry's daughter, Myrna, recently married Robin Weatherford and moved to Man-O-War.

Eleanor visited Man-O-War and spent time here helping her father farm. During one of her visits, a sailing vessel from Harbour Island was wrecked on the reef. The crew made it ashore to Man-O-War. The mate of the vessel was a sixteen-year-old boy named Benjamin Albury, son of another of the Loyalists who had settled on Harbour Island. Eleanor was thirteen; Benjamin was sixteen. They fell in love at first sight. Benjamin stayed here while the rest of crew of the ill-fated vessel returned to Harbour Island.

Benjamin, later known as Pappy Ben, and Eleanor, Mammy Nellie, were married about a year later. Their home was near where Sweeting's Shell Shop is now located. The seashore there has always been called "The Old Landing."

Pappy Archer gave his land on Man-O-War to his daughter, Eleanor. When she was fifteen, their first daughter, Betsy, was born. They had thirteen children – Betsy, Mary, Celestia, Cecelia, Charlotte, Amelia, Margaret, Henry, Benjamin, Joseph, William, Samuel, and John. They all grew up and married except Margaret, who died quite young. What happened after that is shown in the Appendix. Today there are 235 Bahamians on Man-O-War, and all except about five are related to Pappy Ben and Mammy Nellie. However, close relatives do not marry, and my people are both healthy and intelligent.

Before Mammy Nellie died, she set aside land for a church, school, cemetery, and roads. She divided the rest of her land among her children. The local settlement today seems to be just as Mammy Nellie planned it.

Man-O-War: My Island Home

Island Life

Man-O-War: My Island Home

Island Life

SKIPPER ROBINSON'S HOME ON CAVE HILL

ONE OF THE FIRST HOMES BUILT FOR THE AMERICANS

(DETAIL OF INTERIOR)

UNIQUE BUILDING FEATURES OF ISLAND HOMES

HAND MADE SHUTTER

GROUND PIN

LATCHES

"TIE DOWN" OR HURRICANE POST

Man-O-War: My Island Home

The first homes built on Man-O-War had thatched roofs and sides and dirt floors. As time went on, the buildings were improved by wooden floors and weather boarding for siding. Thatch was still used for roofs and lasted for several years. The length of time depended on the skill of the thatcher and the quality of the leaves. Grandpapa Uriah was good at thatching. He said, "Leaves from the Cays, five years; leaves from the mainland (Abaco), seven years."

When anyone was ready to thatch a place, it was "newsed" around in the settlement, and relatives and friends gathered early in the morning to start the job. In case of a replacement of a roof, the men worked speedily and had the thatching done before night fall. This same neighbourly act has continued down through the years. After shingles were introduced, friends and neighbours always joined in and helped. Today if someone has to reshingle, you will see a group of men working together to get the job done quickly. In most cases now the workmen are paid; but, in general, they are loaned from other jobs.

Wooden ground-pins were used both to hold up and support the buildings. The ground-pin hole was dug about eighteen to twenty-four inches in the rock, depending on the size of the building; and special wood such as bull-wood, and the heart of native pine or fat-pine, cedar, dog-wood, and madeira were used. Some of these ground-pins are still seen under the old houses today. Cement was unknown here in those early days.

Kitchens were separate buildings because of the danger of fire. They had rock fireplaces built up from the ground without chimneys. The fireplaces were used for cooking. Later on after people got wooden buildings with wooden floors, some people built fireplaces like a big box, filled with sand and stones, with legs. Others did not consider this safe; and even though they had wooden floors, they still built rock fireplaces with the foundation starting from the ground. This type of kitchen with a dirt fireplace in the corner is what my parents had. One of my chores as a boy was to help to get wood for the wood-box. Sometimes we stored it under the floor of the house, dining room, or kitchen to keep it out of the rain. Usually we gathered dry wood; that is, wood from trees that had died or had been cut down when making fields. One day my brother, Cyril, and I were getting wood from the mangroves on the southwest side of the creek. We were sawing a large piece of hollow mangrove. After cutting across the hole, the tail of a rat came out, sawn off! We did the rest of the sawing carefully, trying to keep the hole covered by the saw when the branch timber was cut through. I got a stick and stood ready for action as Cyril removed the saw. To our surprise, there were several rats there. We succeeded in killing a couple of them, but some took a dive into the sea and swam like fish through the mangrove roots until they were well out of our reach.

During the hurricane season while the spongers were home, large quantities of wood were collected and stored for the families' use during the absence of husbands on their long voyages to the sponging grounds. This eased the burden of the housewives, especially those who had no sons to do this manly chore.

To start a fire, kindling (usually fat pine and shavings from the boatyard) was used. Some people used other methods. I have often watched my Uncle Wesley

Island Life

start a fire by putting a wee bit of kerosene oil on the ashes in the galley, as the fireplace was called, and then lay on the kindling.

In the early 1900's larger homes were built with better materials. My parent's first home was built out of lumber from Wilson's City, the lumber camp near Little Harbour, Abaco. A fair-sized home was of the following dimensions: the main house was eighteen feet wide and twenty-four feet long with two bedrooms upstairs; one bedroom, a parlour and a workroom, sometimes called a sittingroom or shed, downstairs. The dining room was also a separate building. So, each home consisted of three buildings: the main house, dining room, and kitchen, plus an outhouse.

The parlour furniture usually consisted of six straightback wooden chairs, one wooden table generally holding a kerosene lamp, a rocking chair, and a cradle all homemade. The baby slept in the cradle during the day. Evenings a courting couple sat in the cradle with their legs over the side. This doesn't sound very comfortable, but there was no other seat for two. There was a poem often repeated or written in autograph albums:

> In the parlour there were three;
> He, the parlour-lamp, and she.
> Three, of course, is a crowd no doubt,
> So the parlour-lamp went out.

The bed frames were also homemade, and the mattress covers were made from ticking and stuffed with a special kind of grass or feathers. The pillows were the same. Quilts used as spreads and warmth were also homemade. A young woman was not considered eligible for marriage until she could make a quilt and a pair of man's pants out of blue denim. Sheets were made from unbleached cotton or, sometimes, flour sacks were sewn together. There were usually a bureau and a basin-stand in the bedroom which was used as a washing and dressingroom. The basin and pitcher in the downstairs bedroom was china and, in most cases, was a wedding set and generally kept for guests. Upstairs there were enamel pitchers and basins which were for ordinary use. The furniture in the shed consisted mainly of a rocker, a few odd chairs, and maybe a bench or two. Shelves sometimes took the place of tables; and there was often a shelf for the lamp, one for the children's school books, and one for a glass pitcher of water and some tumblers.

In the dining room there was a large table with homemade chairs or benches, enough to seat up to about a dozen people. There was also a safe or wooden cupboard with screening for china and food.

Wood and open fireplaces were used from the early days until the late 1920's when the kerosene stoves were brought here. For several years just a few families could afford this luxury. The woodburning ship's stoves were introduced about the same time. Other people used homemade stoves. These were called cookers. They were fifty-five gallon drums with the top cut out and almost filled with sand. They had a grill across the top, and an opening near the top to let air in. Of course, wood was the means of fuel. Really, they were fireplaces in a smaller form. In the early

Man-O-War: My Island Home

Island Life

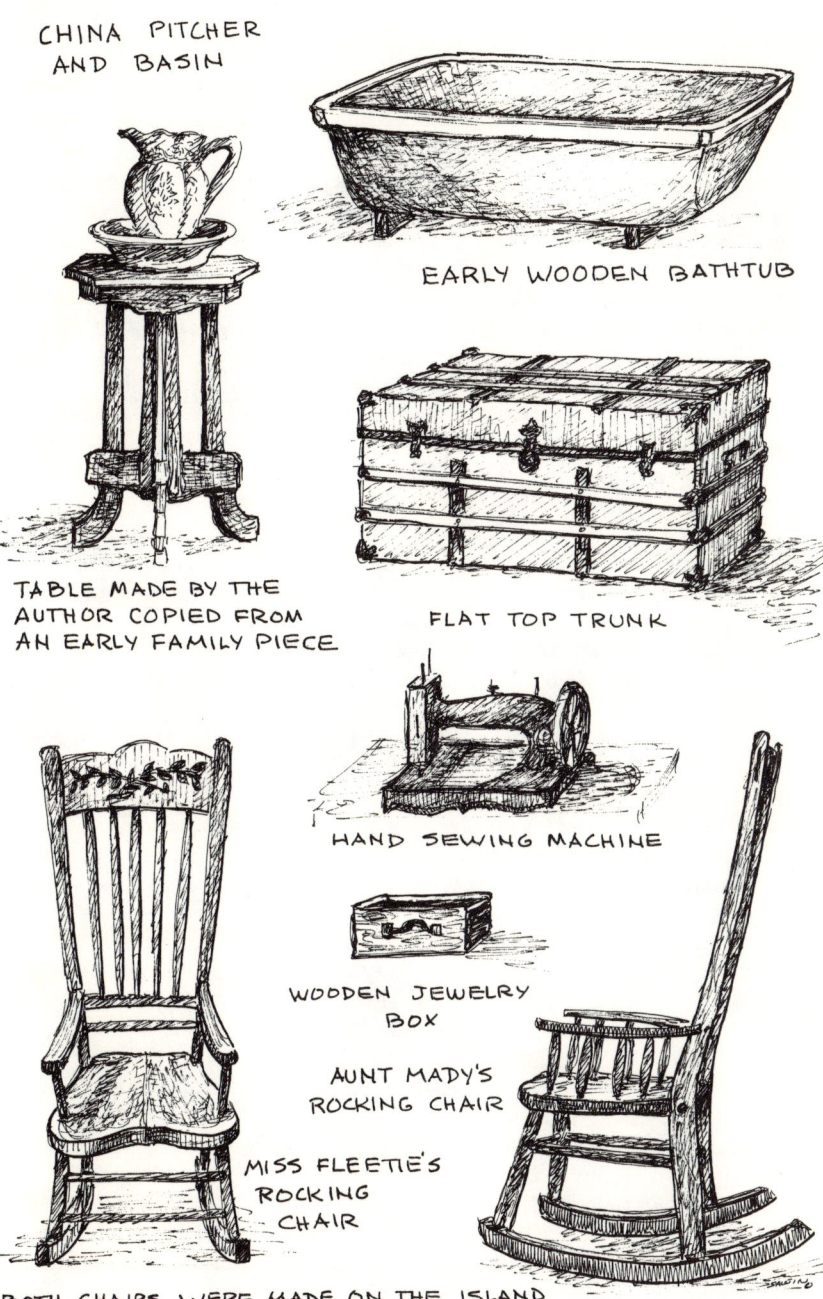

1950's gas stoves began to be used; and except for a few electric ones, gas stoves are still used for cooking today.

Bread was baked in outdoor ovens made of stone or brick and mud. This mud was dug from special places in our harbour. As time went on and cracks appeared on the outside of our ovens, we got more mud and put on another coat of this sticky stuff which hardened in a short time. The base of the oven was built up from the ground about two feet. The oven itself was igloo shaped with a door in the front. When it was time to bake bread, a fire was made in the oven. After a good blaze, the coals were left scattered on the bottom to simmer for a while. Then all the coals were raked out with a wooden rake which is a polelike stick about six to seven feet long with a three- to four-inch by six- to eight-inch piece of wood nailed to the end. The bread was then placed in the oven with a peel, a stick about the same length as the rake with a flat board at the end large enough to hold a one- or two-loaf pan of bread. The wooden door was then put in place with the rake or peel leaning against it to keep it shut. The door was not hinged. The rake, the peel or the door sometimes caught on fire, but it was put out either by rubbing the burning tool in the dirt or by dipping it in a container of water usually kept there for that purpose. The bread was left in the oven for about thirty minutes during which time the baker, in my case my mamma, would now and then move the door, peep in, and sometimes have to rearrange the pans of bread depending on the colour of the loaves. Baking days Mamma usually made a pan of buns and sometimes a ginger-bread man all out of the same dough. These soon disappeared if the children were around when they came out of the oven. They smelt good but tasted better.

An incident I'll always remember is the day Mamma had just raked the coals out of the oven and turned around to get the bread to put in it. A little goat came jumping and dancing into our yard and right into the hot oven! It jumped out quicker than it jumped in or else, I suppose, we would have had baked mutton!

Bread was also baked in a Dutch-oven. This was a flat-bottomed iron pot with an iron lid. There was a fire on the top as well as the underneath. Only a few people could make good Dutch-oven bread that was brown all over and cooked inside. Papa was an expert Dutch-oven bread baker.

I have been writing about baking bread only, because as a boy we could not afford cakes. At Christmas, most families had homemade coconut pies, sweet potato pies, pumpkin pies, and rice puddings. These were a treat. In this day of plenty we have bread and cakes and enough to spare.

Black irons, heated by an open fire, usually in the yard, were used for ironing clothes. Special hardwood, such a button-wood, was used in order to give the minimum of smoke. On each side of the fire there were one, two, or three irons, depending on the size of the family and how many were at work ironing. When the iron was hot, it was cleaned with a piece of old cloth. My sisters helped Mamma and often there were two at this difficult task, but to borrow the words of another: " 'Tis so sweet to labour for those we love. . ." The black irons were greased after use to prevent rusting. The grease used was sperm from the sperm whale. This sperm floated to our beaches; however, we no longer see it today. As a boy, quite often it was my job after school to grease the irons. It was done while they were still warm.

When I see any wear the dripdry pants now, I often think of the many hours spent by Mamma washing and scrubbing by hand on a wooden wash-board, starching, but mainly ironing my white pants with the black irons. She had to take the hot iron from the fire, sometimes test the heat with her face, and rub it or wipe it on the cloth to make sure it was perfectly clean before she started to iron. It was customary in those days for school teachers to wear white pants and sometimes white suits. There was a saying: "Pupils, beware of your teacher when he comes to school on a Monday morning dressed in a white suit!" I am not fond of that saying for my pupils need never beware of me. However, it is only a joke. It was not by choice that I wore white pants as a teacher. The white drill, as the cloth was called, was cheaper than any other material. Mamma made my white trousers with a hand-turning sewing machine.

Black irons were also heated by coal and later kerosene stoves. In the early 1950's irons with a small tank attached were used. These were operated on white gas and worked fairly well. Then came electricity, and so electric irons are used for the small amount of ironing done today.

In the early 1950's there was quite a change in the architecture of our homes. They were built as a single one-story unit. Generally these homes had two bedrooms, one bath, living room, dining room, and kitchen. Some of the modern homes now have more bedrooms and bathrooms. The floors are poured concrete; the sides are usually cement blocks, and the roofs are cedar or asphalt shingles. Most of the furniture in the local homes is imported. I hope someday all our furniture will be made here. I am fond of it. With our good wood, our skillful men make something that is outstanding in appearance and endurance.

From the early days until about the middle of this century, our people generally ate the foods that were available here such as: seafood, pigs, goats, chickens and their eggs, fruits and vegetables.

Seafood was the same as we have today – conchs, turtles, curbs, whelks, crawfish, and many varieties of scale-fish. But without the modern facilities, sails and motors, it was sometimes difficult to procure a meal of these delicacies. Even after sails became available, if there was a calm, the men or boys sculled to and from the fishing grounds. Fortunately, conchs were plentiful and near the shore of our island. They were taken from the bottom of the sea with two-pronged L-shaped hooks, fastened on a pole twelve to sixteen feet long.

Although not as plentiful as they used to be, conchs are still found in deeper water farther off shore. However, large quantities are collected by divers and some by the old-fashioned method. Conchs' shells are their homes. The conch and shell grow together. When the conchs die, the shells die also!

To take conchs from their shells, the pointed end is cracked around with a conch-breaker or an old axe, machete, or chipping hammer. Then with a clever twist, the conchs are taken from their shells. Another way of doing it, is to crack a tiny hole near the same pointed end, and with a narrow knife or ice-pick, release the conchs' hold or grip on the inside of the shells. They are then pulled out of the front of the shells. The "slops" are taken off, and the conchs are skinned or scraped and cleaned, ready for the salad bowl or pot.

Conchs, sometimes called "Bahamian Ham" helped to make the regular diet. They were and are eaten raw, boiled, steamed, and stewed. Later conch fritters were made. About the mid 1940's conch chowder was introduced, and now we make cracked conch and conch salad.

There are three kinds of turtles, as I mentioned earlier, in the waters surrounding our island. There are several ways of capturing turtles. Some of the earliest methods were by using harpoons – striking them into the victims when they came to the surface of the water to breathe. Another way of getting them in the early days was by means of hooking them from the bottom of the sea. Three fairly large fishhooks were set in a cone-shaped piece of lead and fastened with a strong line. This was done by the fishermen. A water-glass was used to sight them. The "turtler" usually waited for his prey to come to a stop before throwing the hooks overboard. However, there were some which would not come to a complete stop, so the hooks might be thrown ahead of the turtle to get to the spot just in time to do their job. There was a battle between turtler and turtle and if the turtler won, the catch was placed into the boat.

After some years a bulley-net was introduced and was commonly used when I was a boy. The turtle bulley-net was cone-shaped somewhat like the crawfish bulley-net, but much larger so as to cover the largest turtles. A line was fastened to the small end of the bulley-net which is referred to as "the bulley." It was let down over the turtle which, trying to escape, tied itself up in the net. The two men in the dinghy then dragged the bulley and catch into the boat. There is another way of netting turtles, and that is by stretching a long net, something like a fish-net, except for the larger size of the mesh, in the feeding areas. The fishermen with long poles make splashes on the water. When the turtles try to run away, they find themselves tied up in the net. By this method, several turtles may be caught at one time. Turtle-nets are still used by a few people, but most people get them with spears.

After the turtles have been butchered and cleaned, the meat, some boney parts, and the liver are ready for the cook. There are several ways of preparing this palatable food: steamed, stewed, broiled, as soup, meat fritters, and meat-balls.

Curbs, or chitons, and whelks live on the rocks of the seashore. For a good catch of these, it is best to go in search of them during low tides. Although the curbs cling firmly to the rocks, they can be easily taken off if the first attempt to move them is successful. However, if they are disturbed, they immediately take a stronger grip and the getting becomes much more difficult. The whelks, except for the very large ones, are picked up off the rocks with little effort. Both curbs and whelks have to be taken out of their shells and cleaned, before being made into that good native soup and stew.

I will describe the way crawfish are caught in another chapter. Suffice it to say here, a meal of crawfish is now a very expensive dinner!

No doubt, scale-fish have been used more often than any of the other sea-foods. The early settlers caught some with hand-lines, and speared some with what were called "wire-pegs." The most of our local people still use hand-lines, but our

American residents and visitors prefer the rod and reel. Our young people are choosey and like to go down to the fishes' territory and get the fish they want by spearing them. There are many varieties of scale-fish. As I mentioned earlier, some of the best are: groupers, red and mutton snappers, hog-fish, burbots or trigger-fish, jacks, runners, porgies, and grunts. There are different ways of cleaning the various fish. Some are scaled; others skinned and filleted. There are also many ways of cooking this great sea-food. Perhaps that is one of the reasons the fish are used so often. Most families had a pig or two which were fed on corn, coconuts, conchs, and potatoes and, of course, left-overs if there were any. The pigs lived in sties made of drift lumber and slender tree-trunks and in some cases out of the sisal masts. Most of the pigs were so tame and mild that they could be let out of the sty to get a little exercise. When it was time to be back inside, a little food was thrown in, the sty lifted and in he or she went. During the rainy seasons, the sty might be moved to several places in the backyard to prevent unsightly and unhealthy muddy-puddles. Usually, Cyril, my older brother, had the responsibility of putting grass in the sty, which helped to keep the pigs warm during a wet wintry night. Sometimes I might take care of the feeding and watering.

It was a big day in the Settlement when a hog was killed. Preparations were made the day before. Wood was collected and stored in a dry place. Axes and knives were sharpened. Before day-light next morning, just about second "fowl-crow," or the crowing of roosters, the butcher started a fire in an open area, sometimes near the sea. Generally, there were two large pots of water. Sometimes a half of a 54-gallon drum was used. When the water was boiling, the hog was killed, either by shooting or a stab in the heart with one of those sharp knives!

The dead hog was now placed on one or two gunny-sacks which had been spread on the ground. A couple more spread over the victim. The boiling water was then poured over the sacks which soaked its way into the skin. At the right time, the sacks were gradually removed and the hairs scraped off. In most cases this method worked well; but, if the animal was having new hair coming out, it could be very difficult. When the hog was cleaned, it was hung up and sawn in halves.

Some adults and children were usually around to see this operation, and to buy or borrow some of the pork. They brought their own containers including plates, bowls, and bake-pans. With money scarce, pork was exchanged; that is, families borrowed some until they killed their own.

Pork was pickled in a wooden tub. The big grain salt, as it is now called, was the only salt we knew. It was brought here all the way from Ragged Island, another of the islands of our Commonwealth, a distance of about 300 miles. The Ragged Islanders came in large sloops, anchored outside the harbour, and brought their bushel and half-bushel baskets ashore in small dinghies. They peddled their wares from house to house.

Goats have never been reared in large quantities here. However, there have been a few from time to time. I had one when I was a boy, and it became such a pet that I cried when it was killed! I could not eat any dinner that day! My Cousin, Thomas, had some pet goats. I often helped to care for them. They were not allowed to roam, but were tied with a rope – one end around the neck and the other to a ground-pin of the house at night so that these animals could be sheltered. Each morning they were loosed from the ground-pin and led out to a patch of grass or weeds, where they were tied to a tree for the day. Sometimes the loosing was difficult, as the goats might have gone around many times. If the rope was long enough, they might have gone around the second ground-pin or tree.

Some years later Uncle Will had some pet goats on Sandy Cay. They were not tied, but were allowed to roam over the cay. At first, they thrived very well. Suddenly, they became sickly and finally died. We often wondered whether they were stricken with a disease, or whether they ate a poisonous plant. There are no goats on our island now.

As mentioned earlier, chickens and their eggs have been part of the diet from the early settlers until now. For many years chickens were allowed to roam and roosted in the trees, but today most people who have them keep them in coops. Each family kept a rooster which was in charge of a yard of hens and biddies. If a rooster from one yard fell in love with a hen from another yard and trespassed, there was always a fight! As a boy I thought this funny. The trespasser was usually defeated and had to retreat to his own territory; but, as if to give the last word, he gave a loud crow if he was strong enough after the battle.

Some hens laid their eggs near the house, and some under the house, hence there was no trouble in finding the eggs. However, sometimes a hen "stole her nest" and might not be found out until she had been "sitting" on them. The eggs were not edible then, so mamma hen was left to finish the three weeks required for the eggs to hatch. A hen's nest was sometimes found by keeping the hen in a coop or box until she was ready to lay the egg. Then a long piece of fishing-line was tied to one leg, and she was let to run. Usually, the hen ran to her nest. By following the line, the nest with the eggs were found. It was the rule to leave one egg in the nest or else the hen might make another elsewhere.

The old common way of preparing chickens for food was stewed with dumplings, or doughs, and homemade soup. Most people now prefer fried chicken. Eggs have been eaten raw in times of illness. They are very nourishing! Now-a-days eggs are boiled, fried, and used in cakes, pies, and salads.

Fruit-growing has never been done full time by anyone on Man-O-War. However, since this lovely island was settled, fruits have been grown by almost every family. In some cases just a few trees in the back-yard for the family's use. Others have grown enough to sell. During the hard times of 1930 to 1945, I often helped to pick the famous cay limes, which were sent to Nassau for sale. The price there was about 12 cents per hundred.

Uncle Norman had a good orange grove at one time. It was a treat to me when Vernon and Marcell and I were allowed to help ourselves to some of these juicy fruits. Uncle Norman received twelve shillings, or about $3.00 at that time, for one shipment. This was 1,200 oranges, and he considered he did well.

The rough lemons and the cay limes are some of the natural fruits. These seem to thrive best when left to grow wild, especially the rough lemons. Other citrus fruits have been cultivated. In recent years there have been a greater variety; that is, various species of oranges and grapefruit, and also tangerines and the very juicy tangeloes.

Island Life

Pawpaws or papayas, as some call them, are grown here; and, if seeds are planted regularly, can be a year-round crop. There are many species of pawpaws. They are a good food. From my experience I would say, "A piece of pawpaw a day will keep the stomach ulcers away!" Other fruits that are grown here are avacadoes, sugar and Jamaica apples, sour-sops, hog-plums, guavas, gunnaps, mangoes, carissas, peaches, cherries, and bananas.

The vegetables that are grown here help the families' budgets. They might be found in some backyards; but usually in small fields away from the home. Tomatoes, beets, carrots, cabbage, turnips, cauliflower, and radishes grow best in the winter. Sweet potatoes might grow year-round. Melons are raised in the summer months.

To go back to the early settlers and even up to the 1940's, when money was more available, there were a few things purchased at the little store, or shop, as it was called: flour, sugar, lard, baking-powder, sweet milk, canned corned-beef, soap, and starch. One day Grand-mamma, Sarah Ann, returning from the shop with her arm full of groceries and three pennies in her hand, said to someone: "Ah, child, you don't get much for a shilling now-a days" (24 cents at that time).

During World War II, Uncle Will opened and started operating a small grocery store. At first, he used his dining room for the sales, intending mainly to keep a supply of the staple products for his workmen in the boat yard. There were times when cash was not available to meet the payroll, but the men were so glad to have a job and to get groceries, they were willing to wait a while for the extra money.

Uncle Will later erected a building to serve as a grocery store, with a small office in one corner. This proved to be an asset to many who were not on Uncle Will's payroll including some from other settlements.

Today, there are two well-kept and well-stocked grocery stores, where just about anything one could desire, is available, including frozen meats. Of course, the prices are somewhat different from those in the days of Grand-mamma, Sarah Ann!

During the years of "The Great Depression," a large family might divide into different teams. Papa and one son went off to the field; a couple of the others went fishing, while some got the wood for cooking. Mamma and the daughters took care of the domestic work. They had no electric machines. Neither did they have many clothes. The gadgets were all operated manually, and they didn't break down.

During this period, a week generally went as follows:

Sunday was observed as the Lord's Day. There were Sunday Schools and sometimes Church Services. Some of the young people gathered in certain homes for group singing and Bible reading. In some homes, husbands and wives sang hymns of praise! In those days, the mammas rocked their babies and sang to them, often composing their own lullabies — maybe different ones every day. Between four and six in the afternoon most of the children and young people, as well as some of the older ones, took a stroll to the cemetery. Greetings were exchanged, and it was a joyous occasion.

The food on Sunday was a breakfast of boiled, salted fish with fresh lime or lemon juice, homemade bread, and coffee with sugar. Sweet potatoes might be substituted for bread. The mid-day meals were always called dinner and consisted of home-grown baked beans, native cane syrup, and duff. At supper, we usually had left-over fish from breakfast, bread, and coffee.

When the sun arose Monday morning, the men and boys went to their duties: some maybe building boats; some cutting or cleaning sisal, even though the price was very low at that time; others to the field. Fish were caught almost every day, and there had to be the wood for the fire. If it was not hurricane season, some of the men were off on a sponging trip.

The men's schedule for the rest of the week was much like that of Monday. The children were in school during the normal hours. In most families like ours, the older boys often had to go fishing after school to get enough for supper. We hurried home from school, and sometimes when I reached home, my shirt was already unbuttoned. After putting on old clothes, we went around Dickey's Cay, and, usually in a short time, we had enough fish for the entire family.

Monday was washing-day for the women. The clothes were washed in a zinc or wooden tub of water. Generally, lye was used instead of soap. A supply of lye-water was kept in a wooden tub, sometimes a half of a barrel, near the cistern. Ashes and water were put into the tub when necessary. After the clothes were scrubbed on a wash-board or scrub-board, they were rinsed and hung on the clothes-line to dry. Then they were taken off the line to await the starching.

Week-day meals were generally breakfast with native fruit, a boiled or fried egg, bread, and coffee. However, many times it was only bread and coffee; and we were thankful. It might be of interest to know that there were no tea-drinkers on Man-O-War when I was a boy, but now more people drink tea than those who drink coffee. Dinner might be one of the following: stewed guavas, native cane syrup, sug-n-egg, native bean or pea soup, sweet potato soup, chicken soup, stewed or fried chicken, thickened chocolate (a drink made with chocolate and flour in boiling water), turtle, scalefish, crawfish, whelks, or curbs. When available, homemade bread was eaten along with most of these foods. As already mentioned, several varieties of cooked sweet potatoes often took the place of bread. The Solomon potato is the best of all.

The supper for each day was similar: Fish, either boiled, fried, baked, stewed, minced, or roasted with bread or sweet potato. There are so many varieties of scalefish, and so many good ways of preparing these for food, that I could enjoy a meal almost every day. A relative of mine, when questioned about the food in the early days said, "It was like this: fish and potato for breakfast; fish and potato for dinner; fish and potato for supper, and for a turnoff, or change, next morning, it was potato and fish for breakfast!"

Sugar-cane tea was used instead of coffee many times. The cane was scraped, cut into pieces about eight inches long, bruised, and boiled with water in a pot. That was very nutritious.

Only raw or green coffee, as we called it, was available. We parched it in an iron pot and either ground it in a coffee-mill or beat it in a wooden mortar with an iron pestle. We were able to use either Mrs. Laura's mill, or Mr. John Sands' mortar and pestle. There was no charge for the use of these valuable inventions; but when we had them, we usually gave the owner a penny, at that time two cents.

Island Life

For the women, Tuesday was baking and starching day. Our clothes were starched to stiffen them — giving them or keeping them in shape. Starching also helped to resist dirt, made the clothes last longer, and the washing much easier. I often watched Mamma do this job. First, she boiled water, and then added powdered starch and a small amount of blueing, a solution used in laundering. When the temperature of this mixture was right, Mamma soaked the clothes in it, and hung them on the clothes-line until they were dry.

Wednesday was ironing day.

Thursday was mending day. Other sewing was done including making new clothes when one could afford to buy material. Shirts and under-wear were often made out of flour bags. The bags used for shirts were generally bleached so as to get the lettering off, and sometimes they were dyed. Small scraps of cloth were sewed together for making quilts and spreads. Mamma carded cotton for her own use in making quilts. She also carded cotton for others, especially Mrs. Patience, who made quilts to be sold in Nassau. In doing this job Mamma used a pair of cards or toothed instruments for combing cotton to make smooth layers.

Cotton was locally grown. There were two species, one with many more seeds than the other. Seeding cotton was one of the several jobs done in the evening and on rainy days. Mrs. Patience had an old-fashioned cotton-gin, which she loaned to other people. I used that invention or machine when I was a boy, and now I am the proud owner of that valuable item. (Lord willing, when I am finished this book, I hope to start a small museum and that cotton-gin will be an important item.) Sometimes an old quilt might be "quilted over", or it was covered with a patch-work of bits or scraps of cloth (already mentioned) with just a little carded cotton added to the parts to fill in where the old quilt was worn through. Naturally, it was more difficult to "quilt over" a quilt than to make a new one, as it was more difficult to get the needle through. However, money was not available to buy blankets so the work had to be done like many of the other seemingly hard chores. School songs, love songs, and hymns were often heard while the women were at this work. Both adult and baby quilts were made. There were several sets of wooden quilting-frames. They were loaned around. Sometimes the owner might be given a penny for the use of them. Generally, when a quilt was in the making in a home, the women and girls of our community freely gave a hand. It was a kind of recreation to them — a chance for little jokes and discussion!

Plating or plaiting during these early years helped a great deal in our economy. The young women did the most of the plating. Only a few could really sew the plat into hats. I learned to plat, and some of the first money I made was doing this work of art. Some of the other boys also earned money in this way. Generally, the young women or girls would gather in groups to plat after the other domestic work was done. It was also done in each home at night. "No rest for the weary" was a common expression. The women platted, the men and boys shelled peas and beans; corn was taken off the cob; old rope was taken apart and the good was spun into yarns for rope-making. But there were the bright spots, peeling and eating oranges and grapefruit or peeling and sucking those juicy sugar-canes. These were the things done in the spare times in the day or night and during rainy days. I am reminded of a saying we had and still use it. It did not happen in Man-O-War, but in a neighbouring settlement. The story is told of one day when it began to rain, a servant said to his master, "More rain, more rest, master." The master replied, "More rain, more shelled corn!"

To get back to the plating, some of the hats were sold by members of the crew on the mailboats. Then for a longer period the hats were sent to Nassau to a very dear friend and relative. She was Mrs. Lela Albury. She had a little store, and she sold the hats for our people. In some cases she sent the cash, but sometimes she sent the items ordered by our people like cloth, including blue denim, for making the men's work pants. Some of our young people were able to maintain themselves in clothing by the platting industry. Mrs. Gladys was one of the best sewers of hats.

Baskets, used as containers for reaping potatoes, corn, beans, and other produce, were also made. A different kind of plat was used – something stronger.

Gourds, which grow on a vine, were often used, the small ones for dipping water out of the water-bucket for drinking or cooking, the larger ones for bailing the water out of our boats. The gourds had to be ripe, though not edible, sawn in two, and then the pulp and seeds taken out.

Friday was cleanup day. Of course, the houses were kept clean by daily dusting and sweeping; but on Friday the floors were not only swept but scrubbed with the workers on their knees with one hand on the floor and the other holding firmly a turbot or trigger fish skin that had been left out in the sun to get hard for that purpose. This skin was used instead of a brush and did a better job. Sometimes, one could smell the pine while the scrubbing was being done. Lye water and fine sand from Sandy Crossing, Dallas Bay (now Ruthie's Bay) and Corn Bay, were used instead of soap and soap-powder. After a good scrubbing the floor was washed with water and dried with a "rag," an old piece of cloth. Small portions of the floor were scrubbed at a time, until the whole floor was so clean that you could eat your food off it. One of my dear old cleanly Aunts often made the remark when I visited her: "Come in, child, if you can get in for sake of dirt." Her floor seemed to be always spotless!

During the scrubbing, like all other chores in those days, it was common to hear the workers or scrubbers singing a song of praise. When we first had our chapel, we did not have tile on the floor. It was scrubbed about once a month. One day I heard a dear old saint on her knees helping to do the cleaning, and singing that lovely Chorus, "I'll do it all for Jesus; He did so much for me!"

There were no glass windows, just shutters. When all the rooms were clean, and, by the way, we were not allowed to walk on the floor until it was dried properly, the dirt yards were swept with a broom – the stick made out of a natural slender stem of a tree. The bushy part was made of the small branches of the broom brush tree. The trash or compost was put out in the back-yard. This served as fertilizer for the fruit trees. In mid-afternoon, a group of women, girls, and boys, went to the north beach and got some of that lovely white sand. This was brought from the beach out through the narrow dirt-paths in pans, cans, pillowcases, and other containers on their shoulders and heads. Then the sand was sprinkled in the yards to make them look cleaner.

Chapter II.
The Wild Life of Our Island

The beauty of Man-O-War is enhanced by a covering of natural and cultivated growth of trees, plants, shrubs, vines, and flowers.

Some of the natural trees are: button-wood, seven-year-apple, sea-grape, wild fig, madeira, dog-wood, broom-bush, sage, tamerind, almond-beef-wood, black and white torch, poison-wood, machineel, old-man and old-woman, pigeon plum, stopper, gumelemi, bloli-wood, silver and thatch palm, and mangroves. Natural or wild fruits are: cocoplums, sea-grapes, figs, sapodillas, wild dillies, tele-berries, ben-giants, stoppers, almonds, and wild cherries.

Many tropical trees have been imported. Some of the fruit trees that thrive here are: orange, grapefruit, tangerine, tangelo, lemon (which seems to produce more fruit if left to grow wild), lime, gooseberry, sugar and Jamaica apple, sour-sop, hog-plum, guava, gunnap, avacado, mango, carissa, paw-paw (papaya), peach, cherry, and banana.

There are many lovely coconut palm trees. Some of the first trees were started here after a boat named *Belize* from British Honduras, carrying a cargo of coconuts, was wrecked on the tiny island No Name Cay, which is near Green Turtle Cay. These coconuts were of all sizes, barked or had all husks removed, and had pitch on the eyes, which the seedling grows through. Some of the coconuts were brought here and used for food; some were planted and multiplied. Others have been imported from various islands of our nation.

The magnificent royal poinciana is now becoming popular. The first two trees were brought here by Brigadier and Mrs. Thomas Robbins in May, 1951. These trees were planted, one in the school yard and the other in our yard at Sunset Cottage, which is now owned by Malvern and Pat Morse, American residents. Brigadier and Mrs. Robbins commemorated the launching of the motor sailer, *McCoy,* built by Uncle Will for Lucien and Stewart Stratton of Marsh Harbour.

Casuarinas also thrive and are often used as hedges. If not pruned, they serve as excellent land marks. I can remember when the first casuarinas were planted on Man-O-War. It was in 1940. Azaleas also grow very well from stems stuck in the ground. They also make good hedges.

I remember when papa brought the first cork tree from Green Turtle Cay. He thought he had something special, but later changed his mind because they multiplied too rapidly. Their long roots damaged the roads and cisterns, and fruit trees could not grow well near them.

Some of the wild flowers on Man-O-War are: sailor's caps, lilies of many varieties, morning glories, four o'clocks, blue flowers, cat-nip, and wild potato flowers.

About the beginning of the year 1940, there were only two hibiscus, five oleanders, and several crotons here. Today, these and other flowering shrubs and plants are so plentiful that our island is a mass of beautiful colours. It is very refreshing to walk along the roads and paths and see the colorful flowers. In the early morning or evening the air is scented with jasmine, roses, and other sweet-smelling flowers.

The waters around our island abound with many species of scale-fish, shells, crabs, and coral. Conchs, crawfish, and turtles are also found here.

Scale-fish, which has been a staple diet since Mammy Nellie and Pappy Ben settled here, continued to be the favourite food of most of our people. The best liked fish are groupers, red and mutton snappers, hog-fish, turbots, jacks, runners, porgies, and grunts.

Shell-collecting, by most people, is now a hobby. However, a few people collect them for sale. Captain Milton Sweeting has a shell shop and both local people and visitors find many attractive gifts there. When I was a boy, we collected shells for sale. We were glad to do anything to earn a few pennies. Some shells, such as kings, queens, screw, and pink conchs, were taken out of the water and left to die. Then they were washed clean in the sea-water. Some, like the panama and the bleeding teeth, were boiled and then picked clean with a large needle or pin. Today, some people freeze them and then do the cleaning. Coffee-beans, limpets, turkey's wings, cowries, sun-shells, and others wash up on the beach already cleaned by the sun and water.

Sea-crabs are not used for food here. They are collected, cleaned, and used as ornaments.

Only a few special pieces of coral are taken from their homes. Most of it is left in the sea garden and is one of the great attractions for our visitors.

About twenty-five years ago the old Cracker Pinder who lived at Lubber's Quarters, Abaco, said that crawfish was rich men's food. That statement could be used truthfully today. The demand is great, and the price is high. However, my island relatives and friends often think of me by giving me this rich men's food, and I appreciate their generosity.

We have three kinds of turtles: hawk's-bill, logger-head, and green-turtles. For many years the hawk's-bill turtles were caught mainly for their valuable shells which are used to make lovely ornaments. Of course, their meat, known as the mutton of the sea, is palatable. The meat of green-turtles, known as the veal of the sea, is also very tasty.

Turtles lay their eggs on our beaches during the months of June, July, and August. I watched a logger-head lay her eggs one night. She crawled up the beach near the cemetery. She settled herself in a suitable spot, and dug a neat round hole in the sand with her hind fins. Then with tears trickling down from her eyes, she dropped over a hundred eggs in the hole. After she finished laying the eggs, she

The Wild Life of Our Island

covered the hole very carefully. She then stood on all fours or fins over the nest and several times let the weight of her body, which was about 150 pounds down to pack the sand tightly. Before returning to the sea, the turtle threw dry sand with her fore fins on the spot, seemingly doing this to try to hide her treasures which would hatch in about two weeks.

There are many kinds of birds here. Some of them stay year round. Some come during the migrating season, when they change climates from cold to hot or cool to warm and vice versa. They generally migrate in search of food which consists of insects, grain. Naturally, those that stay here, nest and reproduce. The common ones are: mocking-birds, several species of humming-birds, yellow-breasts (banana quits), tobacco-doves, pick-peters, wood-peckers, sand-pipers, rain carrion and long-tail crows, and man-o-war or frigate-birds.

The character of the mocking-birds is most interesting, especially in the building of their nests and care of their young. The male and female work together and might start construction of several nests before completing the one they use. This is done to get the attention of bird-watchers on the wrong place. If anyone touches the nests, the mocking-birds will abandon it; and, if the young are not able to fly, the parents take them away. The mocking-birds, as the name implies, imitate other birds. They often perch on the highest tree, building, or antenna, and sing very sweetly as they view the fair creation.

During depression days, or hard times as they were often called, I helped to plant sweet potatoes. The "Lizzie" potato was known to grow quickly. One day while I was in the field, a mocking-bird seemed to say: "Plant Lizzie, plant Lizzie; come quick, come quick."

Yellow-breasts, some of our year-round friends, are very friendly and easy to tame. I keep sweetened water on our porch, and I appreciate their visits. They sip their water while I enjoy my tea, the cup that cheers. They build their nests with a door in the side. After the young ones fly, the mother might still use the nest as a sleeping-room until it is building season again, which is usually spring.

Tobacco-doves, like some other birds, are cunning in the protection of their young. One day, when a boy, I was standing under a tamerind tree on our property near the sea-shore. A tobacco-dove dropped down beside me. Boys will be boys, so I tried to catch it. Each time, just as I was about to cover it with my hand, it rolled over and over on the ground away from me. It appeared to be lame. This was repeated until we were about two hundred and fifty feet from the tamerind tree. The tobacco-dove then took merrily to flight leaving me wondering! I went home and told Papa about my experience. He smiled and told me that was the way the dove acted when they had young ones. Sure enough, I went back and there was the nest with lovely babies. I did not destroy them!

The humming-bird is our smallest and the man-o-war our largest bird. The humming-birds may be seen flying from flower to flower sucking the sweet juices. They move about in a remarkable way, their wings so propelled, that they travel speedily forward and backward, up and down. The humming-birds, like all the others, build very strong and pretty nests.

Man-O-War: *My Island Home*

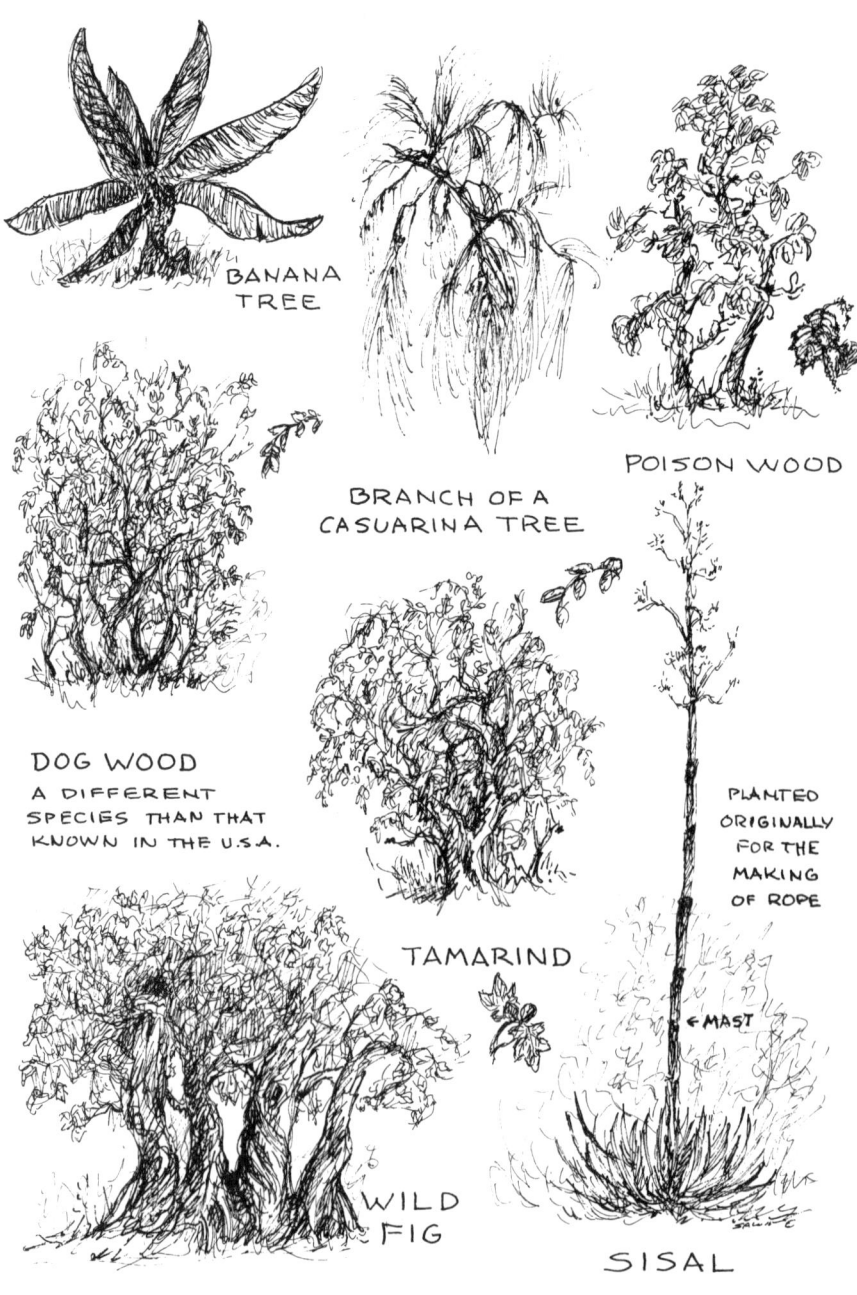

The Wild Life of Our Island

SUNRISE TELLIN

COWRIE

QUEEN OR PINK CONCH

KING'S CROWN OR CROWN CONCH

HAIRY TRITON

BANANA-QUIT (SIZE OF A WREN)

MAN-O-WAR OR FRIGATE BIRD

TERN OR "GULLY"

SEA OATS OR RUSHES

SPIDER LILY

OLEANDER

The man-o-war birds have a forked tail and extremely narrow wings. The male is all black; the female is black with a white breast. Unlike many other sea-birds, they never go into the sea. They get their food by putting their long beak, which has a crook in the end, into the water when the fish are very near the surface. For its weight, about four pounds, it has the largest wings of any bird. The wing spread may be as much as six feet. These birds soar in the air with speed and grace. They have excellent eye-sight often watching some small fish from great heights. When some larger ones like tuna, dolphin, mackeral, jack, or blue runner force them to the surface of the water, then the man-o-war birds descend very rapidly, pick up their prey and ascend instantly in the air again. We have a saying: "Man-o-war fly low, sign of blow; man-o-war fly high, sign of clear blue sky!"

Some of the migrant birds are: great blue-herons, generally called morgan; small white and blue herons, gauldins, bitterns, king-fishers, fowl and fish hawks, cat-birds, painted bunting, red-winged black birds, pinks, and a host of others. All of these are referred to as "winter birds." I always look forward to the seasons when these lovely birds visit us. I find a great delight in feeding and taming them.

The killer-ke-dicks arrive in the month of May and spend the summer with us. After a shower of rain, when termites come out of the ground, dozens of killer-ke-dicks, our good friends, fly swiftly through the air feeding on these destructive insects. They also feed on other insects mainly during the late afternoons and early evenings.

The sea-gulls also arrive in May bringing a welcome sound with their cry or song. This makes us feel that summer is here, and then comes the desire for boating, fishing, and swimming.

Certain other sea-birds including shanks, killem-pollies, noddies, and egg-birds often fly over and around our island fishing for food for themselves and their young which they have on the nearby uninhabited cays and rocks.

The wildlife on our island is still plenteous and it is our hope that it will remain so.

Chapter III.
The Government of our Island and Our Country

For many years Hope Town was headquarters for the Abaco District, and, of course, for Man-O-War. The Commissioner was stationed there and visited our settlement periodically. Some of his duties were to make payments for cleaning, repairs to roads and docks, and other government work.

The Commissioner was and is still the Chairman of the Local Board of Works and School Committee. In fact, he is the general administrator. In the year 1910, Mr. Brooks was Commissioner, and he married Papa and Mamma.

Commissioners also have helped our people with documents, such as wills, conveyances, and others. Another of the Commissioner's duties is to settle law-suits. Fortunately, in Man-O-War, we have had only family quarrels, and these have been settled by the individuals or families concerned, usually by apologizing. There also have been occasions when some greater problem, such as illness, has arisen and the trivial matter was forgotten. The three major law-suits here have been concerning animals: a goat, a chicken, and a dog!

My first experience was with Commissioner Kinnear Cross. Before his arrival in Hope Town, after his appointment as Commissioner of this District, we heard that the new Commissioner was "Cross by name and cross by nature." I found this to be untrue. Rather, he was very kind and helpful in all my dealings with him as I shall explain.

On his first visit to Man-O-War, he and his wife were taken around our settlement, as was customary for most visitors in those days. They were given fruits and vegetables, so much that Mrs. Cross said or was heard to exclaim, "The next time I come I'll have to bring my basket!"

Lewis, my brother, was Postmaster at this time, and when he resigned in 1940, I was asked to act until there could be a replacement. I was only a teenager, and Papa took me to Hope Town in his sailing dinghy to talk to Mr. Cross and get some help in this work. I went into his office trembling, but he was so kind and helpful that he put me at ease and assured me all would be well. His instructions put me in good stead for the office of postmaster which I later held for about twenty years.

I was relieved as Acting Postmaster when Mr. Ivan Russell was appointed school teacher and Postmaster here. Mr. Cross sent me a copy of his letter dated 5th

November, 1940, to Mr. Russell together with a note requesting "please give Ivan Russell whatever help you can until he becomes familiar with his new work."

In 1945 when I was appointed school-teacher and postmaster, I began to work with the Commissioners of the District, and since that time have enjoyed each and every one of them. I was also appointed Justice of the Peace in July 1948. Mr. Lucene Pinder was the Commissioner at that time.

The Board of Works, the Town Planning Committee, and the Board of Pilotage, chaired by the Commissioner of the District represent the government of the Commonwealth of the Bahamas. I have had the privilege and honour to serve as a Government member of the Board of Works for over thirty years and am still active in this capacity.

Man-O-War does not have a police officer stationed here, nor a paid constable. Uncle Will served as a "district constable" without pay for over forty years. At one time Robbie Weatherford was a paid constable, but it was for a very short period. The police officers at Marsh Harbour visit Man-O-War periodically and inspect vehicles in March of each year.

I often think of one outstanding favour done for me by Commissioner Michael Gerassimos in my early years as teacher. I had gone to Hope Town in a small dinghy to make a usual visit to the Commissioner. While I was there, a strong "Norther" came down. Mr. Gerassimos hired two men with their sloop to bring me home. My parents were grateful to him and often spoke of this kindly act.

In the year 1961 headquarters was transferred to Marsh Harbour. Instead of heading my boat southeasterly for five miles to Hope Town, I now changed course and headed southwesterly for five miles to Marsh Harbour. It has been my privilege to assist the Commissioners and Police Officers in their duties here as well as help my people.

Man-O-War, like the rest of Abaco and the Bahamas, is governed by the Government of the Commonwealth of the Bahamas with headquarters in the Capital, Nassau, in the Island of New Providence. We have always had representatives or a representative in the House of Assembly. In the 1950's Party Government came into being. In 1962, both parties, the United Bahamian Party and the Progressive Liberal Party, known as the U.B.P. and the P.L.P., felt the need for a new Constitution. Both parties were at a Conference in London the following year when the "Fourth Constitution" for the Bahamas was settled. This new Constitution which came into effect on the 7th January 1964 did away with the Executive Council, and the Legislative Council became the Senate. The real power was thus placed in the Ministers of a Cabinet from the majority party of the Assembly. At this time, Sir Roland Symonette became the first Premier of the Bahamas. This Constitution was celebrated here by teachers and pupils who marched through the settlement with flags, singing the new Constitution Songs. Each child received a Constitution Day Medal.

In 1967, the P.L.P. took over the reins of Government, and the Honourable L.O. Pindling became the Premier. In 1969 a further step was taken with the "Fifth Constitution." The Premier became The Prime Minister, and the Government was

The Government of Our Island and Our Country

given the majority in the Senate. The Bahamas was then officially named "The Commonwealth of the Bahama Islands."

The next step was Independence. Britain seemed in favour of this, although many Bahamians including the people of Man-O-War were not satisfied with this move. Therefore, it was to become an issue in the 1972 General Elections. Much prayer was offered here, seeking God's Will. In fact, a special prayer meeting was held in the School house the night before the Elections and again our prayer was "Lord, Thy Will be done!" The results of the Elections showed that the majority of the Bahamian people wanted Independence, so the 10th of July 1973 was announced as "Independence Day."

I was appointed to serve on the Independence Committee to represent Man-O-War. I attended most of the meetings which were held at Marsh Harbour. Commissioner Carroll Storr was in charge of the Marsh Harbour District of Abaco at that time. Each meeting began and ended with prayer for guidance and peace in the celebrations as well as in the future. There was still some opposition to the move.

On the morning of the 10th of July 1973, a goodly number of Bahamians and visitors gathered for our Flag Raising ceremony. As a representative of the Bahamian Government and a loyal subject to Her Majesty, Queen Elizabeth II, I hoisted the new Bahamian Flag. The Bahamas was now the 33rd Member of the Commonwealth and the World's 143rd Sovereign State. It was a solemn occasion. The Bible was read, prayers were offered, and God was thanked. One visitor, while shaking my hand expressed it thus, "I enjoyed it very much; you read and spoke from the Word of God and gave Him the praise."

Prince Charles, the eldest son of Her Majesty, the Queen, represented his mother at the Independence Celebrations at Clifford Park in Nassau at midnight on the 9 July 1973. The following morning he handed over the Constitutional Instruments to the Honourable L.O. Pindling, Prime Minister of the "Commonwealth of the Bahamas." The Queen's Message was read and with that the Colonial era in the Bahamas ended.

As a result of a recent agreement made by Governments of the Commonwealth, "Commonwealth Day" is to be observed on the second Monday in March of each year. The following are notes from H. M. Queen Elizabeth's Commonwealth Day Message 1977: "I am glad that the new date for the observance of Commonwealth Day should have been introduced in my Silver Jubilee year. It will be an important reaffirmation of our faith in the Commonwealth if the peoples of such diverse countries and traditions are able to join, on the same day every year, in remembering the objectives which we all share."

The First Governor to visit Man-O-War in my experience was Sir Robert Neville with Lady Neville. Since that time all the governors of the Bahamas have visited us. The last to visit was Sir Milo and Lady Butler in August 1974. All dignitaries who have come to our shores have received a royal welcome. Our people are so pleased to have Government Officials visit us that they turn out and try to make the visitors feel at home. We give them items made on our island and show them our means of livelihood.

Chapter IV.
A Religious People

When Mammy Nellie divided her land among her children, she gave a piece of land for a church building. The first church built there was the "Church of England." For some time it was very active with regular church services. Our first school was also kept in this building.

In the late 1890's the church people became fewer, and the building was deteriorating. Some arrangements were made by the "Church of England" and the "Methodist Church," who by that time had some prominent members here, and the Methodists took over the building.

Shortly afterwards, some of the members, Mr. John Sands, Mr. Robert (Bob) Russell, Uncle Emanuel Thompson, and others took down the old building. With some new material and the best of the old building, the present Methodist Church was built. It was dedicated in April 1912, and for a number of years church services were held there regularly.

For many years the Methodist minister of the District lived in Hope Town and visited Man-O-War periodically. When I was a boy, a boat named the *Atalanta* was used for transportation. Later, another boat named the *Trot* was used.

The Methodist minister of the District now has headquarters in Dundas Town near Marsh Harbour. There are no regular services held on our island now. However, the minister continues his periodical visits, sometimes for church services and sometimes doing visitation work particularly among the sick.

In the late 1890's, the work of the Gospel among the Assemblies of "Brethren" began in Man-O-War with open-air meetings. A Gospel Hall was built in 1902. This was up on the hill, and just like the "Church of England" was used at several different periods for a school. Some of the evangelists who visited here in the early days were Mr. B. C. Greenman, Mr. Christopher Knapp, Mr. Hugh Campbell and his brother John, Mr. August Van Ryn, Mr. Robert Stratton, Mr. Stebbins, Mr. A. H. Stewart and his son Sam, Mr. Walter Kendrick, and Mr. James Fraser.

Services were held for children as well as adults. As a result of these services many were blessed, and I think we have the evidence in our community today. The hurricane of 1932 destroyed this building; but shortly after, the present Gospel Hall near the Post Office was built.

Man-O-War: My Island Home

A Religious People

GOSPEL HALL

THE CEMETERY

GRAVE WITH FLOWERS

UNCLE WILL'S GRAVE

For a period of time the services continued here. This was the place of worship my parents attended. However, sad to say, difficulties arose by outside influence, resulting in the closing down of this Gospel Hall; and for some years there was no Assembly of Brethren here.

After the closing of the Gospel Hall most of our people attended the Methodist Church and open-air meetings held by visiting evangelists. On one occasion, I was given a penny to go around the settlement and tell the people that there was going to be an open-air Gospel Service.

In addition to the evangelists already mentioned, Mr. and Mrs. Murdo MacKenzie and Mr. and Mrs. Bernard Fell visited here. The meetings were well attended, and people seemed glad to listen to the teachings of the Word of God. At one of these meetings held by Mr. Fell in 1939, my brother, Cyril, was converted.

During this period, Sunday School was carried on in the Methodist Church by two faithful, godly women, Mrs. Reca Russell and Mrs. Eliza Sands. Most of the children of Man-O-War attended this Sunday School. I hold very dear those times with Mrs. Reca and Mrs. Eliza. They made a lasting impression on me.

Some years after Cyril's conversion, I also became a believer in the Lord Jesus Christ. When Mrs. Reca and Mrs. Eliza were no longer able to carry on this work, Cyril and I started a Sunday School, first in the Gospel Hall, and later in the school-house. In addition to the Sunday School, we also had a Sunday evening Gospel service. The Lord blessed us abundantly, especially in the school house, during meetings held by Mr. William H. Farrington, a well-known Bahamian preacher.

As the numbers increased, we felt the need for a building to accommodate our congregation. By the kind help of many Christians, a Gospel Chapel was built. It was dedicated on the second day of May 1954. This building was extended in the summer of 1966.

Our Assembly of Brethren continued to grow, and by the latter part of 1975, there arose a "good problem", the need for more space. The lot of land adjoining the present Chapel was available. It was decided to build the new chapel on this site. By the generous and united efforts of interested men, women, boys and girls, the building was completed and dedicated with much praise and thanksgiving on the twenty-seventh of June 1976. There were about five hundred people present for this "great day" in the history of our Assembly. Among them were many visiting preachers, including Mr. Cecil Simms, the first Bahamian to go into full-time gospel work many years ago, and also Mr. August Van Ryn, who first visited Man-O-War with Mr. Robert Stratton.

It is planned that a part of the old chapel will be made into a two-bedroom apartment to replace the small one-bedroom cottage built in 1958 for the visiting preachers. The other part of the chapel will be used for prayer and children's work.

About the late 1930's, Captain Roland Roberts and his brother, Hartley, of Green Turtle Cay, members of the "Church of God" there, came to Man-O-War and held meetings in a home. Mr. Porter White and Mr. Horton were some of the ministers who continued the work. They had meetings in several homes until a church building was erected. My dear school teacher, friend and brother in Christ,

Mr. Robbie Sands, was in charge of this Church until his death. A new church has been built and services continue there. The Christians of Man-O-War, although of different faiths, I feel manifest a real Christian spirit to one another, and also to our visitors.

Most of our visitors are impressed with our community and say it is unique. I believe this uniqueness is a result of the religious activities of our people from early days. They were God-fearing and read the *Bible*. We always had the *Bible* and prayer in our home, and we were taught the things of the Lord. Sunday was observed as the "Lord's Day." All work stopped, and our minds were focused on religious things.

I also believe that the teaching of the *Bible* to the young has had a great influence. I have had the privilege of teaching the *Bible* in our Day School as well as Sunday School. Also through the years Christians from other places have worked with our children in Daily Vacation Bible Schools and Children's Meetings. A regular children's meeting is now held every Wednesday at our Chapel by some of our own young women.

Every Christmas evening we have a Sunday School programme. The children sing or recite some religious pieces. Some of the adults also take part. Everyone looks forward to this. They have new clothes and are anxious for this occasion, because those who have attended Sunday School receive gifts. All present at this programme have refreshments and rejoice in the performance of the children.

This Christmas programme was started by Mr. Walter Kendrick many years ago. He always gave presents to everyone: clothing, thread, razor blades, and toys. Many of the girls got their first doll at one of Mr. Kendrick's programmes.

I often thank God for the freedom of worship, protected by the law of our nation, and pray for those in authority that they may be given the wisdom and understanding in the ways of God.

Our wedding services are similar to those held in most Christian churches. The bride and groom if they wish a large wedding will invite not only people from the Settlement but from the other islands nearby. The service is held in the chapel followed by a reception in one of the parents' homes.

Smaller weddings may be held in the home or a chapel and the immediate family and close friends are included. In some cases a wedding will be a very quiet one with just a Commissioner and two witnesses.

Funeral services usually involve our entire community, as I previously mentioned. Mammy Nellie also left a lot for a cemetery. It was very near the beach in sandy ground. Until 1965 when this cemetery, now almost full, was partly destroyed by hurricane "Betsy," grave digging was easy. When a person in the settlement died, almost all work stopped for burial took place the same day. Three groups of people help in the "laying to rest" of the loved one: one group of men goes to the cemetery to start digging the grave; the second group goes to the boatyard to make the coffin, and there is always some suitable lumber kept for that purpose. The third group prepares the body for burial. In each group there is one or more who takes the lead. These individuals have changed through the years. Some became too old or passed away and younger ones take their places. The three groups complete their job about the same time and the exact time for funeral is set.

The funeral service is generally divided into two parts: the first part is held at the home or the Church and the second at the cemetery. A funeral on Man-O-War is usually conducted as a joint service shared by speakers from each church group. It is decided beforehand who will speak at the home or the graveside.

The first part of the service consists of prayers, hymns, and scripture reading with words of comfort for the bereaved. The coffin, having been left open, is now closed after loved ones have had their last look. We now walk to the cemetery, the speakers walking in front and the close relatives following immediately behind the coffin. The rest of the community including children follow close behind.

There are no appointed pall-bearers. People just willingly take over. Some start out at the home, and there is a continual change with hardly any words being spoken. In this same manner the grave is covered after the second part of the service is completed.

At the cemetery we read scriptures in connection with death, and try to tell people that death is an appointment all must keep, and that we must prepare for it while here in this life. We usually sing several hymns and the service is closed with prayer. It was customary, when I was a boy for the procession to sing all the way to the cemetery. Like most other countries people carry flowers to the grave.

Since 1965 when we got the new cemetery which is in the coral rock above the beach, it is necessary to keep two graves dug as this cannot be done in a day. Nearly all the coffins since that time are bought made, and are called caskets. I guess we are getting modern as time goes on.

Chapter V.
Training Children for an Abundant Life

The first school teacher at Man-O-War Cay was Mr. John Russell, Mrs. Eliza Sands' father. He started teaching in the late 1890's in the Church of England, and was paid a small salary by the Church. Mr. Russell taught for about two years.

The following is a little story told me by Mrs. Eliza when she was a pupil in her father's school: Mr. Harry Sands, one of Mr. Russell's senior pupils, who later became Mrs. Eliza's husband, always blew the conch shell as a signal for the children to come to school. One morning Mrs. Eliza went to his home to tell him to blow the shell. Instead of the two of them going up to school, Mr. Harry swung Mrs. Eliza in his swing in the yard—making both of them late. Mr. Russell punished Mrs. Eliza. She told me that she was so embarrassed that she spent the rest of the day up behind the altar!

Mr. Post, an American, was the next teacher. He taught for about five years in the Gospel Hall up on the hill above the quarry. Papa went to this school, and I have often heard him talk of going to school up on the hill. Then Mrs. Berdina Roberts, better known as "Mrs. Birdie," taught in her daddy's home for about a year. Later Mrs. Eliza, daughter of Mr. John Russell, taught in the same Church of England where her father had taught before. After Mrs. Eliza resigned, Mr. Richardson Sands (known as Dick Sands) of Great Guana Cay, came here and again school was held in the Gospel Hall up on the Hill.

Mr. John Malone of Hope Town (known as John Skinner) was the next teacher, and he carried on in the Gospel Hall for about four years. Many stories were told me by Uncle Will and some of the other pupils of that time. Mr. Malone was an outstanding, strict, but very humorous teacher!

One day during recess, some of the boys began to tease another boy and with a piece of rope pretended to "haul him in" as fish is hauled in a net. Uncle Norman, who was older than these boys said as he passed by, "Haul him in, Boys, haul him in!" He then, pretending to be innocent, walked into the school.

Mr. Malone saw and heard all this from the school window. When the pupils came in school after recess, he called the boys including Uncle Norman up to be tried and punished! He gave each boy about six 'cuts' with a switch in the hand. When it came to Uncle Norman's turn, he said to Mr. Malone, "I didn't do anything."

Mr. Malone replied, "No Nor, you didn't do anything, but you being the oldest and encouraging it, I give you punishment the same as the others."

On one occasion, when Mr. Malone was testing the pupils on the Roman notation table, he asked one of the boys the table 600. The boy replied mischievously, "DC!"

Mr. Malone said to him, "Put out your hand for a switching!" Switching in the hand has always been a means of punishment in our school.

"Didn't I say it," said the boy.

"Yes," said Mr. Malone, "but in what manner did you say it?" The reason Mr. Malone was annoyed and punished the boy was because the 'DC' was a by-word of the boys meaning an old man whom the boys thought funny.

No one got away with anything in Mr. Malone's school if he saw it. I've often heard Uncle Will say: "When Mr. Malone motioned with his crooked finger, punishment was sure!" Another means of punishment in those days was to be kept in school while the others went for lunch. One day a girl missed in her spelling test and she was heard to whisper, "I knew it; mamma has sweetened beans for dinner today." Apparently, sweetened beans were her favourite.

When Mr. John Malone was transferred from Man-O-War Cay School, Uncle Norman was appointed teacher. He taught for one year here; and during the following four years, he taught both here and Great Guana Cay — one week here at Man-O-War and one week at Guana Cay and so on. Uncle Norman also used the Gospel Hall. He found his wife, Mrs. Selina (Lina), at Great Guana Cay. He says the first day he opened school there, he fell in love with her. She was then a pupil, eleven years old. They were married a few years later.

The next teacher here was Mr. Maitland Malone of Hope Town. He taught for about a year in Uncle Joe Albury's house, which was formerly owned by Mr. Henry Fisher, Sr.

When Mr. Maitland Malone was transferred, Mr. Robbie Sands, son of Mr. Richardson Sands, kept school in our first school house. One of my uncles donated this small house which he bought at Jericho, Wilson City, then a famous lumber camp on Abaco. The house was taken down and brought here about 1921. The school was put on the land Mammy Nellie left for that purpose.

I started school in that building in 1929, and I have many pleasant memories of those early days. Mr. Robbie Sands was very kind to me. I would often go to his house in the morning just to have the privilege of walking to school with him.

They say "Boys will be Boys," and one day I tried to deceive Mr. Sands. I went to his desk with my slate full of writing. In those days, and for many years, all our work was done on slate. During my early teaching years, slates were used for most of the lessons. He praised me for the writing, and told me to go back to my seat and write some more. I went to my seat; but instead of cleaning my slate, I played around a while, and then took the same work to him. He took one look at it and said, "This is the same writing you brought to me before." I should have been punished, but was not. However, I went to my seat with a lump in my throat and hung my head in shame. I never tried that again. Mr. Sands and I were very close friends after I became a man, and often enjoyed a little chat together usually about spiritual matters.

Training Children for an Abundant Life

The school house was completely destroyed in the severe 1932 hurricane! Mr. Sands carried on school in the Methodist Church. In 1933, my eldest brother, Lewis, was appointed teacher; and he also had school in the Methodist Church.

Shortly after Lewis began teaching, a part of the present school house was built. This one was also of second-hand material. The Board of Education offered the old Teacher's Residence at Hope Town for a school at Man-O-War, if our people would go and take it down. They went to Hope Town, took down the building, leaving the property clean and in good condition as was requested by the Board of Education.

Although this building was old, there was enough good lumber, Long Leaf American Pine, to build the school house and also to make the desks. This is one of the many community efforts which our people have been noted for down through the years. When the boat arrived from Hope Town, even the children joined in and helped to carry the material to the school grounds. It was my responsibility to stack some of the lumber in order. New cedar shingles were used for the roof; and when they arrived on the mail-boat from Nassau, a group of men went to work and the building was shingled in a matter of hours.

I spent about six years as a pupil under my brother, Lewis. We enjoyed good teacher-pupil relationship. His teaching helped me in many ways, for which I am thankful.

As mentioned earlier, the first school teacher was paid a small salary by the Church of England. Later, Man-O-War School became a Grant-in-Aid School. 'Grant' meaning a small salary from the Government (Board of Education), and 'aid' meaning help from the parents or pupils. The 'Aid' might be in cash, 2 cents or 3 cents per week for each child; or produce, potatoes, beans, corn, or a meal of fish. After some years, the 'Aid' was discontinued; and the teacher was obliged to live on the 'Grant' plus part-time work elsewhere.

In a Grant-in-Aid School, the teacher had no paid staff. It was customary for the senior pupils to help teach the lower classes or grades. I had the privilege to do this, and I stayed in school until I was fifteen. This teaching experience and my love for the children helped me in the decision to accept the post as teacher later on, and also gave me the ability to get started on such a wonderful career.

Lewis was the teacher here for about seven years, and then Mr. Ivan J. Russell of Marsh Harbour was appointed teacher. He did well and continued to raise the standard of our school. He was here for about five years and then was transferred to Pine Ridge, a lumber camp in Grand Bahama.

Some of the Man-O-War people suggested and encouraged me to apply for the post. After some consideration, I sent in my application together with a recommendation from Mr. Ivan J. Russell. I received the following letter:

Education Office,
Nassau, Bahamas.
April 17th 1945.

Sir,

With reference to your application of March 24th 1945, I am directed to inform you that your application is accepted, and you should begin your duties as Grant-in-Aid Teacher at Man-O-War Cay at 6.48 per annum plus War Bonds at 25% as early as possible.

The School Committee has stated that you are acceptable and Mr. I.J. Russell recommends you, therefore it rests with you to do your utmost for the Education of the children.

Please inform me, by cable if possible, of the date you opened school.

> I have the honour to be,
> Sir,
> Your obedient servant,
>
> Mary B. Albury
> Chief Clerk, Education Office.

Mr. Haziel L. Albury
Man-O-War Cay, Abaco.

I opened school right away. Walking to the school house, I unlocked the door. I am now using the same lock and key after a period of more than thirty-two years. Returning to school after five years' absence, during which time I worked at Uncle Will's Boatyard, I was a bit nervous. However, I immediately went to work to carry on the school, endeavouring to teach the children to the best of my ability, and to prepare them for future life.

Mr. T.B. Neilly, of Spanish Wells, who was head teacher at Marsh Harbour at the time, was a great help to me during those early years. Teachers' Conferences and Summer Courses have also been important.

As time went on, our school grew in the number of students and it achieved higher standards. During the latter part of 1949, Mr. T. Hutchinson, Director of Education, visited us. He told me he was pleased with the school; and as a result of his recommendations, we were promoted to a "Board" school on the 1st January 1950. Betty, the only daughter of my brother Lewis, was appointed Monitress or teacher at that time.

As a result of a visit to our school by our good friend and Member in the House of Assembly, Mr. Harold Johnson, and by his recommendations, Vashti Albury (now Thompson) was added to the staff. With Betty's and Vashti's help the wheels of the school's machinery moved more smoothly. Betty resigned in August 1961; and by some misunderstanding, I could not get permission to take on a teacher to replace her right away. However, my wife, Mary, with her willing heart, started teaching in September 1961 and taught for one year without pay! Thanks to Mr. John Bethell, M.H.A. and Mr. Rodney Bain, Director of Education, Mary was officially appointed Subordinate Assistant Teacher in September 1962.

Vashti resigned in August 1962; and my eldest daughter, Minerva, succeeded her and started teaching in September of the same year. Minerva resigned in August 1966, and Lily Albury succeeded her in October the same year. There has been no change in staff since Lily's appointment. Lily, Mary and I work well as a team. Lily teaches Grades I – III, Mary teaches Grades IV – VI, and I teach Grades VII – X. Along with our duties as teachers, we have to be prepared to render First Aid. Lily is referred to as the 'Nurse,' Mary the 'Doctor' as she had one year in Nurses' training in Nassau, and I the 'Dentist.'

In 1952, an extension was built to our school house. The Board of Education offered the material for the building and desks, if our people would be responsible for the labour. We agreed; and, like all such projects at Man-O-War, free labour was available.

Our School Year usually starts the first Monday in September and ends the latter part of June. It was not always this way, for in earlier years the Summer Holidays were eight weeks or less. During my term of office, when there were only eight weeks' holiday in the summer, we closed school for the week mid-day on Fridays. With the longer holidays, school closes at three o'clock on Fridays, the same time as other school days. The School Year is divided into three terms – Christmas, Easter, and Summer. We have two weeks' holiday at Christmas and one week at Easter or in the Spring if Easter is late in the year, plus midterm breaks and public holidays like Discovery or Columbus' Day, Good Friday, Whit Monday, and Labour Day. Our Independence Day, the 10th of July, is also a public Holiday. Of course, we are out of school at this time.

School starts promptly at 9 a.m. The 'first bell' at 8:50 a.m. is a signal for the children to head for the school; though by this time, the most of them are playing in the school playground. The 'second bell' is a signal for them to line-up and walk in an orderly manner to their places in school. At noon school is let out for lunch, a one-hour recess. The pupils and teachers go to their homes for lunch. The school house is located in the central part of our charming community.

Our school bell was brought here by Mr. William D. Lee, better known as "Bill Lee," one of the first of the Americans to build a home here. This bell was used on the farm of Mr. G. D. Pope in Bloomfield Hills, Michigan. Mr. Pope and the Neil McMaths were very close friends; and through them and Caroline Lee Pope, daughter-in-law of Mr. Pope and sister of Bill Lee, the bell was offered to our school. It was accepted with many thanks.

In the early days when blowing a conch shell was the call to school and I was a student, I had the great privilege of making this sound many times. Then there was a period when the hoisting of the Union Jack was the signal. This was discontinued when we received the bell. Of course, we still have the flag; but now it is our Bahamian flag waving over the school house.

The bulk of our school supplies come from the Ministry of Education. Some text books are bought with school funds. We are indeed thankful for all the supplies given to us by visiting friends.

We teach all subjects required of an "All-age School": Religious Knowledge, English Language, English Literature, Arithmetic, History, Geography, Health Science, Art, Poetry, General Science, Nature, and Physical Education.

We are thankful that we can teach the *Bible* in our school, and we feel there could be no substitute for our Morning Devotion period. The pupils really enjoy the hymns, choruses, Bible-reading, Bible Stories, and Bible-Quiz. Even some of the children under school age, if they are passing by, want to come in for what they call the "Sunday School part."

Man-O-War: My Island Home

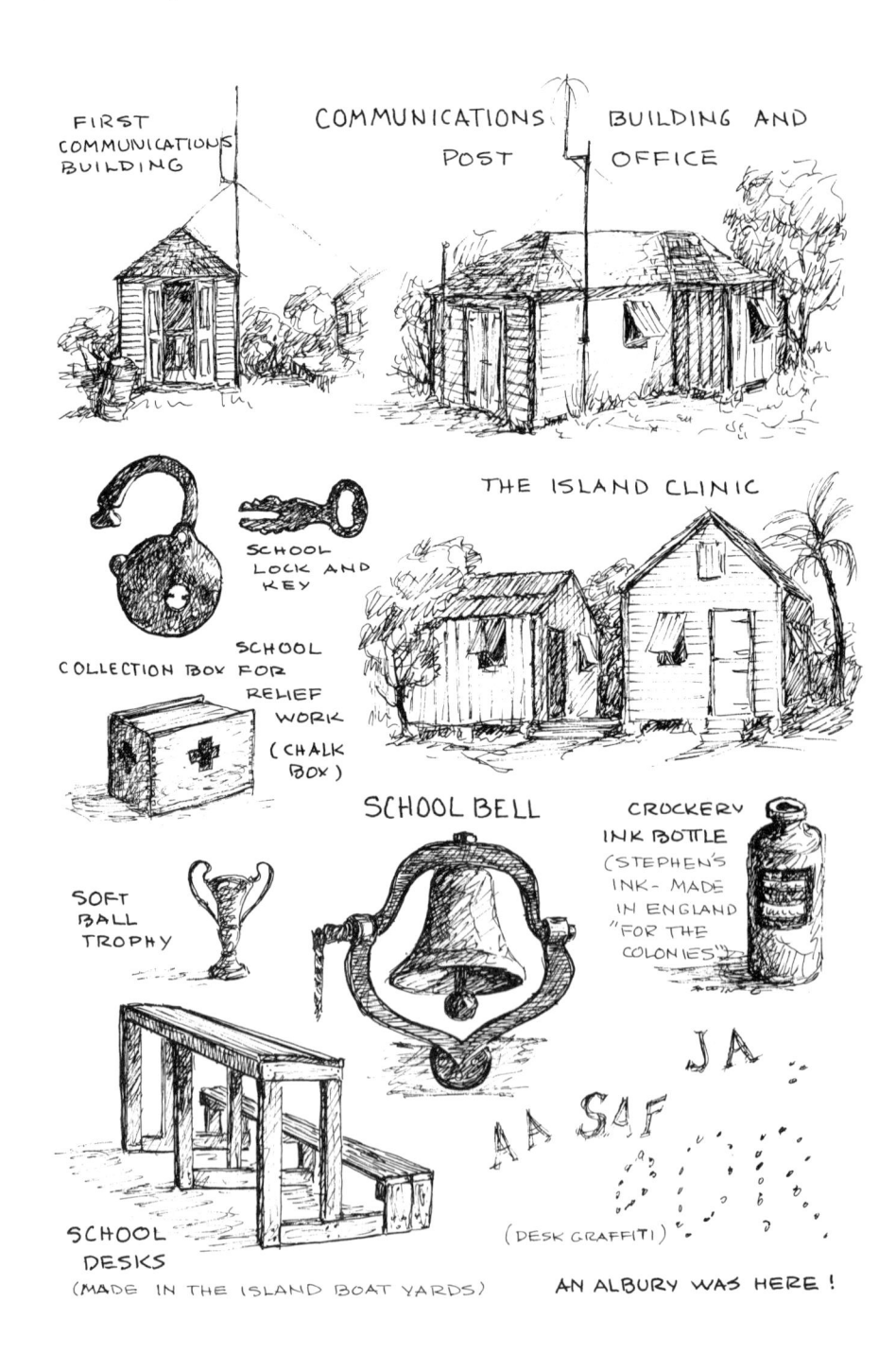

Training Children for an Abundant Life

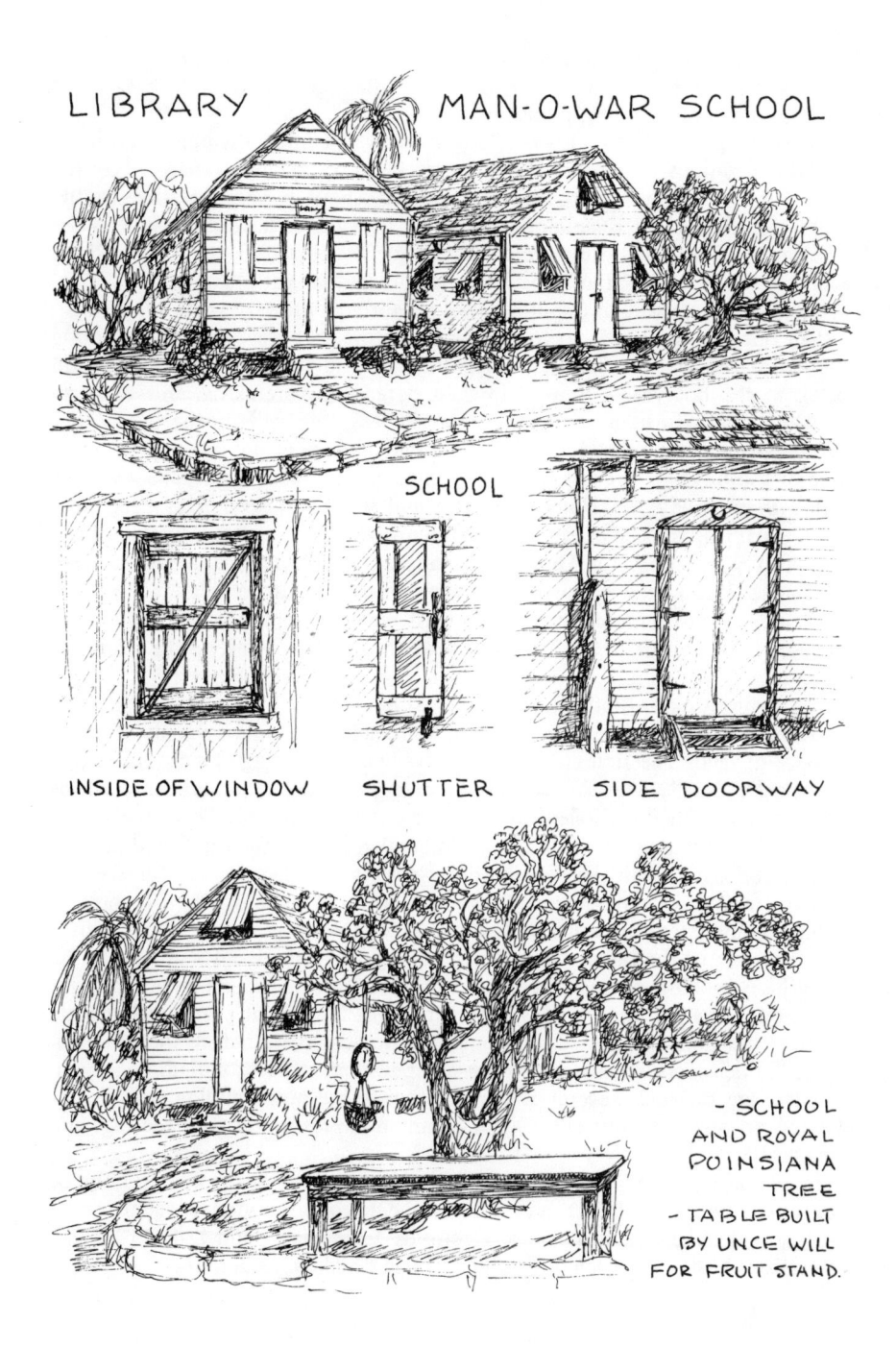

LIBRARY   MAN-O-WAR SCHOOL

INSIDE OF WINDOW   SCHOOL SHUTTER   SIDE DOORWAY

- SCHOOL AND ROYAL POINSIANA TREE
- TABLE BUILT BY UNCE WILL FOR FRUIT STAND.

We do not have a great discipline problem. The little "cane" spends most of its time on my desk; but once in a while, when the school gets noisy, it does its work! Writing lines is still one form of punishment.

School is compulsory from ages five to fourteen years, but some pupils remain in school until they are fifteen. Our aim is to get them up to the standard to get the Bahamas Junior Certificate, so the last year of school is very exciting to the candidates for the B.J.C. Examinations and for myself. We have done well in the B.J.C. Examinations. The results are encouraging! Of course, we try to train them to become good citizens. Grandpapa Uriah taught us that with "good manners" in one pocket, and "honesty" in the other we'd get through life very well!

Most of our boys and girls go to work even before they leave school – working after school hours and on Saturdays. The boys help in the construction work on houses or in the boatyards; some help their parents in caretaking, and some go fishing which they consider a pleasure. Nevertheless, this helps in the family diet and also by giving them a few dollars from the sale of some of the fish.

Some of the boys go straight to work from school. Others might take a year or so to find their steady job. Some stay here and work and become grocery store managers, boat captains, mechanics, fishermen, gardeners, and the boat builders that Man-O-War is famous for. One young man went away to the U.S. to take a six weeks' course in the maintenance of Mercury motors, but completed it in two weeks. Some go into the construction business building homes for the Americans and Canadians and acting as caretakers. A few who live here work on the Mainland of Abaco.

Almost without exception, the young men at Man-O-War Cay have a home when they get married. In most cases by the time a boy leaves school or shortly after, he gets a piece of land. The first step toward a home is the digging of a cistern, a hole in the rock. He usually does this in his spare time, even nights. Sometimes, relatives and friends help with this project until the cistern is completed. There the young man leaves this and goes to work and earns enough money for the foundation of the house. The cistern and the foundation of the house might be left for a while. After more money is earned and maybe a loan from a bank, the big task of procuring materials for the walls, roof, windows, and doors is accomplished. This is what we call getting the house "closed up." The young man is now usually at the age when he is looking seriously at the girls. By the time he is planning the interior of the house, some fortunate young lady is helping. She might even put her little savings into the home. Many of the homes are not complete before the wedding. However, the necessary rooms, which are one bedroom, a bathroom, dining-room, and kitchen, are finished. Several of our young men are now building their homes on Man-O-War. Some are not engaged. A common expression is "Get the cage and then the bird!"

A few of the young men who leave Man-O-War continue in the construction of houses; others work in banks and offices; or become insurance agents, boat captains, aeroplane pilots, mechanics, electronic technicians, and butchers. Some manage various businesses, such as Kentucky Fried Chicken restaurants.

Training Children for an Abundant Life

Our girls, naturally, help around their homes and also with the domestic duties of caretaking. They are encouraged to cook, sew, and prepare themselves to be good house-wives. Some work in stores, the Post Office, the telephone and telegraph station, restaurants, and others are busily engaged in sewing for the local people as well as for visitors.

From the early days of teaching there were School Inspectors. They tried to visit each school in the Bahamas once a year. This was quite difficult way back in the sailing days, because the schools are spread down through the chain of islands about 760 miles long. The story is told of one of these inspectors who came here on his annual visit. When he landed on the dock and walked up the road, he said: "What's that rotten bosh I smell? It's enough to take one's breath away!" Apparently, sisal had been cleaned in the sea-water nearby and the odour was not like the perfume of roses! The expression or saying of that Inspector has been handed down, and is used even today, when an unusual smell pervades the air.

Even though we try to learn and teach English, we have our own Bahamian and even "Man-O-Warian" language, which we commonly call "conch slang." Seemingly, no matter how hard we try at school, when out of school we nearly all fall into the same pattern, dropping and adding "h's," exchanging "v's" for "w's" and many other peculiar expressions. For example: "Me and you"; "We was taking"; "You ain't"; "What this is?"; and many others which you will find in this book.

The real English accent is not always easily understood by some of our people. Some years ago the Inspector, an Englishman, was giving a spelling test in one of the Abaco schools. He asked a boy to spell "nail", but pronounced it "nile." After repeating it several times, and the boy spelling 'n-i-l-e' each time, the headteacher said, "Boy, spell nail." The boy spelled out "N-a-i-l," the correct word.

Mr. Wilton G. Albury of Harbour Island, no doubt a distant relative of mine, was the first Inspector I can remember. He was fond of telling fables like "Brer Fox," "Brer Rabbit," and "Brer Bear." When he corrected a lesson or a word, you never forgot it. For example, when he heard one of the pupils say "substract," he made all of us repeat "Sub--tract, sub--tract" until he was sure we understood how to pronounce the word.

During one of his visits, while Lewis was the teacher, Mr. Wilton Albury gave some of us who were Boy Scouts a test. Lewis had spent much time and effort in our Club, and Mr. Albury was well pleased with our knowledge of scouting.

Mr. T.A. Thompson, who had been a Headteacher for many years, was our next School Inspector, appointed about the mid 1930's. He was a very kind and gentle Christian. I remember two things that I, as a pupil, learned from him. When answering one of his questions I used the term "dead corpse." He very kindly told me it was not necessary to use the word 'dead' along with the word 'corpse.' Then he asked the question, "What gifts did the wise men bring to the Baby Jesus?" No one answered, so he told us and said the three words in such a way that I have never forgotton it – "Gold, Frankincense and Myrrh." In fact, almost every time I read this scripture, especially in school, I think of Mr. Thompson.

Man-O-War: My Island Home

Mr. Thompson was still our Inspector when I took over the school. He was a great help to me in getting started in this great profession. His last letter to the teachers the day before his retirement has meant much to me, and I consider it one of my treasured documents, and it should be in every teacher's handbook. The following is a copy of that letter:

> Education Office
> Nassau, N.P.,
> Bahamas.
> 29th June 1949.

Dear Teachers,

Tomorrow I shall be saying good-bye to the Department of Education after more than forty years of service. Before doing so, however, I wish to offer you my sincere thanks for the ready and willing co-operation you have given me during my term of office as Inspector and Superintendent of Schools, and also to offer you a few thoughts for your consideration.

Let the development of character be your chief objective in the training of children. Always bear in mind that you are teaching *yourself*, not subjects set out in the Curriculum, and success depends on your character and personality. If I may use a modern expression, you are selling *yourself* to your pupils. See to it that they get good value.

Nearly two thousand years ago, the Great Teacher said, "I am come that they might have life, and that they may have it more abundantly." These words embody the highest conception of service the world has ever known. They should express the ultimate aim of teachers, for the highest service the school can render to humanity is to fit the children to live *more abundantly*.

The development of the *mind* is not to be neglected, for how can one live an abundant life with an undeveloped mind? You should be studious, seeking earnestly to improve your own qualifications, both academic and professional, so that you may inspire the children under your care to develop into honest and intelligent citizens.

In saying farewell I want to express the hope that you will find your career as teachers satisfying and enjoyable. You will do so if you realize your responsibilities and put all your powers into this important business of training children for an abundant life.

> Yours sincerely,
>
> T.A. Thompson
> Inspector of Schools

I am pleased to say that I have found my career as a teacher "satisfying and enjoyable."

Mr. Samuel Guy Pinder of Spanish Wells was our first District Inspector. His first visit to our school was the 8th November, 1961. Shortly after that, the title of the post was changed from District Inspector to District Education Officer. Mr. Pinder

Training Children for an Abundant Life

had been in the teaching profession for many years; and at one time, when I was a boy, he was the Headteacher at Hope Town — just five miles from Man-O-War. He was well-liked in that settlement.

Prior to his appointment as D.I. and D.E.O., I was fortunate to get to know Mr. Pinder at the annual Teachers' Conferences in Nassau. Mr. Pinder's first visit to our school was enjoyed so much by teachers and pupils, that we were always anxious for him to return. We were honoured to have him make Man-O-War his base when visiting the schools in the Abaco Cays. Mr. Pinder and I have had great times together discussing education, and he helped me greatly with my records, as well as many methods of teaching.

Occasionally, when school work was over, we'd go on a short fishing trip and bring home our supper. Whenever it was convenient, Mrs. Pinder would come to Man-O-War with her husband, and both, Guy and Aline, have become great friends of our whole family. He had been D.E.O. for the Island of Eleuthera as well as Abaco, but the responsibility of the two islands was too much for one man; and, to our regret, Mr. Pinder left Abaco.

The present inspector is Mr. Hugh Cottis, and he is most helpful in his work with our school.

We were in desperate need of wash rooms and during the latter part of 1973, the people of our community built two very nice modern toilets for the school. Most of the money for the material was raised by having 'Fairs,' and some of the young men gave free labour and built them. In January, 1974, when school reopened, these conveniences were ready for use by teachers, pupils, and also visitors. I was happy to see some of my pupils and ex-pupils of earlier years work so hard, even at night, on this community project.

There have been two deaths among the children of school age here during my life-time, one when I was a pupil and one during my teaching career! Una, the daughter of Mr. Harold and Mrs. Gladys, died of whooping cough at the age of eleven. She was in my grade at school, a very bright pupil. She was an outstanding girl and loved by all who knew her. On the 8th of February, 1961, Lee, the son of Edwin and Elsie, died at the age of six or seven of a kidney problem! He was a good pupil, and I found it a bit difficult to preside at the funeral service. However, the hymn, "Safe in the Arms of Jesus," requested to be sung by his mother, eased the lump in my throat!

Our pupils are active in many projects, besides sitting in the school room and in the playground. Each year, during Poppy week, there is a house-to-house sale of poppies. We usually get a generous amount of money. At the end of each school term, I take the school boys to collect all bottles and cans, or any rubbish, along the roads. We do this, not only to help to keep our settlement clean, but to try to train our children not to litter, and even to pick up the trash left by others. When there are appeals from the Red Cross for help, our pupils are willing to give a share of what they have to ease the burden of others.

There were times when I could have been promoted during my early years of teaching. On one occasion, when Mr. A.R. Braynen was Chairman of the Board of Education, he and Mr. Hutchinson, Director of Education, visited our school. Mr.

Man-O-War: My Island Home

Braynen said to me, "Mr. Albury, you are like the man sitting by the pool. We are going to take you up and put you in. We have greater things for you to do and more money." Each time I was offered a promotion, when I gave my reasons for not leaving Man-O-War, without any hesitation, those in authority agreed to let me stay. I am grateful to them for their consideration.

The author is also grateful to the parents, his pupils, the school committees, the Governments, and all who have allowed him to serve here in his own settlement. There is a special warm spot in my heart for every pupil who has attended my school. I really love them!

The following letter I received this year:

Mr. Haziel Albury
Principal
Man-O-War Cay
Abaco

Your reference

Our reference
EDU/CRF/

Date
28 February 1977

Sir,

You are to be congratulated for your excellent performance as a teacher and administrator over the years.

We at the Ministry wish you to know that your service is deeply appreciated and we hope that you will continue in the same vein for many more years.

Best Wishes.
Yours sincerely

F. Russell
for Permanent Secretary

ER:new

Chapter VI.
Island Industries

Boat-Building

Boat-building has always been one of the main sources of the livelihood of Man-O-War, especially during this century.

My great-grandpapa Bill began building dinghies when he was a young man. His brother-in-law, William Thompson, commonly called Uncle Billy Bo, moved to Man-O-War from Hope Town. He had more experience in the building of larger boats, and thus helped the industry. The first boat Uncle Billy Bo built here was about the middle of the Nineteenth Century. It was nineteen feet on the keel with a deep draft. It was built for Uncle Ben, Jr., son of Pappy Ben, and named *Faith*. The boys nicknamed her the *Wild Boar*. This boat was used for hauling pineapples from the farms near the Bight of Red Bays on Abaco to the American Cargo vessels, known as Yankees. These vessels, seventy-five feet and over, sometimes called fore-an-afters, took these pineapples to ports on the east coast of the United States. They would come to our Western Channel and lay to until a pilot came out to guide them to the safe anchorage where they loaded the pineapples. The *Faith* was also used to go to wrecks. On one occasion she went to a sugar wreck and got a full cargo of this valuable food.

In the early 1860's, my great-grandpapa Bill and Henry Albury, known as Henry Pack, built a twenty-eight foot keel boat with a well for keeping fish alive. This boat was named *Temperance* and at first was rigged as a sloop but later as a schooner. The fishing business in the *Temperance* was so successful that Grandpapa Bill built a larger schooner named *Valiant* which was thirty-five feet on the keel.

The Temperance was sold and fishing was carried on for a while in the Valiant. However, due to some misfortune, unknown to the author, the latter did not prove successful and she was sold.

All of Grandpapa Bill's sons, except Uncle Winer who died young, were boat-builders. They were: Thomas, Winer, Richard, Joe, Edwin, Jeremiah, and Wesley.

Uncle Joe married the daughter of Mr. Henry Augustus Fisher, Sr., formerly of Green Turtle Cay, and later of Hope Town. Mr. Fisher, who was also a boatbuilder, moved here and helped Uncle Joe and others in the boat-building. One of the first boats Uncle Joe built was a nineteen footer named *Useful*, for his younger brother, Uncle Edwin. Of course, in later years Uncle Edwin built boats on his own.

Most of the men of the following generations were boat-builders or helped in this industry. During my early boyhood days, some of the builders were my papa, Uncle Dick; Mr. George; Mr. Benjamin and his brother, Mr. Napoleon Thompson; Mr. Treason and his brother, Mr. Harry Sands. Occasionally Uncle Norman built a boat, but he was nearly always too busy making the sails.

Boat-building was a tremendous help to our people during those depression days or hard times, 1930 to 1940. The sales were slow, but our people were able to send dinghies to certain merchants in Nassau who supplied groceries, pending the sale of the dinghies. One of the outstanding merchants was Mr. E.L. Sawyer, father of Lem Sawyer of Fashionette, Nassau. The price of a ten-foot keel dinghy was five pounds or $25.00 at that time. The merchants in Nassau also supplied nails, paint, caulking cotton, and ring-bolts. These materials were needed in the building of a dinghy. All the frame and planking were collected on Abaco. The frames were made from the natural crook of madeira, dogwood, and sometimes other trees. The planking was made out of our native pine. The men cut the trees down with an axe and in most cases carried the logs out on their shoulders, one man at each end of the log. Occasionally, the men would take their rip saws over to the pine yard and saw the logs in halves thus making it easier to handle. It was lighter in weight but it had more gum or resin to get on the clothes and hands. Several times I went along with Papa and either my brother, Lewis, or my brother, Victor, to get the pine logs. It was my privilege to do the fishing for the family during the cutting and hauling of the logs, so that when we returned home, we had logs for lumber and fish for food. Most of the lumber for planking the dinghies during the hard times was sawn by hand. Fortunately for our builders some lumber often floated to our beaches. This came from the sailing vessels who had to unload their decks in times of storms. Their loss was our gain. Some of this lumber was also used in the building of homes. It is very interesting to remember in those days no one had a watch or clock on the job. The men worked from "can to can't," or sunrise to sunset.

On the third of September 1939, Britain declared war on Germany. Even though tiny Man-O-War is over 5,000 miles away, there was great excitement here, and machetes were put in action cutting down and clearing bushes for new fields.

We expected harder times; but instead, beyond what seemed to be darkness, lay a new era in the history of our island. Uncle Will began receiving orders for boats from Americans. Some of the first we built were dinghy hulls for Mr. Basil Symonette, Son of Sir Roland Symonette, First Premier of the Bahamas. These boats were shipped to Mr. Symonette, who was living in Miami at the time; and he with some other fellows finished them. There were several different sizes, fourteen to twenty feet length overall.

Then a young man named George Wall came over to see Uncle Will about building larger hulls. These were also completed in Miami. They were sloops, ketches, and motor-sailers. Uncle Will did no advertising and yet became well known. There were times when I had to write letters and turn down orders because we just did not have enough workmen. I did Uncle Will's letter-writing, and he and I with the help of our wives did the book work for the boat-yard and the small grocery store.

The money made by some Americans during World War II continued to find its way to us. Mr. Theodore R. Zickes, who came to be affectionately known to us as Uncle Ted, came here and ordered a thirty-foot Auxiliary Sloop. Uncle Will completed the boat for Mr. Zickes, and it was named *Sweet-heart*. At first, Mr. Zickes did not let his wife know that he had this boat – hence the name. In addition to the *Sweet-heart*, Uncle Will built a dinghy for Mr. Zickes to use as a tender. The *Sweet-heart* was left here year round in Uncle Will's care. I wet the decks each morning when it did not rain and there was no dew. For this job I received two shillings (28 cents) per month! Each year the *Sweet-heart* was given a complete paint job by some of Uncle Will's workmen.

Uncle Will had the privilege of using the *Sweet-heart*. He seldom took time off; but on one occasion in the early 1940's Uncle Will, Aunt Mady, and I went to Green Turtle Cay to visit relatives. While we were there someone told Uncle Will that Mr. J.W. Roberts, Sr., of the Abaco Lumber Company wanted to see him. Mr. Roberts wanted Uncle Will to build a freighter for the Abaco Lumber Company. The appointment was made and the following week Mr. Roberts came to Man-O-War to discuss and complete the plans. Mr. Roberts told Uncle Will that he wanted a freight boat about eighty-five feet on the keel, broad beam and shallow draft for operating in the waters near Pine Ridge, Grand Bahama. He said, "William, instead of paying someone else a fortune for a model or plans, I'm going to leave it up to you. I know you will build a good boat."

The building of this boat meant employment for all on Man-O-War who could work. It was also a great help to some of the men of the neighbouring settlements. They cut and brought timbers here and Uncle Will bought them. The timbers for the frames of the boat were cut on the mainland of Abaco. Our men went on weekly timbering trips to such places as the White Land and Old Robinson's Bight. As there were no power boats in those days, the going and coming was slow, hence the necessity for weekly trips. Also there were no roads and trucks in Abaco like there are today. Generally, each gang of men had one man cut paths with a machete from the sea to the timber areas. The timbers were carried or dragged out by a team of men. The timbers were then loaded into a boat to be brought to our boat-yard. Usually, the timbers were put in the sea-water to season. It helped to prevent worms, and the wood was then easier to cut.

On most of the timbering trips the men slept aboard the boats. Occasionally, some might be fortunate enough to find a lodging with friends who were farming in the area. The food for the trip consisted of a good supply of homemade bread, some plain cake called sweet bread, potatoes, coffee, sugar, canned corned beef, and fresh fish which were caught usually in an hour or so each day by one of the men. There was no official cook. They all gave a hand.

The planking for the boat was supplied by the Abaco Lumber Company. The lumber mill at that time was at Cornwall on the south side of the island of Abaco, near Hole-in-the-Wall. Due to the war, there was a shortage in fastenings and other hardware needed in the construction of the boat. Naturally, this caused a delay in the completion. However, Mr. Roberts was able to purchase some nails in Cuba and other materials in Nassau and the United States. There were many trunals or treenails used for fastening — all locally made. I helped to make them. The trunals were driven from the outside of the plank, through the frame and right to the inside of the hull, with a wedge on each end. There were no electric tools in those days.

This boat, named the *Joyce Roberts*, was towed to Nassau. I went on it with Uncle Will and others. That was my first trip to the City, the capital of the Bahamas. There were several people who came aboard when we arrived in Nassau. Among them was Mr. George Roberts, later Sir George, a great friend of all who met him. He was formerly of Harbour Island where many large boats had been built, and where Pappy Ben came from. Uncle Will and his workmen were praised highly for a job well done by all who saw the boat. The *Joyce Roberts* proved to be a seaworthy, oceangoing vessel.

After the motor was installed in Nassau, the *Joyce Roberts* went to Miami to have the tanks, wiring, and other essentials installed. Emerson and Mr. Maurice went along on the boat to Nassau and on to Miami to finish the woodwork. While Emerson was away on this trip, his second daughter, Dollie, was born.

Captain Leland Albury was the skipper of the *Joyce Roberts*. He was a famous sea-captain, recently retired. Some of his first trips in this boat included the hauling of lumber to Jamaica and Cuba from Cornwall, bringing loads of brick from Miami for the new lumber camp at Pine Ridge, Grand Bahama, and transferring lumbering equipment from Cornwall on Abaco to Pine Ridge. While the lumber mill was in operation, the *Joyce Roberts* continued hauling lumber to Nassau and other ports. When the lumber mill closed down, she was sold. Her name was changed to *Church Bay*, and she performed splendidly as a mail, passenger and freight boat for several years. On one occasion, she substituted a trip for our mail-boat and she came right into our dock. Uncle Will and others went aboard, and I'll always remember the look of satisfaction on Uncle Will's face when he said, "It's the same old *Joyce Roberts!*"

Uncle Will built a 130-foot barge and also a 60-foot tug named the *Donald Roberts* for the Abaco Lumber Company. Both of these crafts were well built. One builder from another island came here while the tug was under construction. After looking it over, this visitor said that it seemed to him that Uncle Will and his men were trying to use all the timbers on Abaco. The *Donald Roberts* was used as a tug off Grand Bahama, even in high winds and boisterous seas. She proved to be everything that could be expected from a vessel of that size. When Owens Illinois transferred its pulp operations from Grand Bahama to Abaco, the *Donald Roberts* was used to tow some of the large barges with houses and other buildings and equipment to the new site.

In addition to the commercial boats and hulls to be towed to the U.S.A. for finishing, Uncle Will and other boat-builders continued to build pleasure boats, mainly for the Americans who came and bought property here. Many boats were built at Uncle Will's yard.

Since Uncle Will's death two boats for racing in the Out or Family Island Regatta at George Town, Exuma, have been built at the William H. Albury

Shipyard operated by Emerson Albury and Scott Weatherford. This yard is now owned by Edwin Albury and used mainly for hauling boats for repairs, drying, and painting.

Some pleasure sloops as well as one freighter have been built by Basil Sands. Basil has also built many dinghies for the Government to be let out on easy terms to farmers and fishermen. This Government scheme has been in operation for about thirty years and has been a great help to both builders and owners of these work boats.

My brother, Lewis, started building boats when he was fifteen years old, and he has worked on both large and small boats. He and some of his sons now build speed boats and occasionally a commercial dinghy.

Mr. Maurice Albury was famous for his small sailing dinghies. Mr. Maurice's sons, Willard and Benny, work full time building speed boats 16' to 22' and installing and repairing motors. They have the agency for Mercury motors. Then generally have orders for boats about twelve to eighteen months ahead.

Edwin's Boat Yard is mainly for hauling boats. However, Edwin has built several boats including the ferries owned by Albury's Ferry Service. He also built the *Malola*.

The two dry docks, Wm. H. Albury Shipbuilders, Ltd. and Edwin's Boat Yard, are now hauling boats from other islands of our Commonwealth as well as boats from the U.S.A. and Canada. Man-O-War continues to be the boat-building centre of our nation. Some of the finest and strongest boats in the world are built here. The last schooner Uncle Will built, the *William H. Albury*, sailed in the tall ships parade in 1976. The dinghy attached was built by Uncle Maurice.

Although most of the hard work is now done by or with electric tools, much still is done by hand. The first electric tools were used here in 1946 when Paul Liskey, an American, brought a small generator for Uncle Will's yard.

The Abaco Freighter

During the summer of 1917, news was received that the freight rates for hauling lumber to Cuba were very high, so by the Fall The Abaco Company was formed by some of the inhabitants of Man-O-War Cay, Hope Town, and a few Abaconians living in Nassau. My uncle, William H. Sweeting and his brother, Ernest, along with others thought it would be well to get in on the freight business as well as sponging, which at that time was one of our main industries.

After the hurricane season that year, instead of all the spongers going to the sponging grounds, some of them went to collect timbers for the building of the three-masted schooner *Abaco*. They went near the southwest side of Abaco in two boats: the *Rester* and the *Lena Grey*. Some of the men who went to cut the timbers were Papa, my three uncles, and a few others. When the *Resource*, one of the spongers, came in from a trip, it was used for transporting the timbers that had been cut.

The keel for the *Abaco* was laid at Man-O-War Cay in front of what is now Captain M. Sweeting's home and shop during the latter part of 1917. The late Mr. Jenkins Roberts, of Hope Town, was the foreman of the job. In later years he said

Man-O-War: My Island Home

SANDS BOAT YARD

TROPHY WON AT FRIENDLY ISLAND REGATTA - 1977
SCOTT WEATHERFORD -- SKIPPER

ROUGH WATERS

WILLIAM H. ALBURY BOAT YARD

ALBURY DOCK AND FERRIES

Island Industries

UNCLE WILL'S BOAT YARD - 1972

FRIGATE BIRD II

WILLIAM H. ALBURY

GAFF AND BOOM

CHEROKEE SMACK AND DINGHIES - OFF THE BIGHT OF ABACO - 1947

Man-O-War: My Island Home

UNCLE MAURICE'S
BOAT SHED AND
WORK BENCH

THE STEM

AN UNCLE MAURICE DINGHY

DINGHY RACE IN THE FRIENDLY ISLAND REGATTA - BAHAMAS

Island Industries

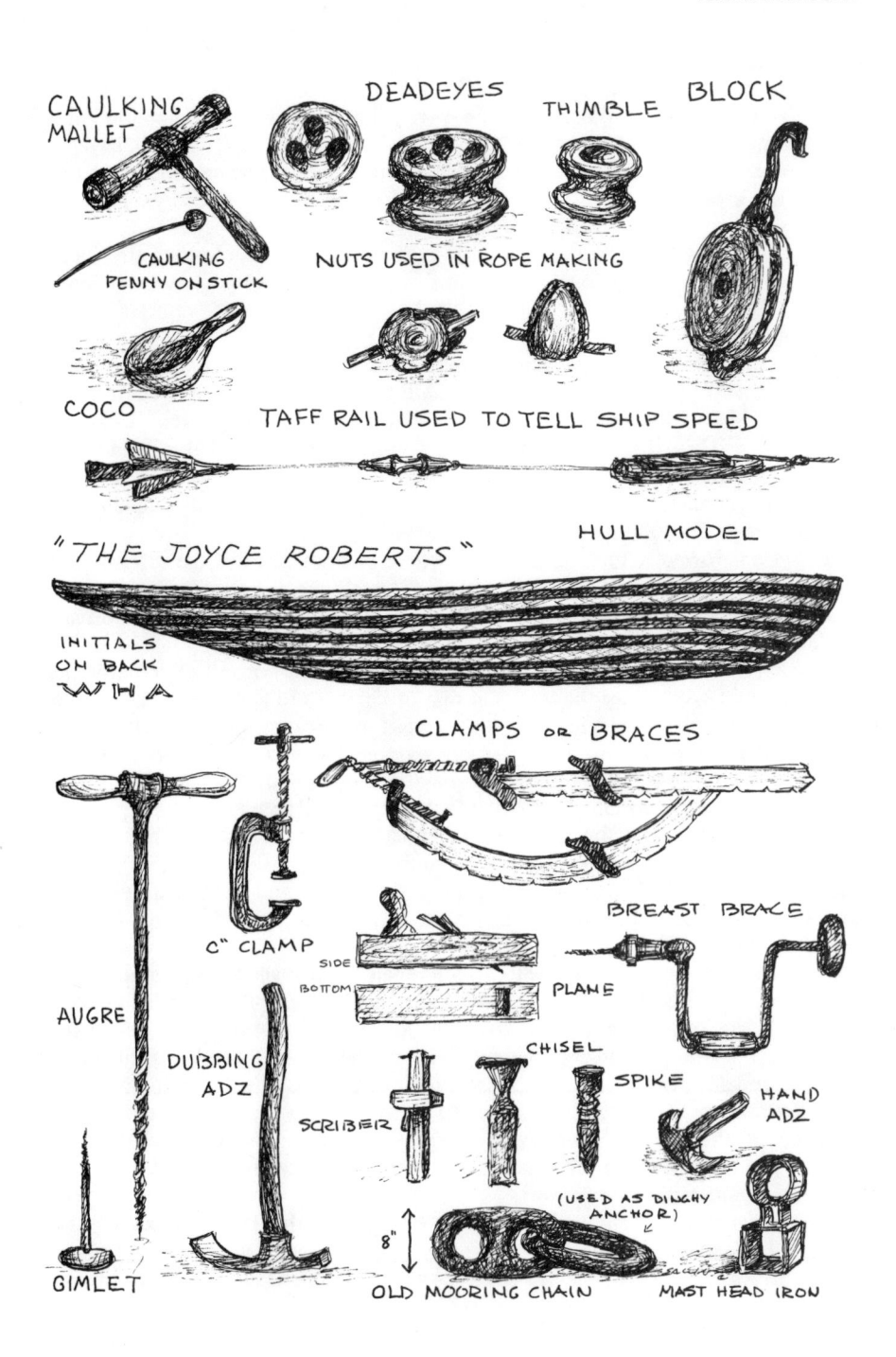

that, if his son, Skip, and his father had not been ill during the time he was at Man-O-War Cay building the *Abaco*, he would have considered this period the happiest time of his life, because he had a group of men whom he did not have to force to work. At one time, he had thirty men working on the vessel; and when the bell sounded, every man went to his job. Except for one saw, operated by a gasoline motor, the *Abaco* was built with hand tools.

At the launching Uncle Norman said, "It's the best launch ever known anywhere in this part of the world—one minute and she is in the water." Refreshments provided were homemade cakes and pies, and two barrels of soda water as no ice was available.

The *Abaco* was a three-masted schooner, with no motors. Dimensions: Keel 112', L.O.A. 130', beam 33', depth 10' (middle). The *Abaco* was used for hauling lumber from Mobile to Cuba, also from Jacksonville to Cuba. Freight rate for about a year was $25.00 per 1,000 feet. She also made several trips from Norman's Castle, the lumber camp on Abaco, to Cuba, but she could not take a full load because there was not enough water in the Moore's Island channel for her full-loaded draft. She could carry 275,000 feet of lumber when loaded.

The *Abaco* proved a successful venture for a year or so until the rates of the freight dropped so low that the owners decided to sell her. J. P. Sands Company of Nassau bought her for the sum of $10,000. She cost $20,000; but as Uncle Norman said, "She had paid for herself; so they had a little money to share."

The story of *Abaco* would not be complete if we did not tell of some of the misfortunes met with along the way. On one of her trips to Cuba after passing the western end of New Providence, the steam boat *Miami* ran into her, striking her about midship. There was no damage under water so the *Abaco* completed her trip to Cuba and then went to Nassau to Symonette Shipyards for repairs which cost $3,000. It was proven to be the *Miami's* fault so they had to pay for the repairs. It is interesting to note that the tug which came to help the *Abaco* into the harbour did more damage than the *Miami*. It smashed the tender (small power boat) on the *Abaco*'s davits on her first approach to take her in tow; and then on the second attempt, the tug struck the *Abaco*'s bowsprit, and it went through her pilot house window and broke off.

My father was one of the men who helped repair the damaged *Abaco* and he had just finished replacing the bowsprit, packed up his tools, and thought the job well done. But he looked in the harbour to the windward and saw the *Abaco Bahamas* getting under way skippered by a Grand Cayman. He was not capable of handling the vessel, and she broke the *Abaco*'s bowsprit off again, also the fore-topmast. The *Abaco Bahamas* had been built in Hope Town by Mr. J. Roberts for some of the same men of the Abaco Company. Unfortunately she never made half enough money to pay for herself, so the expense of this repair had to be paid by the owners of the *Abaco Bahamas*.

The *Abaco* went ashore in Hope Town Harbour in the 1926 hurricane. The owners, J. P. Sands Company, hired a gang of men to put in a ways and the *Abaco* was launched sideways into the sea again. In the 1928 hurricane she was in Nassau and turned bottom up in the tempestuous storm. Uncle Norman says, "I believe they burned what they could and that was the end of the three-masted schooner *Abaco*.

Sail-Making

Man-O-War has been famous for its sail-making for many years. Uncle Norman Albury has been making sails ever since I can remember, which is at least forty-five years. As a boy I was often found in his sail-loft which was a room in his home. I helped by threading needles and waxing twine. On one occasion, Uncle Norman used my pocket knife to do the cutting of the canvas. He had the knife several days; and when he gave it back to me it was as sharp as a razor.

Uncle Norman told me that his papa, Uncle Edgar Albury, began making and repairing dinghy sails in the early 1890's. The first of the larger sails he made was for the twenty-two foot boat named the *Rester* owned by Grandpapa Bill. After that he made a sail for Uncle Ben's nineteen-footer built by Uncle Billy Bo. This boat was named *Faith*, but nicknamed *Dickey's Cay*. All the sails Uncle Edgar made up to that time were Leg-O-Mutton (Jib-headed or marconi).

When Mr. Henry Fisher, Sr., was building the small schooner, *Primrose*, Uncle Edgar dreamed that Mr. Fisher came and asked him to make the sails. His dream proved to be a reality. Uncle Edgar had never cut gaff sails before, but Mr. Fisher had seen it done and he gave the necessary help. Uncle Edgar made the sails and, as usual, they were satisfactory.

Uncle Edgar continued to be busy as various boats were built. Uncle Joe, one of the famous boat-builders, launched three two-masted schooners in one day.

When one of the spongers named Sea Horse was sold and the new owners needed sails for the boat, they came all the way from Grand Bahama to get Uncle Edgar to make another suit of sails. Uncle Norman says he was ten years of age when he began helping his papa.

Uncle Edgar, Uncle Norman, and Mr. Tom Stalin of Hope Town made the sails for the three-masted schooner, *Abaco*. Some of the sails were made from new canvas, but some from the sails of wrecks. Mr. Jenkins Roberts, who was in charge of the building of the *Abaco*, helped in the cutting of the sails by draft. Mr. Roberts took the measurements off the paper, and Uncle Norman helped in the laying out and cutting.

The sails for the three-masted schooner, *Abaco Bahamas*, were also made by Uncle Edgar and Uncle Norman. Like the *Abaco*'s, some of these sails were made out of second-hand material.

By this time, Uncle Edgar was unable to do any more of this work he liked so much. Uncle Norman took over and continued to make the sails for the new spongers, which, at this time, after World War I, were large sloops. He also made most of the sails for the finished boats built by Uncle Will.

In addition to the sails for the boats built at Man-O-War, Uncle Norman made some for Mr. Johnnie Albury, Sr., and Jr., and Mr. Benny Roberts of Marsh Harbour. The sails for these large boats were made out of Woodberry canvas,

Man-O-War: My Island Home

number three, twenty-two inches wide. Some of the smaller boats' sails were made out of number six. Dinghy sails were usually made out of number ten Woodberry canvas. A large dinghy's might be number eight. Uncle Norman began using Vivatex for sails about the year 1955. This was thirty-six inches wide—thirteen ounce for large sails, ten ounce for small ones.

Uncle Norman made two suits of sails for the fifty-six foot schooner, *Windfall*, owned by Mr. Bill Norton of Newport, Rhode Island. The first suit was made out of inferior ducking about twenty years ago. It lasted only about two years. The second suit was made out of good quality ducking and gave long years of service.

When Mr. Norton's brother, who also lived in Newport, Rhode Island, saw the *Windfall*'s sails, he sent down and had Uncle Norman make the sails for his schooner, the *Whistler*. Uncle Norman told me this was the largest mainsail he ever made, twelve hundred square feet.

Uncle Norman's wife, Mamma Lina, and his eldest son, Vernon, helped in the sail-making. Sometimes they might all be busy with the hand-sewing at the same time. Uncle Norman could really push that needle through the canvas very quickly. On one occasion some boatmen were in a hurry to get their sails to start out on a sponging trip. They stood around and watched the sewing. Finally, one young fellow decided that Uncle Norman sewed so fast that the needle seemed not to move from the sewing palm on his hand. During recent years, Uncle Norman has made many awnings and boat-covers. You can see them all around Man-O-War.

About seventeen years ago, my wife, Mary, one of Uncle Norman's daughters, was at the sail-loft one day and saw a ditty-bag that someone had donated for the purpose of keeping the palms, needles, and wax. Mary thought it would be a nice style for a bag to use as a purse and so asked her mother to make one for her. Mary wanted some rope stitched around the bottom of the bag. The style of that bag became popular and many were made and sold. As time went on the style changed from the rope around the bottom to the pocketed ones sold today.

Mamma Lina also makes travel bags, cushion and bed covers. The demand for bed covers and bags increased so Lois, Mary's only sister, joined her mother and added her designs of jackets, hats, and bags to Uncle Norman's Sail Shop. Vernon and his wife, Patricia also help in the shop. They have been very successful; and Man-O-War is now well known for its bags, hats, and jackets, in all the many colours and designs. These items are much liked by the visitors and are so convenient for packing that the machines must be kept on the go, sometimes day and part of the night, to supply the orders.

Lois' daughter, Annie, and daughter-in-law, Melonie, are both working, mainly behind the scenes. They cut and sew at home, and the business could not go on without their assistance. The visitors find it very interesting to go to the shop and watch the work being done by Mamma Lina and Lois. There is always a friendly atmosphere, and Uncle Norman usually entertains with his many stories, poems, and songs.

Sponging

Sponging, as an industry, starting around the mid 1800's, was for many years one of the principal sources of income for Man-O-War Cay, Abaco, and the rest of the Bahamas.

The sponge is a marine animal usually attached to a rock or some other object on the sea bottom. There are many kinds of sponges, a few of which are suitable for commercial use. The commercial sponge, as we know it, is only the skeleton or a small part of the whole sponge.

Man-O-War Cay was involved in and profited from the building of the sponge boats, as well as owning shares in these boats. By the turn of the century there were about fifteen two-masted schooners that had been built and berthed on Man-O-War. They were owned by Man-O-War people. One of the most important boat-builders in those days was Mr. Dalbert's father, Uncle Joe.

About 1914, the beginning of World War I, some Man-O-War people decided it would be more profitable to haul lumber from the United States and Abaco to Cuba. They temporarily stopped sponging and sold the two-masted schooners because a larger boat was needed for hauling this freight. One of the three-masted schooners used for this purpose was the *Abaco* which was built at Man-O-War.

After World War I, when freight rates dropped way down, sponging again became our most important source of income. Sloops were the type of sponging vessels then built.

In those days the size of the ship was described in terms of the length of the keel rather than by overall length. The two-masted schooner was generally thirty-five to thirty-eight feet on the keel, fifty to fifty-five feet overall, with a sixteen-foot beam and a five-foot draft. Some of the schooners built here were the *Magic*, the *Serence*, *Eulah M.*, the *Complete, Doris, Emerald, Resource, Galvanic, Lily S.*, and the *Resolve*.

Sloops were also built in Man-O-War, among them those named *Olive, Louise, Alice, Regain, Lone Star, Signet, Truant, Spray,* and *Stella*. The sloop was a smaller version of the two-masted schooner. It was generally twenty-four feet on the keel, thirty-four feet overall, twelve feet beam and five feet draft.

Other features of both types of boats were low free-board, a bow-sprit, a relatively short mast, loose-footed sails, and a boom almost as long as the mast. Cabins were low. Their tops served as additional deck space for working purposes, to store dinghies or to spread out sponges. Each vessel had sleeping accommodations for her crew. Most of the eating was done on the deck. The schooner had a wood-burning fire-place in a cook-house midships; the sloop had an open wood-burning fire-place aft of the main cabin. The cost of a schooner ready to sail, without dinghies, was approximately $1,500.00. The cost of a sloop, $500.00.

Each year, a couple of weeks before the sponging season started, the captain and mate would paint and ready the boat. The dinghies were usually owned by the individuals who used them, so they were no problem to the captain or the owner of the vessel.

Without benefit of modern conveniences, such as: motors, radios, and early bad-weather warnings, the spongers had a very healthy respect for hurricanes.

Man-O-War: My Island Home

Consequently, the sponging season was limited from about the middle of October to the end of May or June.

By mid October, after hurricane season, preparations for a sponging voyage were nearly complete. The sponging vessels, bright with paint, lay at their anchors or moorings in Man-O-War harbour. Barrels of salt-beef and cans of corned-beef and fried fish were hauled by the men on their shoulders and floated to the mother-ship in the dinghies. To keep the hundred pound sacks of flour and sugar dry, they were carried on boards by two men, with pants rolled above their knees. Fresh vegetables—tomatoes, cabbage, beets, carrots, sweet potatoes, and pumpkins—were the last provisions put aboard. The dinghies were loaded on the deck of the ship and lashed down. Then began the long and often stormy passage to "The Mud" on the Great Bahama Bank. This was one of the greatest sponging areas in the world.

A sponger's working day started at dawn, when the dinghies left the mother-ship. A schooner carried eight to ten dinghies. Each dinghy was manned by a bowman, or hooker, and a sculler. While the sculler propelled the dinghy with his long oar, the bowman looked through his water-glass, a wooden glass-bottomed bucket. When a sponge was sighted, he signalled the sculler to put the boat in the right position. The bowman could then go to work.

These signals had to be known by all scullers in sponging, turtling, or fishing. Signals were "show from you," which meant push away the top of the sculling oar thus turning the dinghy to the right; "pull to you" or "go left." "let her go ahead" or "back her." The sculler used his oar to obey these signals. Then the bowman would push his hooking pole down, hook the sponge at the bottom, and with a clever twist tear or cut away the root from its lodging. A steel L-shaped hook with two or three prongs did this cutting. Made by a local black-smith, it was attached to the hooking pole.

There was much friendly rivalry among the hookers. I heard in later years that my Papa, commonly called Captain Eddie by visiting Americans, was well known as one of Abaco's best hookers!

When the dinghies were out, the cook was the only man left aboard the mother-ship. In addition to preparing a vast amount of food, he also had to tend the ship and keep it close to the dinghies. The spongers were heavy eaters. In addition to the food brought from home, fish, conch, crawfish and turtle, found near or on the sponging grounds, were part of their diet.

Sunday was observed during the sponging trips, and Church Services were held by some, either on board the vessel or at nearby cays or settlements. One of the usual Sunday dinners was home-grown baked beans, salt-beef, duff (steamed sweet dough with raisins), and native cane syrup.

A poor hooker might find it hard to recognize the good sponges, and waste time pulling up the rotten or inferior varieties. A good hooker found the best sponges, which were called the sheep's wool. The hookers nicknamed them "Checkerboards," because white reef sediment sifted over them like flour, but the eyes stayed black. Next in value was the velvet, whose eyes were bigger. Least desirable were the coarse grass sponges. Only the best of these were kept.

Island Industries

Some sponges were not attached to the sea bottom. They were called rollers. I have read that the largest sponge ever taken out of the Atlantic was found in the Bahamas about the year 1910. It was a roller. It weighed ninety pounds when it came out of the water, but only twelve after it was cleaned and dried. It was six feet in circumference and was sold for $23.00.

The dinghies returned to the mother-ship at mid-day, or maybe, not until late afternoon. Then the catch was spread to dry on the deck or on a nearby cay. Before long, the smell was terrible!

After the sponges died, they were put into a fenced-in portion of the sea called a kraal. This fence or kraal was made out of natural sticks from the slender stems of trees driven into the mud or sand. The sponges soaked for several days before the men went into the kraal with bruisers or clubs to get the black gurry out. It was no easy job to jump and stay in one of those kraals on a cold wintry day! After this organic sediment had been beaten out, the sponges were taken from the kraal and put in the sun-light to dry. Then some of them were sweet and soft enough to wash your face with.

After four to six weeks, depending on the weather, a full cargo of sponges was wet down with sea-water for easier packing into sacks and stowing in the hold. The vessel then sailed to Nassau and the Sponge Exchange. At the Sponge Exchange a stall was rented and the sponges were arranged as advantageously as possible to attract buyers, mostly Greeks. Sometimes the sponges were sold in a few hours, but at other times it would take four or five days. Naturally, the spongers were willing to spend a little time in Nassau in order to get the maximum pay for their catch.

In the middle of March, after several trips had been made to "The Mud," and when the weather was warmer, the winds lighter and the water clearer, the sponging fleet worked the Bight of Abaco for a couple of voyages before the hurricane season began again.

Sometimes, when the weather was bad, one of the dinghies tied astern might break away. Then the schooner hoisted her flag as a signal, turned stern, and, wing and wing, began its search for the lost one. If a vessel to leeward hoisted a flag, it was a signal that the lost was found.

When the vessel was returning and in sight of home, the hoisted flag was a signal to loved ones of a successful trip. Often a new flag had been purchased in Nassau and saved for this moment. When a vessel was due, frequent trips were made to the hill-tops. Two of these look-outs were the sites where Sunrise and Sunset Cottages are now situated. The first one to see the vessel might sing out in a loud voice "Sail-ho for the *Louise* coming with a big red flag!" They always seemed to know the exact boat when sighted.

No one made a fortune sponging, but many made a living. Sponging carried our economy from 1850's until the 1930's. There were two rules in sharing the sponge money. One rule was that the two men in each dinghy kept their catch separate for the entire trip. When they reached Nassau, the individual catches were sold separately by each dinghy crew. Although the Captain and Mate each had a dinghy with sculler, they pooled their catches and sold them as a team. When the sponges were sold, the food bill, usually called the "grub bill," was paid by the spongers, each paying their share. Then twenty-five percent of each sale, including Captain's and Mate's, went to the owner of the vessel. The Captain, Mate and Cook were paid out of the owner's share. When each dinghy's money was divided, the bowman received one and a half shares plus an extra half if he owned the dinghy; and the sculler received one share.

The other rule was that all the sponges were put together, and sold as a whole. The "grub bill" was paid first. The remainder was divided into shares: the owner of the vessel might get two or three shares, the captain and mate an extra share for their duties, the cook one share, the bowman one and a half shares plus an extra half for the dinghy, and the sculler one share. One share might be $25.00 to $30.00 for a successful six weeks' trip. A record share was $45.00 for a trip of eight weeks.

Papa, as well as some of the others, gave up sponging on a regular basis before the disease of the sponge, and took up ship-building and carpentry as a full-time occupation. How wonderful this must have been to my Mamma who had been left alone so much. I am one of nine children, and I wonder how she managed without Papa's daily help!

The sponge industry was crippled by overfishing and a series of severe hurricanes during the latter part of the 1920's. Sometimes the spongers would come home with hardly enough money to pay the "grub bill."

In the early 1930's some people tried to cultivate sponges. Cement discs were made. I helped to make some. They were one and a quarter inches thick and six inches in diameter. A four-inch stick set in the centre held the plant in place. One large sponge, cut in pieces, made a goodly number of plants. We planted some here in the Eastern harbour in front of our property.

For a while these sponge plants seemed to grow. However, before they came to maturity, which takes about three to four years, a world-wide blight or disease in 1938 struck and all the sponges died. By the mid 1960's, when sponges were growing again, synthetic sponges, which were much cheaper, had taken the place of the natural sponge. The industry has not been a part of our economy since that time.

Sisal

Sisal, which now grows wild on Man-O-War, has played a part in both our fun and our economy. The plant normally grows about five feet in height with a circumference of about six feet. Its leaves are sword-shaped. Each leaf is tipped with a vicious prickle. The plant reproduces in an unusual manner. An eighteen- to twenty-foot mast, growing from the centre, first blossoms and then drops, not seeds, but fully developed sisal plants.

When I was a boy, we wrote love notes on the leaves using the prickle as a pen. There were many plants along the paths outside the settlement and also on the cemetery road. When we walked these paths on our way to our farmland, and when we took our usual Sunday afternoon stroll, we could read the leaves to learn about the latest romance. It was more exciting than Dear Abby!

Island Industries

In the late 1800's, an Englishman by the name of Abbot, came to the Bahamas and went around the islands planting sisal. He bought some of the plants from the people here. Uncle Norman told me that these baby plants were very valuable and said, "A little hat full, a common measure in those days, of the baby plants would bring ten to twelve dollars. Grandpapa had two plants down on the point land, and he sold many a dollar's worth off those plants."

Uncle Edgar took Mr. Abbot around the islands in the sponging schooner *Complete* to spread the word about this new way to make money. They went to various settlements here in Abaco as well as Eleuthere, Grand Bahama and Andros.

There was a large sisal farm and mill at a place then called Drink Waters near Cedar Harbour on Abaco. Some people from Man-O-War went there to work. The sisal leaves were still cut by hand, but the cleaning was done at the mill. My grandpapa, Uriah Sanders, and his family lived at this farm from 1905 to 1911. Grandpapa was caretaker of the boats there. He took the manager and his friends fishing in the boat named the *Sea Witch*. Grandpapa also skippered the *Enterprise* on several of her trips to Nassau with the cleaned sisal.

There was also a sisal mill, owned by Mr. Benny Roberts of Marsh Harbour, at Bakers on Great Guana Cay. Our people used to sell the raw sisal leaves there. Uncle Norman's boat, the *Stella*, was one of the boats used to take the raw sisal from Man-O-War to Bakers. Often on the return trip Uncle Norman took a load of the cleaned sisal to the mail-boat to be sold in Nassau. The extra four or five dollars he received for hauling the cleaned sisal made it a profitable trip.

Sisal was cultivated on Man-O-War. Papa turned a large part of his farmland into sisal. It was cleaned by hand here. First, the leaves were cut from the plants with a sharp knife, then stripped lengthwise. They were bundled, put in the sea-water and tied to the mangroves to soak and soften. In two to three weeks they were ready for washing. This washing was done by a brisk motion in the water and by slapping the leaves on the surface, which was the way to get rid of the pulp. If the leaves were left in the water too long, the fibre was dark and less valuable.

It was not only hard physical work, but the soaked sisal had a dreadful smell. No wonder our people are now boat-builders and carpenters. Cleaning sponge, sisal, and fish were such smelly jobs!

The mail-boat captains took most of the cleaned sisal to Nassau to sell for our people. Sometimes when the sisal was ready and the mail-boat was not here, Uncle Edwin bought it and later sold it in Nassau. He did not do this for profit, but in order to give our people a quick shilling (14 cents). This was true especially during the hurricane season when the men were unable to go sponging or do anything to make money.

In the early 1900's the price of the cleaned sisal was only two cents. It remained at that price until World War I, during which time the price rose gradually to a peak of fourteen cents a pound.

When the price of the sisal was the highest, people climbed through briars and went into difficult places to get just a few leaves. It took about twenty medium-sized sisal leaves to make one pound of cleaned sisal, but only ten to twelve large leaves were required to make a pound. The leaves varied in size, depending on the soil and the care of the plants.

The price stayed at fourteen cents a pound for a while; but after the War was over, it slid slowly back to about two cents a pound. Even though the price dropped so low, some people still worked at this industry until the late 1930's. Papa and my youngest brother, Eddie, cut and cleaned some of the last sisal sold from this island. They received only seven shillings ($1.00) for the one hundred pounds that they had laboured over. That finished the sisal business.

If the cleaned sisal was not sold in Nassau, it was made into rope here for local use. First, it was spun into yarns on a wooden spinning wheel, and then laid into rope by a three-man team. As a boy I helped the teams by keeping the strands from getting tangled. All too often I found my shirt and hair getting tangled!

Rope was also remade from other rope. Sometimes a piece of large rope or hawser would get chafed or cut, leaving portions of it in good condition. The piece of good rope was taken apart into small strands called yarns, and new rope was made using the same procedure as when we made rope from sisal. Some people who worked around the docks in Nassau, or skippers of boats, saved these pieces of hawsers or dock-lines and sent them to relatives or friends at home.

I helped to take many ropes apart, made the yarns into new rope, and used it in the boats with Papa. Almost all the ropes Papa used were home-made.

Crawfishing

In the early 1930's, when sponges were scarce and the bottom had dropped out of the sisal industry, our people needed a new way to make money. We learned there was a ready market for our delicious crawfish or spiney greenback lobster in the United States of America.

About the year 1935, Captain Eddie Sawyer of Marsh Harbour, formerly of Green Turtle Cay, began buying crawfish in this area and took them to Florida in his fifty-foot boat, the *Remax*. After a while it was discovered that crawfish were more plentiful around the cays north-west of Man-O-War Cay or the area commonly referred to by us as "down the cays." A buying station was set up at Allan's Cay. Later other buying stations were opened at Carter and Fish Cays.

The fishermen from Man-O-War moved to the buying stations for the crawfish season (September through March). Of course, the men all tried to get home for Christmas and an occasional weekend when the wind was favourable. They were at least forty-five miles from home and had to travel in a dinghy under sail. The fishermen always took a supply of food: flour, sugar, dried beans, salt-pork, rice, grits, native cane syrup, lemons, and limes with them. It was too early in the season for fresh vegetables. Additional supplies were brought from Nassau and Florida. Eventually, a grocery store was opened at each station. This was a tremendous help because the boats were not large enough to hold a winter's supply. Sunday was a special day, as always, with Church Services and an extra good dinner. The fishermen lived in thatched huts. The first week they were at the station, known as the Ranch, the men were busy getting their temporary homes habitable.

The essentials for catching crawfish during the early years of the industry was a dinghy, two men, a waterglass, a tickler, and a bulley-net. A tickler is a piece of galvanized rod about three and a half to four feet long bent to a ninety-degree angle and fastened on a pole of the required length. A bulley-net is cone-shaped, about sixteen inches in diameter at the large end and about three feet in length. The large end is kept open by a galvanized rod bent in a circle and also fastened on a pole. The nets were hand-knit by some of the fishermen summer evenings and rainy days at home.

The dinghy and crew started out from the Ranch in the early morning, weather permitting. After arriving on the fishing grounds, the sculler took his stand on the stern sheets and did the sculling. The bowman began his search looking through the waterglass. Crawfish usually stay in shelter during the day and move about to feed at night. Among the shelves, shoals and reefs the bowman used the tickler to dislodge the fish from their hiding place. After the fish was tickled out, that pole was passed on to the sculler who either held it in the water to await further use at the same spot, or he might pull it across the boat. The bowman then took the pole with the bulley-net and pushed it skillfully over the crawfish. It soon entangled itself trying to escape. The bowman then pulled the valuable catch to the surface and placed it carefully in the boat.

After a hard day's work for both bowman and sculler, they returned to the station. The catch was put into a scow made of strips of wood, and left in the sea to await the arrival of the boat from Florida. The crawfish had to be kept alive because we had no refrigeration in those days.

About once a year, usually in the early spring, crawfish march in large numbers in shallow water, sometimes in one area and sometimes in another. They stay one or two days and then resume their normal behavior. Mr. Tweedie, one of the old fishermen, told me about the first march he saw, and which he believes was the first time this phenomenon was observed by anyone from Man-O-War. He said the weather had been very blustery for a couple days, but began to improve the afternoon of the second day. He and his sculler decided to try their luck in a few protected places. They caught some crawfish at the first place they tried, moved on to another, and to their great surprise, they could see, even without a waterglass, hundreds of crawfish marching, shoulder to shoulder, through shallow water. Mr. Tweedie stood in the bow of the boat and without any trouble soon filled the dinghy so full the sculler told him to stop. The crawfish were able to jump back into the water faster than he was bringing them out. Needless to say, when Mr. Tweedie returned to the Ranch, there was great excitement. Early the next morning, all the men were out to fill their boats from the crawfish on march.

The bulley-net has not been used by our fishermen in recent years. The men dive to any depth of water on the banks, channels or reefs and spear the fish. Hiding-places or shelters are old trucks, cars, stoves, refrigerators, washing-machines and drums which have been put down for the crawfish. This has helped tremendously. Sometimes a fifty-five gallon drum of fish is caught at one time.

Man-O-War: My Island Home

At the beginning of the crawfish industry the price was about two cents per pound. The fishermen could not sell all they caught because there were not enough boats in the exporting business. At that time the exporters only bought forty pounds per dinghy each trip. The export boat usually made two trips a week, but when the weather was bad it could not cross the Gulf Stream. The poor fishermen were sometimes left for as long as two weeks with nothing to do but guard their catch and wait for their pay—eighty cents ($.80). The price of crawfish has increased over the years. It now sells for $4.50 per pound. The fishermen can sell all the crawfish they can catch. With power boats and refrigeration the men can come home each night and do not have to endure the long months away from their families.

Some of the other men of Abaco, engaged in the exporting of crawfish were: Captain Rupert Roberts with two of his sons, Max and Oswald; Captain Willie Sweeting; Captain Leland Albury with Horace and Emerson; Captain Charles Sawyer with Mertland Albury; Uncle Norman and Marcell; Captain Lambert and his brother, Morrill; Captain Ernest Sawyer with his sons Roswell and Sylvan; Captain Sammie Sawyer with his son, Fred; and Mr. Harold Lowe and his son-in-law, Gerald Key. Mr. Harold and Gerald, Captain Roswell, and Captain Fred are the prominent exporters in Abaco at this time.

Most of the crawfish caught at Man-O-War now are sold to Victor Bethel of Great Guana Cay. Mr. Bethel is an agent for Abaco Food Supply.

The people of Man-O-War benefited in several ways from the crawfish industry. They built the boats used for crawfishing for themselves and also sold boats to people from other cays in the area. Through the years the sale of crawfish has really helped the income of our community.

Quarrying

One of the most important questions asked by our visitors: "What is the excavation in the rock? How did it get there?" I might explain before I try to answer the question, there were several of these on the island. I built the cottage, known as "Mary's Hideaway" over one and Edwin had one enlarged to make way for boat storage.

The side-stones for our old roads were made in these quarries. The stones are of coral. It was hard work: first, two trenches, about four feet apart, depending on the length of the rock-saw, had to be cut in the rock; then the saw which had two handles was used by two men to cut a slab eight to nine inches thick. Care had to be taken when this slab of rock was ready to be let down to the ground. Ropes were used and generally soil was piled up to stop the deep fall. Like some wood the stones were better if they were cut by the grain of the rock. Of course, the slab had to be cut up in stones of about eight inches wide, eight inches deep, and sixteen inches long. Some along our roads are a little larger. The size seemed to depend on the strength of the worker for these stones had to be shouldered to the needed area.

Quarry soil or small stones were cut by hand in these areas and used in making roads. It was toted to the working area, graded by a garden rake, and then one man beat it down with a dumb-batty or tamp, while another man kept sprinkling the soil, thus allowing the lime in the rock to help keep the soil firm. This was a good substitute for cement and tar on level ground, but not so good on our sloping cross-roads. Heavy rains would do damage to them, but as explained in another chapter, in those days it was necessary to use all available money to help our people in their daily needs. They could not use it to buy cement.

Farming a Field

Bull-dozers and such machinery were unknown by the early settlers and up to my early manhood years. Even now we seldom use anything more than a machete or cutlass to remove the bushes and trees. A few people use chainsaws for very large trees and picks for getting up the roots.

Generally, a machete is used to cut down the trees, bushes, and shrubs. The cutting is called "falling" or felling. After these dry, in about ten to fourteen days, they are burned. In order for the field "to burn clean," the bushes must be placed in the right order, not just to lie where they fall. As the falling is done, the trees or bushes as the case may be, are placed root-part towards the cutter with the top of the tree over-lapping the root-part in each case. The common expression for this is called "lapping." The idea is to have the leaf part of the tree over-lapping the bare part of the stem—hence making the burning right. By the way, the roots aren't dug up during the falling. Only some of them that were in the way were removed, as holes were dug for planting, except for certain vegetables, when the earth was plowed with a pick, grub-hoe or adze. Why burn the bushes? Well, it has its advantages and disadvantages. The advantages are that the burning kills all the worms and pests. This is a great help to the farmer. The weeds are slow in springing up, and a crop of melons or potatoes might be reaped with only one weeding. The disadvantages of burning are that some of the soil is destroyed, and also some helpful insects.

For many years there was plenty of land owned by the descendents of Pappy Ben and Mammy Nellie, so new fields were made almost every year. Insecticides were unknown and no one could afford fertilizer in those days. Cave-earth, as it was called, or bat manure from a cave at Little Harbour and from others near Hole-in-the-Wall, Abaco, were sometimes procured and used. Also wet sand from the beach was especially good for growing sweet potatoes. Seaweed was and is still used. There's nothing better for Coconut palm trees than seaweed. I've tried it. "The proof of the pudding is in the eating!"

During recent years the same lot of land has been used continually. Fertilizer and other manure is added to the soil. Stock-weeds sometimes become a problem because of this, but the vegetable crop is improved greatly.

Man-O-War: My Island Home

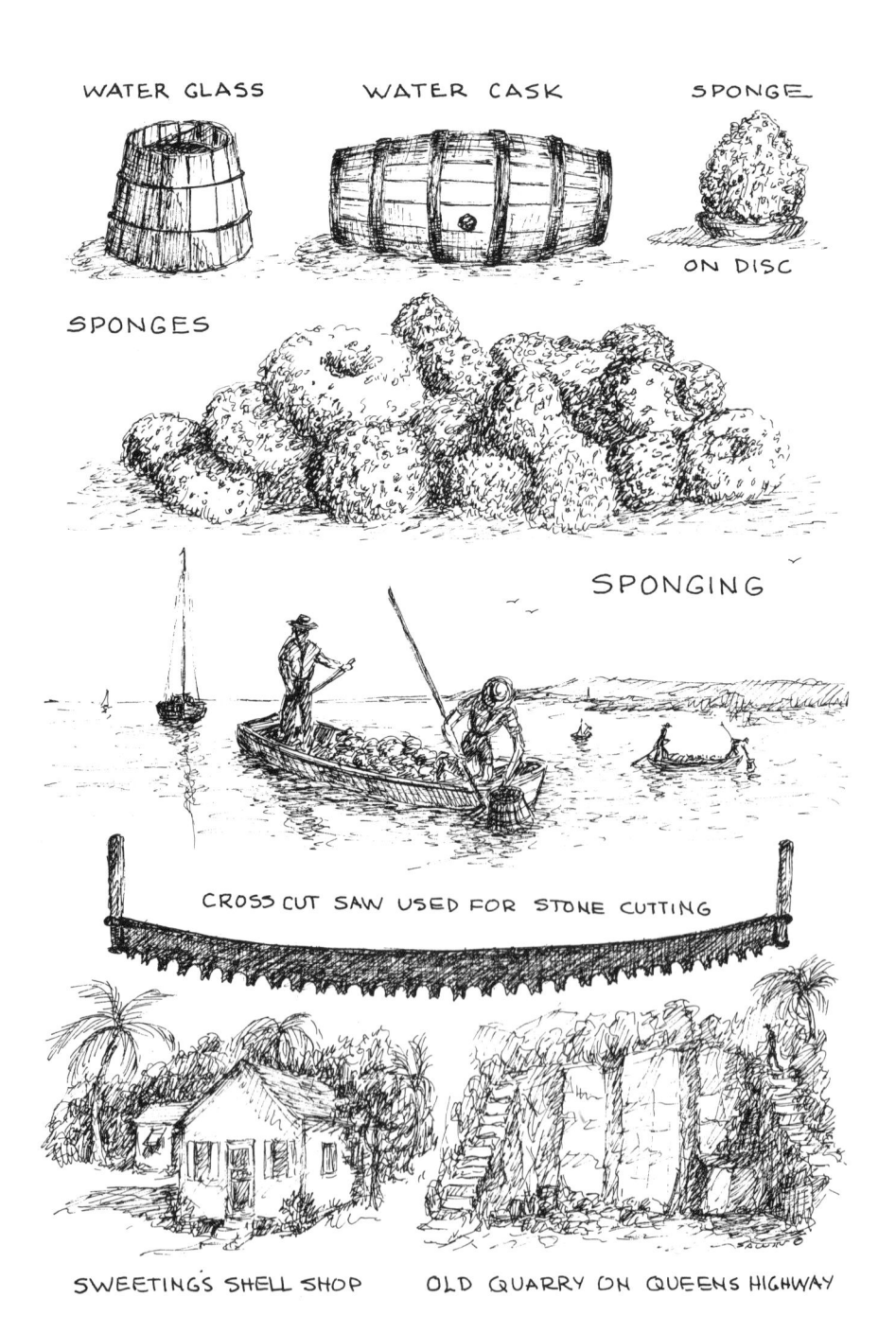

WATER GLASS

WATER CASK

SPONGE ON DISC

SPONGES

SPONGING

CROSS CUT SAW USED FOR STONE CUTTING

SWEETING'S SHELL SHOP

OLD QUARRY ON QUEENS HIGHWAY

Island Industries

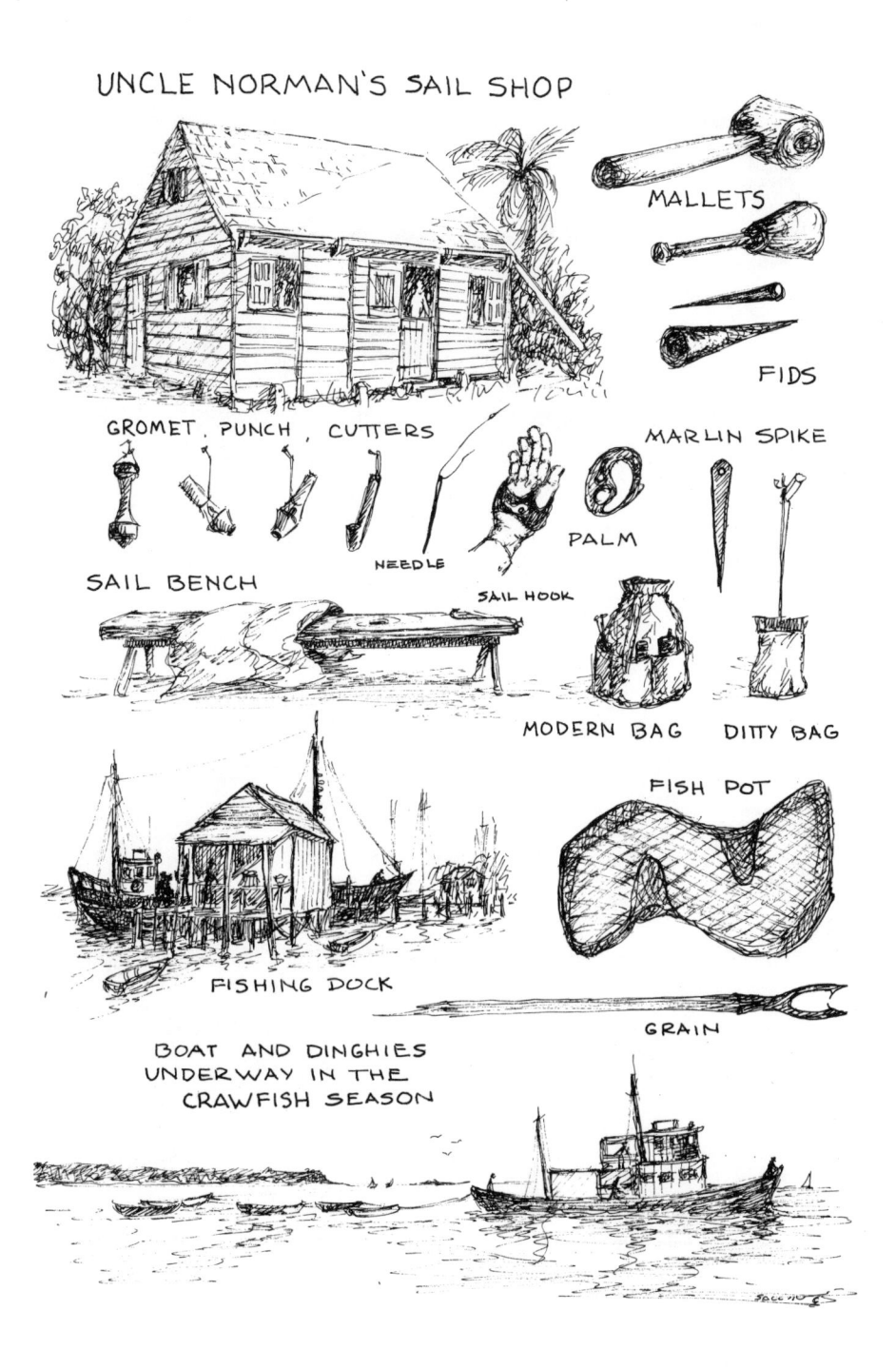

UNCLE NORMAN'S SAIL SHOP

MALLETS

FIDS

GROMET, PUNCH, CUTTERS

NEEDLE

PALM

MARLIN SPIKE

SAIL BENCH

SAIL HOOK

MODERN BAG

DITTY BAG

FISHING DOCK

FISH POT

GRAIN

BOAT AND DINGHIES UNDERWAY IN THE CRAWFISH SEASON

Chapter VII.
The Health of Our People

Medical Care

The early settlers of Man-O-War depended much on home remedies, bush medicines, for their health. Occasionally, a medical missionary visited and helped the sick and needy.

Local midwives delivered the babies, and they performed their duties in a remarkable way. My great grand-mamma, Lydia, was one of the outstanding midwives. Aunt Sarah, Uncle Norman's mother, assisted Grand-mamma Lydia during the latter part of her service. Then Aunt Sarah took over and carried on this work for many years. I remember the last years of Aunt Sarah's service. As a boy when I saw her going with her "little bundle," I knew there would soon be a birth.

The birth of a child was referred to as a "wreck." If the baby was a boy, it was called a "blue denim wreck"; if a girl, it was a "calico wreck!" Blue denim was the cloth that was usually used in making men's pants, and calico was used for women's dresses.

After Aunt Sarah could no longer do this great work, Mrs. Emma, Captain Lambert's mamma, and my mamma did most of the midwifery. Sometimes they worked together and at other times alone. Generally, the expectant mother's mother or the new baby's grand-mamma assisted the midwife. If the mother was not available, another relative might be allowed in the bedroom during the delivery period.

Until about the early 1950's, it was compulsory that the mother stay in bed for nine days after child-birth! The grandmother left her home and spent most of the time, especially during the night with a dim light in the bedroom, to take care of the baby and mother.

If the husband of the expectant mother was at home, he generally went for the mid-wife when necessary. The early morning of the 4th of August 1950, I went to tell Mamma that we needed her at our home. I found out that she had been called to my sister, Florrie, during the night! During anxious moments I walked or ran to Florrie's home as we had no golf-carts then. Just as I entered the door, I saw Mrs. Emma and Mamma both sitting down talking. It seemed that they both were breathing a sigh of relief — another baby delivered! When Mrs. Emma and Mamma saw me, they both said, "I hope you have not come for us!"

I replied, "Yes, we need you up on the hill." They told me that Florrie had a baby boy! Then they came to our home and in a short time our second daughter, Denise, was born. Florrie's baby, Ben, and Denise were born within hours of each other. I often tell them they are twin cousins.

In 1954, a government nurse, Jean Griffin, was sent here and lived in the small clinic which was built by the local people and American friends. Later, Jean was transferred and Nurse Peet replaced her. For a period these nurses used Man-O-War as headquarters and served Hope Town — five miles by water to the South-east, and Great Guana Cay — seven miles to the North-west.

Our present nurse is now living in Marsh Harbour, and with the good transportation we are able to have her here in a very short time. I might add that after our nurse was transferred, while Mamma was able to do it, she was called to the home of an expectant mother, pending the arrival of doctor or nurse. Sometimes upon arrival they found the job done!

Doctors to Our Island

One of the first doctors to give Man-O-War regular service was Dr. Mallet who was residing in Hope Town. This was about the turn of the century.

Uncle Norman spoke highly of Dr. Mallet and told this incident: "Papa went to Guana Cay one very calm night. Mamma and I went to visit Grand-mamma. On our way home, Mamma told me that she would make us a little drink of coffee before going to bed. Then as we walked towards our home, she said she could smell the swamps on the Mainland or Abaco! At that time Malaria was raging in Marsh Harbour. We came home and had the drink of coffee. Nine days later we were flat on our backs with malaria. We got so bad that Papa and Uncle Edwin decided that they should send for Dr. Mallet. It was a stormy day! Mr. Napoleon, Elsie's daddy, and others put on their oilers and went to Hope Town to get the Doctor. He came down and gave us some medicine. Mamma's was stronger than mine, because I was just a little boy. The medicine did us good, and we were soon rid of malaria!" Fortunately, there were no more cases here.

Dr. Sam Johnson was the next to practice in this area. Also in the early 1900's Dr. and Mrs. Walter Kendrick of Birmingham, England, came to Nassau and then lived in Hope Town. He was known as a medical missionary, and practiced medicine as well as preaching the good news of God's free salvation. He was a great help to our people here. However, like all doctors, there are some patients whom doctors and medicines cannot help. Dr. Kendrick was called here when Aunt Ida, Uncle Will's mamma, died in childbirth November, 1912. When he arrived at the home and saw the condition, he got down on his knees and prayed. The people said this was a sign that he had no hope or help of his own. After some years in Hope Town, Dr. Kendrick moved to Green Turtle Cay. He still visited Man-O-War at times, and our people went to Green Turtle Cay for medical aid.

As a baby, two years and eight months to be exact, I was taken ill. Papa and Mamma took me to Doctor Kendrick, and he diagnosed the case as infantile paralysis. His advice to my parents was to keep my body warm, wash in hot sea-water, bandage the swollen joints and take special nourishment. All the many forms of vitamins we have now were not available at that time. Occasionally, Virol could be purchased and this proved to be very helpful. I highly recommend "Virol" even today!

Doctor Kendrick told my parents that there was a chance that I might out-grow the disease. After many years of severe pain, when I was about fifteen years of age, I suffered the last attack! I have not been bothered since. Some people today question whether it was polio or not, because no one took it from me. Some think it was a kind of arthritis as this is common in our Albury family. Whether it was polio, arthritis, or any other disease, I know not. One thing I know, that whereas I was a cripple, now I am not! Thanks to the kind care of my parents, relatives, Doctor Kendrick, but above all thanks to my Heavenly Father, the great Physician!

Dr. Kendrick's charges were very low, and sometimes none at all. He, like the other doctors before him, were not dentists, but often practiced the extraction of teeth. He had a medicine, a formula all of his own, which proved successful in drawing out small cancers! He died on 30 July 1969.

Dr. Robert Stratton, born in Dunkirk, New York, moved to Marsh Harbour in the year 1915. He became famous as a doctor and preacher of the Gospel, and was also a tremendous help to the people of Man-O-War for many years. Many times the charges for his services were nil. He used three boats during his service – the *Evangel I, Evangel II* and *Witness*.

After the severe '32 hurricane, during the typhoid epidemic, Dr. Stratton generally made daily visits to Man-O-War, sometimes twice a day, to render services to those suffering with that dreadful disease. Instead of charging for his services, he often put his hand in his pocket and left some cash to help the families during those "hard times," as that period was called.

Dr. Stratton was very good at pulling teeth. He was so strong and clever that Uncle Will called him the "horse doctor." On one occasion when his son, Lucien, was trying to get a tooth out for Uncle Will and it was no easy job doing this, he told Lucien to go for the "horse doctor." This was done and out came the tooth!

Dr. Stratton continued to practice until he became ill himself. He died on the tenth day of July 1975. I was honoured to be one of the speakers to take a part in that great funeral service.

Dr. Evans Cottman from Indiana, U.S.A., author of the well-liked book, *Out Island Doctor*, began treating patients here about the year 1953. He married a distant relative of mine, Viola Sawyer of Marsh Harbour. During the years while he had his boat the *Green Cross*, he often visited Man-O-War and tied up to our public dock and held clinic aboard. He also came in emergencies or when the patients were not able to travel. He was always very kind and calm. He never rushed with his work; and in any case that he thought he could not help, he suggested the patients to go to someone more qualified.

For many years Dr. Cottman was called "the poor man's friend." He dispensed medicines, and his charges were so little that it seemed he made no charge for his services. For example, shortly before his death, the bill for sending a pair of glasses to Nassau to have a pin put in the frame was 50 cents. This did not even pay for the postage. This "poor man's friend" was a personal friend of mine. When our eldest daughter, Minerva, was six years of age, she had eye problems. I took her to Dr. Cottman to have her eyes tested. The test showed that she needed glasses. He ordered them for her. These were a great help to Minerva. He often told me how good Minerva was during the tests, but I think it was the good doctor and his kind attitude towards her.

Dr. Cottman had a sense of hunour as all readers of his book will agree. Some years ago he told me the difference between a doctor-fly or stinging doctor, and a real doctor. The stinging doctor gives you his "bill" first, and a real doctor his "bill' last.

He also told me about a man he helped with glasses. This was told me while he was testing my eyes. He told me how glad he was when he could really improve a person's eyesight. He said a certain man came to him and told him he was blind. Before doing the usual test with the card, he asked the man if he could see the hinges on the nearby door without glasses. The patient replied: "I don't even see the door!" Dr. Cottman carried out the test; and when he was about finished, he said to the man: "Do you see the hinges now?" "Yes," he replied. "I can see the screw-heads in the hinges." Dr. Cottman's sudden death 15th February 1976 was a shock to all who knew him. He cannot be replaced!

In November, 1959, when Owens-Illinois, transferred their pulp operations from Grand Bahama to Abaco, Dr. Ejnar Gottlieb and his wife, Mrs. Gottlieb, also a nurse came with them, and for about three years Dr. Gottlieb's clinic was aboard the *Robert Fulton* at Owen-Illinois's port at Snake Cay. He, or I should say they soon became famous for their medical work.

Dr. and Mrs. Gottlieb began visiting Man-O-War periodically and treated patients using our small clinic. To show our appreciation, the people of Man-O-War gave Dr. and Mrs. Gottlieb a new Man-O-War-built speed boat, which they used for transportation for several years. The boat was named *Doctor Fly*.

After about three years on the *Robert Fulton*, Dr. and Mrs. Gottlieb moved much nearer to us locating at the present clinic in Marsh Harbour. They continue to hold a clinic here fortnightly unless the weather is too bad or if they are on an emergency case. The Gottliebs are a great asset to Man-O-War. Besides treating people for the daily and common ailments, they are called upon for various emergencies and operations.

My wife, Mary, spent one year in Nurse's Training in 1954. Though only one year, she gained enough knowledge to put her in good stead to help in our community. She has been called upon in cases of sickness or accidents rendering First Aid, giving advice, or, if she thinks necessary, getting a doctor.

From the beginning of our settlement, there have always been some outstanding person or persons with "a good nerve" or "strong heart" in times of accidents, such as cuts at the boatyards, burns, and other wounds. Uncle Will was this kind of person during his lifetime.

One funny incident comes to mind just now. About a quarter of a century ago, one beautiful morning, Mr. Carl Russell was fishing out in the channel between the south-eastern entrance of our harbour and Sandy Cay. Somehow he got a large hook stuck into his hand. He managed to get his anchor aboard, sail up, and was

The Health of Our People

scudding his way through the harbour to get in for help. He passed a boat in the harbour where Captain Leslie, Tony's daddy, was working. As Mr. Carl passed by, the usual call came from Capt. Les, "How's the fish?"

"I've got a hook in my hand, and I'm going to see if I can get it out!" replied Mr. Carl. He sailed on and came into Uncle Will's boatyard. Mr. Russell, Uncle Will, and others came up to Uncle Will's house. While efforts were being made to remove the fish hook with the floor as the operating table, a voice was heard, "I got here as soon as I could!" In wonder and amazement, Uncle Will looked to see who this doctor could be, wondering where he could have come from and how he got the news. It was none other than Captain Les, who had sculled ashore, grabbed an old satchel, and put on some spectacles and a ragged jacket – pretending to be a doctor! Uncle Will often spoke of this as one of the surprises of his life.

Now back to First Aid and helpers. My brothers, Lewis and Eddie, and brother-in-law, Emerson, have also given valuable help and continue to do so in time of accidents.

We have been very fortunate to have among our American residents some famous doctors who have given great assistance during the absence of our doctors. Three of the outstanding ones are: Dr. Reginald Smithwick of the Massachusetts Memorial Hospital in Boston, Dr. Hermon Howes of South Yarmouth, Massachusetts, and Dr. Herman Pearse of Strong Memorial Hospital, Rochester, New York.

Dentists

In general the people on our island lose their teeth at an early age. It is believed that the rain water we drink causes this. So it was necessary for the doctors in the early times to pull or extract teeth. Some of the early settlers pulled their own teeth and also those of their relatives.

In 1913, Mamma needed an upper "plate of teeth." Papa went with her to Nassau on the mailboat, *Albertine*. The dentist, Mr. Johnson, whom she intended to go to was too busy, so another young dentist named Dr. Bleeby was recommended. Mamma went to him on 22 May 1913 and in three days she had the teeth. She tried them out for one night, and then went back to him the next morning. When the dentist saw Mamma and Papa coming into his office, he said with a smile, "Come in and bring your troubles." Mamma told him that there was one sore spot. He took the denture, touched it up on a small wheel, and gave it back to Mamma. That was over sixty-four years ago. Mamma still has the same teeth, and there have been no troubles since. The price for the teeth was three pounds ($15.00 at that time).

In the early 1940's Lucien Stratton of Marsh Harbour became a resident dentist. Prior to that time, other dentists might come here and work during brief visits, but the visits were few and far between. Lucien often visited Man-O-War in his boat the *Witness* which was equipped for dental work.

On the first day of January, 1943, I got my first upper denture from him. The price was four pounds ten shillings. That was during World War II and the pound had devalued, so it was about $12.60. Lucien and his Dad had taken out or extracted my teeth previously. Those were the days when the waiting period was three months! Some years later I got a lower denture from Lucien. We were sorry indeed when Lucien stopped this work. For after Lucien closed down his dentistry, there was another period when our people had to go to Nassau or elsewhere for dental work.

In 1964, Dr. Norman Cove of England came here, and started a practice in Marsh Harbour. He rented our cottage and after a short while his wife, Yvonne, joined him. Dr. Cove had his own boat and this was used as transportation to and from Marsh Harbour for four years. He then moved to his new home there.

Within months after the arrival of Dr. Cove, there was a complete change in the teeth and appearance of our children, and of course, some of the adults. Most of our people now visit a dentist regularly.

Our Little Clinic

One day in 1953, Bill Lee came to Uncle Will and expressed his concern about the need for a building where visiting doctors and nurses could help the sick and a place where First Aid equipment could be kept.

Bill Lee, Uncle Will, and I walked around the settlement looking for a good location for the desired building. I offered a portion of our land near our home, now called "Sunset," but as it was not in the central part of the settlement, it was considered not suitable. Finally, we decided to build on a lot owned by Uncle Will, who freely gave it for that purpose.

In a short time, the building with a homemade operating table, cupboards, and a rain-water cistern was completed. The American friends gave the money for the material, and the local people gave free labour.

Mr. Seward Johnson of Johnson & Johnson visited Man-O-War about the same time, and kindly donated a couple barrels of First Aid and other medicines to our new clinic. Needless to say, these were very helpful!

In 1955 our friend, Seward, proposed a memorial to Bill Lee, who died in July 1954. Other friends of Bill's, American and local, wanted to join in with the suggestion. Education and medical help seemed the most needed and were both of great interest to Bill. The result was the addition to the clinic which Bill had helped to establish. This addition is now used as a waiting room for patients during the visits of doctors, dentists, and nurses.

The clinic is situated on one of the hills on Man-O-War. I recall the words of my friend, the late Boris Leonardi, the first time he saw the place: "The beautiful view will be a great help to all the patients who have to come here!"

Home Remedies

As in any community, some home remedies are still in use.

For pains in joints, muscles, and persistent headaches, the remedy is called cupping. First, put some paper in the bottom of a medium-size tumbler, or drinking glass; then light the paper with a match. Place tumbler with fire over any of the thick muscle area of the body, except over the kidneys! The flesh or muscle will draw into the tumbler in a lump like a cup-cake. The tumbler is then taken off and three small cuts, deep enough to bleed, are made with a razor. Repeat the

The Health of Our People

procedure with the glass and fire, making sure to cover the same area and get about a tablespoonful of blood from the patient. Uncle Norman is a great believer in cupping and says that this causes the blood to circulate better.

For coughs, wild geranium is the cure for a long drawn-out cough, when all other remedies fail. This is a lovely, lacey-looking vine that grows on the sandy ridge or dune just up from the beach. Get some of the young branches; wash and put in a pot. Cover with water and boil for about fifteen to twenty minutes, or until the water is the colour of strong tea. Sprinkle a little salt and drink about a small tea-cup full morning and evening.

For upset stomach, mint tea, made from the mint vine, is a good soother. This is especially good for babies. The mint vine is boiled the same as the wild geranium.

For appetite, cat-nip is another remedy used by boiling the catnip weed and drinking the tea.

For strength and energy, another tea remedy is "old-man and old-woman." These are trees and so only the leaves are used for boiling.

For fever, a grass called "fever-grass" is boiled with water.

For boils, place a leaf of the weed called Blue Flower, with vaseline, in boiling water and leave until the leaf dries and place on boil.

For tooth-ache, a piece of hard-a-port tobacco, a lump of salt, or a piece of cotton wet with mother's or sister's perfume placed in the cavity of a bad tooth usually gave relief. Someone has said that the only cure for a bad tooth is to turn it root to the sun or take it out.

For ear-ache, blow pipe smoke into the ear. Repeat until patient gets relief.

For stiff neck, place castor-oil (Idle-bob) leaves around neck and rest.

For a laxative, eat a small portion of aloes, or cut it in small pieces and steep it in water. Take a small portion for a few days. Aloes is also good for the circulation of the blood. A few of our jokesters still try lemon juice in ebb-tide salt water.

For a sprain, put oakum and turpentine around injured part.

For relief when a fish or any bone is swallowed, chew piece of dry bread and swallow it as quickly as possible.

For arthritis, swim in the sea-water. If water is too cold, get a good supply and heat it and bathe in it.

For sore-throat, gargle sea-water in the throat.

For sinus problems, take sea-water in through nostrils. Sea-water is good for many other ailments. Someone has said it is free like Salvation; that's why so many people do not try it!

Thomas Albury
3rd generation

Sarah Ann Albury
Ne Sawyer
4th generation

Norman Albury, Uncle Norman
Selina Albury, Ne Weatherford
Aunt Lina

Uncle Norman's sail shop many years ago.

Skipper Robinson
& Ted Zickes
"The First Americans"

School House
a few years ago.

Haziel Albury

Uncle Will's boat yard in the 1940's.

Mary Albury

Uncle Will and Uncle Morris.

Front Row

Eddie Albury and his wife Fleetie

Back Row

Lewis, Cyril, Victor, Haziel, and Eddie (Jr.)

Mady Albury
Ne Saunders
"Aunt Mady"

William H. Albury
"Uncle Will"

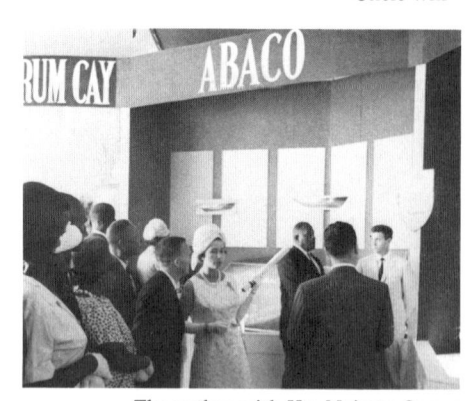

The author with Her Majesty Queen Elizabeth II in Nassau discussing boat building on M.O.W. Feb. 1966

Harcourt Thompson as a boy.

Haziel and his "Office on Wheels"

Uncle Will and his able assistants
at his boat yard in former years.

Uncle Will and one of his boats.

Tug-of-war
"Sports Day"

Vernon Albury in
action with grain
and water glass.

Chapter VIII.
Transportation and Communication: Then and Now

It was about the year 1918 when the sixty-foot schooner *Albertine*, skippered by Captain Augustus Roberts of Green Turtle Cay, already on the Abaco-Nassau run, made Man-O-War a regular stop. Before that time the Captain would kindly have the vessel "lay to" in Pointed Rock Channel to receive or deliver mails, freight, and passengers. Papa and Mamma with baby Lewis went to Nassau as early as 1913. Their round-trip fare and board on the boat while they were there was one pound ($5.00 at that time).

When Man-O-War was included in the scheduled run, the "mail-boat," as it and others that followed were called, had to anchor outside the harbour entrance and the cargo was brought ashore in a small boat powered by sculling with one of those famous sculling oars or by a sail. Before there were any docks, the crew had to get in the water, with pants rolled to the knees, to convey the cargo from the small boat or tender to the shore.

After the *Albertine* had been used for several years, Captain Augustus Roberts and his sons operated the fifty-foot schooner *Edna M.* for the mail service. (The *Edna M.* had been built as a sponging vessel at Green Turtle Cay for Captain Roberts by Mr. Johnnie Albury, the well-known builder of Marsh Harbour.)

These sailing vessels were successful and all went well until power boats came on the scene. Naturally, our people wanted a motor-boat. It was about the year 1924 when the hundred-foot steel hull *Priscilla*, which was converted from a sailing yacht to a motor vessel, powered by a 115-h.p. Fairbanks Morse Diesel became our mail-boat.

At first the *Priscilla* was skippered by Captain Leland Albury of Hope Town. He ran it for a while and it gave good service, but as the lay-over period for the mail-boat was at Green Turtle Cay, Captain Leland thought that Captain Augustus' sons who had helped their father in the *Albertine* and the *Edna M.*, should take over; and so for many years the *Priscilla* was skippered by Captain Osbourne Roberts, Captain Hartley Roberts or Captain Roland Roberts. Occasionally, Captain Cromwell Curry, also of Green Turtle Cay, and who served as mate, would be in charge.

There were no stores as we have today at Man-O-War, so the Captains of these mail-boats would generally do some shopping in Nassau for our people when money was available for such things as food, clothing, paint, and nails. They would also take to Nassau some things to sell for the people here, such as sisal, turtles, sponges, boats, and hogs. Some of the crew took hats made out of the silver-top and pond-top thatch and sold them for a commission. Some of the first money I made was by this hat business. The Roberts gave good service and those of us who were fortunate enough to know them, hold them in high esteem.

For a long time, we had a fortnightly mail-boat service. The *Priscilla* would spend one week on the Nassau-Abaco run and one week on the Nassau-Eleuthera run. After the *Priscilla*, there were other subsidized mail-boats. I'm not sure if I have them in the order they ran, but will try to mention most of them.

The *M.V. Lady Dundas*, skippered by Captain Calvin Sawyer of Green Turtle Cay; the *M.V. Content*, skippered by Captain Stanley Weatherford of Great Guana Cay: the *M.V. Richard Campbell*, skippered by Captain Robley Russell of Hope Town. The *M.V. Stede Bonnet*, built for a mine-sweeper by Symonette's Shipyard during World War II, was our next mail-boat. Captain Lloyd Albury of Great Guana Cay was the skipper of this vessel during most of her service. Other Skippers were: Captain Ancil Albury of Marsh Harbour and Captain Leland Roberts of Cherokee Sound. Then came the *M.V. Deborah K.*, our present mail-boat. It was first skippered by Captain Archie Bethel of Cherokee Sound, but now Captain Garnet Archer of Marsh Harbour is in charge.

The Agency at Man-O-War for the mail-boats was for some years run by Uncle Wesley's family. His daughter, Lilian, did most of the book-work. Then Mabel Sands became the agent and holds that post now.

We appreciate the kind services rendered by Captains and crew of all the mail-boats down through the years. There have been many hard and rough nights on that Northeast Providence Channel. I've heard Papa talk about some of these when he came as a passenger. Sometimes, when the entrance from the ocean to the smooth water inside was seemingly blocked by breaking waves, kerosene oil was dumped from either side of the ship to make the going easier.

All the mail-boats' departures from Nassau have been in the late afternoon, usually about five o'clock. It was, and still is, considered a night's run from Nassau to Abaco. These boats generally come in from the ocean at Little Harbour Bar on North Bar Channel. Occasionally, they come around to our Man-O-War Channel because of a "rage" or high seas.

In addition to our Government-subsidized mail-boats, we had excellent freight service on boats owned and operated by Captain Sherwin Archer of Marsh Harbour. From April 1940 to January 1950, Captain Sherwin used his sponging sloop *Arena*. At first the *Arena* had no motor, but later a small one was used as an auxiliary. He also had many rough crossings on that Northeast Providence Channel. I saw him come to our harbour entrance many times fully loaded with freight piled high on the deck, with just enough room for the Captain and crew to stand.

Like the Robertses of Green Turtle Cay, Captain Sherwin did quite a bit of shopping for the Man-O-War people as well as others in Abaco. At first the orders were small, but with increasing prosperity the lists became longer. He would come ashore here on his way to Nassau, walk the whole of our sea-road with his note-book, taking orders for anyone who wanted anything from a thimble to a sewing-

Transportation and Communication: Then and Now

machine, a pound of nails to an anchor, a pair of shoes to a suit of clothes, a tin of baking powder to a one hundred pound sack of flour, a bottle of aspirin to a tin of bandaids, and a pair of sun glasses to a wedding ring!! He did our banking also as there were no banks in this area in those times. With the building of boats for the Americans, cheques were introduced. Captain Sherwin took the cheques to Nassau to the bank and brought back the cash as a favour!

In January 1950, Captain Sherwin got a larger boat, the *M.V. Tropical Trader II*, and continued on the Abaco-Nassau run until 1957, when he bought a larger boat, the *M.V. Almeta Queen*. He skippered the *Almeta Queen* until 1968, when he gave way for his nephew, Captain Garnet Archer, who was skipper until it went down in a storm on the way from Nassau. Fortunately, there were no lives lost; and as already mentioned, Captain Garnet is the Captain of our present mail-boat, the *M.V. Deborah K*.

Captain Sherwin Archer was a Justice of the Peace for many years. He served as a Senator for a term; and when he was nominated as a Candidate for the Honourable House of Assembly, the people of Man-O-War gladly voted for him. He was a member (M.H.A.) in the House of Assembly for one term. He received the Queen's Certificate and Badge of Honour for his services in this country and was privileged to have Her Majesty Queen Elizabeth II pin the badge on him during her visit to Nassau in February 1966. Captain Sherwin died suddenly at his home on 2nd November 1976 and Man-O-War lost a good friend. Even though he never lived here, he was always interested and helped our people in many ways.

The first sea-plane landed here in the year 1937 during an election campaign. Edison Russell, formerly of Hope Town, was running against Frank Christie for a seat in the House of Assembly at Nassau. The plane was one of those double-winged birds and landed in the harbour just before nine o'clock. The entire community turned out to see this new way of transportation, and it was such an important event that the school children were excused for the day!

When Bahamas Airways Limited, known as B.A.L., started its operations in 1947, the people of Man-O-War had to go either to Hope Town or Marsh Harbour to get on the plane, as it did not stop here. Later, Man-O-War became a "flag stop." I had a flag-pole in my yard; and if we had a passenger or passengers, I'd put up a blue denim flag. This was a signal for the plane to stop. Of course, they stopped here if they had passengers from Nassau. The number of passengers soon increased, and Man-O-War became a regular stop. Air Mail service began. The eight-seater Goose and four-seater Widgeon were used and would splash down in our harbour, twice a day; sometimes more often when there was a charter!

There were very few boats moored in the harbour in those days, sometimes only one or two, sometimes none. It is easy to see that it would not be safe to land a plane in our harbour now — so many boats.

After some years, the Goose and Widgeon were replaced by the Catalina, a twenty-one-seater sea-plane which had to land outside the harbour. Captain Leonard Thompson of Hope Town, who served in the Royal Air Force during World War II, was one of the early plane captains. He was a great help in getting the Abaco air service. In 1957 an airstrip was built at Marsh Harbour, and scheduled

Man-O-War: My Island Home

flight to Man-O-War and the other outlying cays were discontinued.

Bahamas Airways folded its wings the 9th of October 1970, and now Bahamasair is the flag carrier of the Bahamas with daily flights from Nassau to the Marsh Harbour International Airport. There are also daily flights by Mackey International between Miami, Fort Lauderdale, West Palm Beach, and Marsh Harbour.

Passengers for Man-O-War Cay take a taxi from the Airport to the ferry dock. Albury's Ferry Service operates between Marsh Harbour, Man-O-War, Hope Town, and Great Guana Cay. Marcell and Ritchie Albury own this business and employ several of our young men, not only in the passenger service, but in the inter-island freight carrying. Apart from the scheduled flights, a goodly number of private planes – American, Canadian, and local – now use the Marsh Harbour International Airport.

Communications

In the early days, there were no communications by telephone or telegraph. Sometime after Hope Town became the Headquarters for this District, a telegraph station was located there. If anyone at Man-O-War wanted to send a telegram, it meant a trip to Hope Town by sail boat. If there was a light wind or calm, the sculling oar was used. When a telegram was sent to Man-O-War, via Hope Town, the sender would have to pay an additional four shillings or $1.00, the fee for bringing it here. This was usually only done in cases of emergency. For a few years prior to our own communications installation, we would also have to go to Hope Town to make an overseas call.

In May, 1952, Mr. R. E. Knowles and Mr. Jack I. Albury, two prominent men in Bahamian Communications, arrived here on the *Trot*, a famous motor boat for transportation in those days. At one time she was brought here for repairs at Uncle Will's boat-yard, and after inspection, one skilled workman said, "The first 'T' should be taken from the name!" These men came to install a V.H.F. (Very High Frequency) system to operate through Hope Town. The building, which cost two hundred pounds or $560.00 at that time, had already been built, and the bulk of the radio equipment had arrived by the previous freight boat out of Nassau. I well remember the words of Mr. Knowles when he stepped on the dock, "At last we are here!" There had been many delays; hence this remark. Mr. Knowles and Mr. Albury worked very hard, even many hours overtime, to get us in contact with Nassau and the outside world.

On the 24th day of May, 1952, the first telegram and overseas phone-call was made from Man-O-War. This first telegram was to thank those responsible for this great step forward in our history. The V.H.F. equipment through Hope Town was used until 1961, when we began to use H.F. (High Frequency) radios direct to Nassau.

In January 1965, we were connected with the new Forward Scatter System at Marsh Harbour. This is the present system, and we get very good reception with all parts of the world. Whenever there are problems with the equipment, the technicians at the Scatter Site at Marsh Harbour rush to help us, and we are usually on the air within a few hours. To date, we have not had the necessary equipment to do our

Transportation and Communication: Then and Now

own dialing. This is done for us by an operator at Marsh Harbour or Nassau. It is hoped that by the end of 1977 we will be able to do this.

The installation of a public booth outside the radio building some years ago has proved to be a great asset, especially to our visitors or winter residents. They can have their pleasure during the day, and then check on their loved ones at home, and also discuss business transactions. There are many times we could use a second booth — the line-up is so long!

Citizen Band radios and Walkie-Talkies have become very popular at Man-O-War and the nearby settlements. They are in most of the homes and boats operating in and around the Cay. They are also used by the taxis at Marsh Harbour. Our stand-by channel is eleven. For a conversation, we usually switch to another. The new CB's have twenty-three channels.

During the sponging days, when Papa left home for six to eight weeks at a time, he would not hear from home unless another vessel came out to the sponging grounds. In that case, when they sighted the boat coming, there were very tense moments of suspense while all waited to hear news of loved ones at home. Of course, the people at home had a similar experience!

Today, I hardly ever make even a fifteen-minute run in my boat without a Walkie-Talkie so that I can be in touch with home if necessary. What a contrast to those former days!

Chapter IX.

Firsts: The Coming of New Fangled Gadgets

Like most of the early settlers of the Bahamas, the people of Man-O-War used shark oil for lights. They twisted an old piece of felt hat, or something similar, and placed it in the oil, and lit it.

Home-made candles were also used. They were made by using cans, pieces of drift bamboo and paw-paw (papaya) stalks as forms and with a cord or piece of soft cloth for a wick. They melted the sperm found on the beach from the sperm whale, and poured it into these forms. When the sperm hardened, the form would be taken off and placed on a base or home-made candle-holder, sometimes a can or an old saucer or bottle. I made candles when I was a boy and used them when learning my lessons at night.

My Great-grandpapa Bill, commonly referred to by us as "Grandpapa Bill," brought the first kerosene lamp to Man-O-War. He bought it in Hope Town together with a can of kerosene oil with a nozzle. A supply of them had been imported from Jacksonville, Florida, brought over on one of the freight boats used for exporting pineapples and other freight. Grandpapa Bill invited all the family to be present on the night of this historical event – to see the new light! He warned them that it could be dangerous and said, "That's real oil you know!" They all stayed outside the house, peeping in at the door and windows. It is said that when Grandpapa struck the first match he trembled so much that the flame went out, and he called for some of his sons to come and light this new gadget!

They said to him, "No, no, you brought it here! You've got to light it!"

Grandpapa lit it, and at first the wick was turned down very low. All the family were excited with this first lamp; and as they drew nearer and turned the wick higher, the beams of this brilliant light added new life to the people of the island who had often strained their eyes in the flickering candlelight.

Shortly after this, the hurricane kerosene lantern was introduced and was used mainly on boats. Most families began to get kerosene lamps. The kerosene at that time was of excellent quality and gave a brilliant bluish light! It came in five-gallon cans in a wooden case, until about the mid 1940's when fifty-four-gallon drums were used. It continued this way until the late 50's when it was brought here by a tanker. As people changed from kerosene lights, stoves and refrigerators to electric ones, the demand for kerosene became much less until today very little is sold here.

When I was a boy and even up to manhood, money was very scarce, so we could not afford to keep any extra kerosene on hand. As it was one of my jobs to have the lamp ready for the night, I would often take it to the store and buy just a pint at a time. Of course, the wick had to be trimmed properly for the best results.

The way Grandpapa Bill and his family handled that first lamp may seem funny to us, but down through the years I have known kerosene lamps, stoves, and refrigerators to explode, and on one occasion, this caused the death of a young bridegroom who came here with his bride on their honeymoon. He tried to adjust the flame in a kerosene refrigerator, but in doing so he pulled the tank out too quickly. He was slushed with the oil, his clothing ignited, and he caught on fire, ran down the hill and collapsed. His dear bride ran to the caretaker in the local settlement, who, with many other people rushed to the scene. The young man was taken to the Princess Margaret Hospital in Nassau, but died shortly after. So it was wise of Grandpapa Bill to be cautious!

In the late 1940's, Aladdin lamps with mantles became available here. These gave a good light and also great heat. There were a few privately owned generators, operated mainly for lighting purposes. I had one of these which helped much with my paper-work.

In the late 1950's Chester Bethel of Nassau, and Vernon Albury of Man-O-War Cay, had diesel generators installed here to supply Man-O-War with electricity. Street lights were installed that same year. These generators, along with others as the need arose, were in use until 1974 when the underwater cable was laid. Now we get electricity from the Marsh Harbour Power and Light Company.

The first navigational light, located on the South-east end of Dickey's Cay at our harbour entrance was installed in 1949. It was a kerosene lamp which had to be attended to every evening by filling it with kerosene and trimming the wick. Mr. Isaac Roberts was our first light-keeper, followed by Mr. Arthur Weatherford. The installation of this light was a great step forward in navigation for all, especially our visiting yachtsmen. We now use an electric light instead of the kerosene lamp.

The first phonograph, or "talking machine" as it was called at that time, was brought here in 1930 by a visitor, Mr. Beuel. After visiting Man-O-War for a while, he left, intending to return very soon, leaving here most of his luggage, and the talking machine. The latter he left in the care of Mr. Nelson and his wife, Mrs. Therese. It was a portable set. Even though a small boy, I was allowed to use it or play it. I always enjoyed listening to the songs and hymns.

Later in the early 30's Mrs. Patience Albury had a very good talking machine, and people would gather respectfully on Sundays to hear the records played. Near the same time Uncle Norman brought one from Nassau, and didn't we have fun with that? Uncle Norman not only had singing records, but records with funny stories, some of which are still remembered with pleasure today. I recall Uncle Will saying he wondered why Uncle Norman bought a talking machine. He didn't need one!

As time went on, other talking machines were brought here. Later they came to be called record-players and were fairly common, and they were followed by Hi-Fi and Stereo sets. Today we have all sorts of tape and recording equipment.

"Firsts" – The Coming of New Fangled Gadgets

The first radios were brought here during World War II. Mr. Maurice exchanged a small dinghy for a radio owned by Larry Ptak of Cleveland, Ohio. Uncle Will had one and by this time Captain Lambert Sands, while away on a freighter, had sent one to his parents.

Every evening people gathered around these radios to listen to the news which at that time was war news. Elmer Davis, Lowell Thomas, and Gabriel Heater were some of the American reporters we looked forward to hearing. We also heard the B.B.C. News from London through ZNS at Nassau. The famous speeches of Sir Winston Churchill were encouraging, and the reports of the morale of the British people were outstanding. I remember one night a reporter said that a bomb had fallen in a large store, and the owner put up the sign: 'Hitler was our last customer! Will you be the next?"

Even during these sad days of war, we enjoyed various other programs on the radio – like "Amos and Andy." Of course, the highlight of the week were the Religious programs on Sundays.

Many radios have been brought in since that time and now certain homes at Man-O-War have two or three. Television found its way here about twenty years ago and now there are sets in many homes.

The first refrigerator was brought here by Skipper Robinson in about the year 1949. It was a kerosene refrigerator. Later that same year, through the kindness of my good friend, Mr. Max Feinberg, who loaned me the money, I was able to get one for our home. Later more kerosene refrigerators were bought. When gas stoves were introduced, some people then bought gas refrigerators and as soon as we had full-time electricity, some people changed to electric ones.

The first known camera was brought here by a friend of Mr. F.O. Thompson, who was my mother's school teacher at Green Turtle Cay. It was about the turn of the century during the time that Mr. Post was teaching in the Gospel Hall up on the "Hill." Uncle Norman was a small boy and a pupil at that time. The man took his camera out of a bag, and then covered his head with a black rag and said to the pupils, "Now everybody sit still. I'm going to take you!" About seventy-five percent of the pupils began to cry. They thought he was going to take them away with him. However, they found out differently. He went away alone, but after a time he sent them one of the pictures he had taken. There were the children with their hands up to their brows crying! This may seem funny, but I wonder what we might have done if we had been placed in the same circumstances. I suppose some of us would have tried to find a hiding place.

The first camera I saw was brought here about the year 1930 by Miss Malvena, the adopted daughter of Mr. and Mrs. Lanford Sands. I well remember that Sunday afternoon when the dear lady was surrounded by people requesting pictures; but she did not have enough film to "take" everybody. By that time, our people had learned to know more of the camera and the meaning of the word "take" in connection with pictures. of course, being a little more modern, she did not use the black rag over her head!

My brother, Victor, and Uncle Will were the next to have cameras. Then, during the latter part of World War II, when Uncle Will was building the auxiliary sloop

Sweetheart for Mr. T.R. Zickes, he sent a camera for us to "take" pictures as the work on the boat progressed. I had the privilege to operate that "gizmo." Cameras are now popular here with our local people, but especially with our tourists!

Today it seems strange to think that all of these changes have been so recent. We lived for many years happily without these modern inventions, I hope we can live happily with them.

Chapter X.
Sports and Recreation

The first settlers and the earlier generations to follow did not have much time for sports. They certainly had good exercise in clearing the bushes for the fields, and also the digging of the holes for plants – all done with hand tools. However, as time went on, certain games or sports were introduced.

Wrestling was one of the first sports, followed by "Rounders", a game similar to baseball. On stormy days some of the spongers might enjoy a game of rounders if they happened to be near a cay with suitable cleared ground. Children, especially the boys at home, found great delight in playing this game. They had to play in the roads or some open garden. Wreckers, the men who went to the cays near the reefs where ships were wrecked, often passed away the waiting-time by wrestling or playing rounders.

Swimming in the harbour and jumping from the decks of the sponging vessels, and other boats and also from the docks, have been done as a sport down through the years. Diving also is a sport, swimming through the water or holding to a piling of a dock under the surface, and testing who could "hold the longest breath" were and still are island sports.

Sailing, during the sponging days, served as a recreation. Although very seldom they took time to sail in races as such, the men found great delight in the sailing of those schooners and sloops. They often raced to and from the sponging grounds, or in the crossing of the N.E. Providence Channel between Nassau and Abaco. I've heard Papa talk about the fast vessels, such as *The Lily S., Doris,* and the *Galvanic.* Dinghy racing was done when I was a boy, but later faded away. However, it is being revived, and our young boys seem eager to get in on this sport.

Sloop racing has been part of a Bahamian way of life for many years, and in recent times there has been an annual race in April. During the early part of 1975, a sloop named *Abaco* was built here by the "William H. Albury Ship-builders, Limited," to enter the races at the annual Bahamas Family Island Regatta at George Town, Exuma. Stewart Stratton of Marsh Harbour was the skipper, and I was fortunate to be a crew member.

The *M.V. Fendo*, owned by the Marsh Harbour Shipping Company, Limited, and Captained by Lewis Key, kindly towed the boat to George Town, and boarded most of the Abaco's crew and other visitors for the week of the races. The *Abaco* was also towed back by the *M.V. Fendo.*

I was invited to board on the Trawler, *Sea Lark*, and I received royal service from the owners, my friends, Phil and Dottie Sawin. I had some meals on the *Fendo*, and I enjoyed them very much. I commend Captain Lewis Key and his crew for their kindnesses.

This was our first experience in these races which have been going on for twenty-two years. After we arrived at George Town, we realized that the only chance we had was if it blew a strong wind, because the other boats had almost double the sail area. The kind people of Exuma and other visitors said they felt sorry for us. "You Abaco people have the best built boat," said one man, "but you can't win the race with a handkerchief for a sail!"

Before the races, some of our boys challenged another man, saying, "We are going to take the Cup to Abaco!"

He replied, "You might take a cup to Abaco, but you'll have to go back by way of Nassau and buy yourselves a cup from the "Nassau Stop-N-Shop."

There was a strong wind until the day the races were due to start. They were postponed because some of the boats had not arrived, but on that day we raced some of the boats which were there. We kept up with the sloop *Good News*, the 1975 winner. Judge how we were encouraged. However, we noticed that the more we sailed, the more the Abaco's sail stretched. The material was very poor. By the way, that sail was not made at Man-O-War.

On the morning of the first race, the exciting moment arrived. The signal was given, and with each man trained well by our Skipper, the *Abaco* was the first of the fleet to get underway. The wind was still fairly strong. We crossed the *Good News* on the first tack. Unfortunately for us, the wind gradually decreased. The other boats let out their reefs and away they went in the light wind!

The *Abaco* did much better the second day. For a while, we sailed tack and tack with the *Thunder Bird*, a former winner, which went around the buoy just seconds ahead of us. But when we should have gone around it, the *Stormy Weather* was now under our lee, so we could not keep off as she stayed until we were some distance out of line. She swung off without even going around the buoy. We ran off and rounded the other buoy ahead of the *Stormy Weather*. We were now in fourth place. When she came to the buoy, she hooked it in her keel, rudder or something, and carried it with her. The other boats which were behind us, seeing what had happened to the buoy, heaved to, thus putting them to windward of us. Well, to make a long story short, it was fun and did not matter too much unless we could have made it first. That race was for the Prime Minister's Cup, and the first boat was the winner—no seconds or thirds, no points taken into account. Without any mishaps, we might have third or fourth place in that race.

At the end of the second day, the sails on the *Abaco* were stretched badly. It was decided not to attempt the last day. My nephew, Scott, one of our crew, asked the Skipper of the *Tidal Wave* if he could go with him as crew. The skipper and crew welcomed him aboard, and he enjoyed their friendship as well as the sail on the boat. Taking the points of the other races into consideration, we came seventh in a fleet of eleven boats.

Sports and Recreation

Well, what our friend said about the "Cup" was right. However, we did not bother to buy a cup. It was hoped that we would win it someday. The skipper of the *Good News* trying to encourage us said, "Don't give up; I came last for the first three years, but I kept at it, changing this and that; now these two years, the *Good News* won!"

We returned home, not at all discouraged. All who saw the performance of the *Abaco* felt that, if given another chance, a larger sail, and by moving the mast forward and putting more lead in the keel, she could make a better showing. Some thought she could be the "Winner." However, it was decided to build another boat and try it in the races. It was built and completed in time for the 1976 races.

When the owners of the *Abaco* decided to change the name they offered a $10 prize to the pupils of our school for the best one given. All of the names were very good but finally the three best were put into a bag and the one pulled out by one of the pupils was *Rough Waters*. A very suitable name as this boat performs best in heavy winds or rough waters.

In the meantime, the *Abaco* was refitted and given the name *Rough Waters*. The new boat was given the name *Abaco II*. I was invited to be a member of the crew of the *Rough Waters*, but had to turn it down due to other duties.

As in 1975 so in 1976, the skipper and owners of the *M.V. Fendo,* were very generous in the transportation of boats and people. Again some boarded on the *Fendo* during the stay in George Town. Because of a rage both boats were put on deck for the crossings.

In November at our first Annual Abaco Regatta *Rough Waters* performed well and on the last day crossed the finish line ten minutes ahead of the other boats.

Rough Waters proudly crossed the finish line *first* in five consecutive races in Class A at the 1977 Out Island Regatta at George Town, but under the handicap rules received a second place in overall performance. She was first in the Prime Minister's Race and brought back his cup to Man-O-War this same spring.

To celebrate the victory, more than 250 people gathered here for a buffet dinner celebration to honor the crew, designer, builders, and supporters of the sail boat *Rough Water* which made history when it crossed the finish line first in five consecutive races in class A at the recent Out-Island Regatta at Georgetown, Exumas.

I acted as master of ceremonies and led the group in cheering for and congratulating the Man-O-War captain, crew, and the builders. The festivities were attended by local residents and visiting boaters and tourists. All enjoyed the spirit of the affair and the excellent food prepared on the island.

A short period of silence was observed in memory of William H. Albury, the "Uncle Will" of Abaco boating, who for years set the high standards in boat building which proved themselves in the recent performance of the *Rough Waters*. The children sang the Bahamian National Anthem and every one felt warm and appreciative when told of the wonderful friendly spirit and welcome that all who attended the Georgetown Regatta were shown by the officials of the races the competing captains and crews, and the residents of the lower islands.

Man-O-War: My Island Home

As young children we had many games. One of our great excitements as boys was to get a half of a coconut, use a stick for mast and sea-grape leaf for a sail and let it go sailing along the sea-shore. Occasionally, one got out of our reach and away it sailed all the way across the harbour to Dickey's Cay. Believe me, that seemed a much greater distance than it does today.

For many years kites and tops have had their seasons, and it could be any time of the year. During my boyhood days we made our own kites from strips of some light wood, pieces of wrapping paper and glue made from flour when we could affort to use the wee bit for that purpose. It was tricky business to get the right length and weight of the tail. It was common to use the plat of an old hat. Sometimes a branch of a tree might be used as a tail. When line was available, we would send the kites up in triplicates. We would mount one kite and let it go up, then tie another line to the top of the second and then the third. As time went on, we were able to purchase different colours of tissue paper and some kind of glue. We really made beautiful kites then. Today, we see other kinds of kites which are bought-made. Some of these are beautiful and bring pleasure to the owners as well as the kite-watchers.

Spinning tops were also homemade until recent years. Dog-wood and lignum-vitae were the best woods for making tops. A galvanized nail with the head cut off was used for the peg. Although our boys can afford to buy tops now, I am pleased to see some of them making their own as well as some for their friends.

Marbles was a great sport when I was a boy. With no vehicle traffic we often "played marbles" in the roads, and sometimes in our yards. After the "32 hurricane," our family spent about eight weeks at Green Turtle Cay. Papa and Victor rebuilt Uncle Dawson's house during that time. I often played games with the boys near my age there, and we were able to exchange ideas. I really enjoyed that visit as the friendships started there have continued down through the years, and most of my friends have done well in business. The present Postmaster of the Bahamas, Mr. Harris, is one of them. I am wandering now so let me get back to the point I want to bring out.

With no police here, we could spin our tops or play marbles in the road; but in Green Turtle Cay, the police, in carrying out his duties, could not allow this. Sometimes, we took a chance, but generally we used a cleared lot of land or a yard to have our fun! Playing marbles seems to be a "thing of the past" as it has been a long time since I have seen any quantity. Occasionally, I see a marble when clearing one of the old house-lots.

Hiding was one of our games. One of the hiding games was called "Run, Sheep, Run." A group of boys would divide into two teams, each with a captain. The last of my years of playing this game, we often flipped a coin to see which team went off to hide first, but in the early days, coins were scarce, so we said a little rhyme, with all the boys standing in a circle or a line, until we got the required number. One of the famous rhymes was: "Two, four, six, eight; Mary at the garden gate, Picking Cherries ripe and green. Two, four six, eight." The team captain then called his group together to give them instructions what to do. I might explain the gist of this game. First there was a home base. The boys who were sent off to hide tried to

Sports and Recreation

get back to base and put a foot on it before anyone of the opposite team could see him and get to the base first. If the searching party touched the base first, then the other was "Out!"

After giving his group their orders and they had disappeared in the bushes, the team captain crossed his fore-fingers with one of them in the direction of the hiders. The searchers chose their course by pulling a finger, and then began looking, not daring to go far from the base. The team captain called out certain phrases, a code to let his friends know how to creep, and what to do, such as "Lay flat," "Creep slowly," "Fried fish," "Ripe bananas," and so on. If or when one of the searching group saw one of the hiders, he shouted, "Run, sheep, run!" If the hider got to base first, that team had another turn; but if it was one of the searching team, then it was their chance to hide.

"Cow-boys and Crooks" was a game brought here from Nassau by my Cousin, Thomas. This was popular for a while, and it is similar to the American game of "Cops and Robbers."

Now, what about the girls? Skipping has been one of their favourite sports for many years. "Sweet-bread and butter, come for supper," was once played here. This game was played by one girl hiding an object, usually a small branch of a tree called a "switch". The one who found it had the chance to hide it and so on. Other games were "Pass my gold ring", and "Miss Jennie Jones".

Games by boys and girls were: "The Farmer in the Dell," "Go in and out the Window," "Bluebirds through my Window," "Here I Stand in the Well." Some of these games or sports are still carried on by the children. However, ball-games seem to be the most pleasure during the last two decades for my senior pupils and the young people.

About the year 1956, we got our first school playground. My school boys and I did the clearing with machetes, axes, picks, and rakes. Games and sports became more interesting. Although much too small, the first soft-ball games were played in this playground. The balls were often collected out of the adjoining bushes and trees. Later we got our basketball court. My pupils still play soft-ball on the school playground. Basket-ball and volley-ball are played by both my present pupils and my ex-pupils who are really the young people of Man-O-War.

During the year 1965, our young people became so enthusiastic that they realized the need for a ball-field. By the kindness of Uncle Will and my son-in-law, Billy, the land became available. By the hard work of our men and the help from our Government, we had a field for day-playing by the end of 1965. Lights were installed the latter part of 1967. This has been a great asset to our community. Our young men have learned to play without quarreling. There are no games on Sundays nor on the Church Service nights. This is again indicative of our God-fearing people! Teams from the other settlements come here. We have had teams from Hope Town, Green Turtle Cay, Marsh Harbour, Dundas Town, Cherokee Sound, and Spring City. The Man-O-War Team has also enjoyed playing return games at these places.

There are many other games and sports which our children enjoy. On the 10th July, Independence Day, is our sports day. At eight in the morning, old and young, meet at the main public dock. School songs are sung, followed by a prayer of thanksgiving. All are welcomed, especially the visitors. Then the fun begins! An old-time washing tub is put on the ground, usually in the road, enough water to cover a child's head is poured into the tub; a small amount of evaporated milk is added, not much—just enough to make the water cloudy! The children then take their turn diving into this solution and collecting coins which have been put there for this purpose. The hands are not allowed in the tub. The money must be picked up with the teeth. By-standers or spectators continue to throw in coins as others are taken out. Near the end of this sport, two children might be allowed to dive at the same time. What a splish-splash!

With the money diving over, the swimming and diving races begin for all ages. In the meantime, a greasy pole is being prepared. A part of this is lashed to the dock with the greasy part extending out over the water. A piece of canvas is nailed into the end of the pole. The fellows slide out trying to get the canvas. Do they work or really play? They line up on the dock and after trying and falling into the water many times, one finally succeeds and tears off the canvas. Then a stick is nailed on the pole and the fellows have to walk out and break off the stick. There is also a sculling race. I had not done much of this since my young days. However, I managed to finish in second place.

When the water-sports are over, the crowd then moves to the school premises, where we have sack races, three-legged races, skipping, running, and last, but not least, tug-of-war between married and single men and women. Generally, the married ones win; but on the 10th July 1975, the single ones defeated the married. This was a record in our tug-o-war history.

After these activities, everyone is tired and ready for refreshments. By the generous donations of money, cakes, pies, and fudge, there is a great feasting time. The prizes, consisting of different sizes of hams, chocolates, and other sweets, are presented after the meal.

There is a dinghy sailing race in the late afternoon. I came in second two years ago in my dinghy, which was the last boat built by my Papa.

Fishing is a great sport, and is enjoyed by young and old. Fishing is done from the docks, beaches, along the rocky shore, in the channels, reefs, and the Atlantic Ocean. The famous bone-fish are caught in the harbour or near the harbour's entrance. Groupers are caught in the channels and near the reefs. Snappers, blue runners, and many other fish are caught in almost all the waters surrounding our island. Tuna, sail-fish, king-fish, and others are caught in the ocean.

Beach-combing is now a hobby by many people, and the net-covered glass-ball is one of the most valuable items found on our beaches. It floats all the way from Portugal, and no doubt other places as well. After a couple weeks of northeast to east winds, one or more might wash or roll up the beach. The first one at the right spot is the finder and owner. Some time ago one was found in front of our property. When we saw our friend walking out with it, Mary said, jokingly, "That should be mine! It was so near our home!"

I said to her, "My dear, it will never float to your bed!" The early risers are likely to be the finders. However, Mary did find one about mid afternoon one day.

Sports and Recreation

In the early days, beach-combing was not a hobby, but rather a means of helping to earn a living. Lumber, sometimes in large quantities, from freighters, sometimes washed off their decks, or unloaded at sea by the crew because of storms. This lumber was used in building houses and boats. I have often heard Papa talk about the excitement when the beaches were covered with good yellow pine.

Ambergris, a waxlike substance from the intestines of the sperm whale, was another valuable item found here years ago. Valuable, because it was used in the manufacture of perfumes. Sperm was also found on our beaches, but this was not valuable like the ambergris. However, it was good for greasing black irons at the end of ironing day. Would I know!

During World War II and a few years after, bales of rubber were found on our beaches. These found a ready market in Nassau, and the price was considered to be very good. Rafts, loaded with food, were also found during World War II.

Conch pearls used to be very valuable. Some people would go and gather conchs in search of the pearls. These are not so valuable today. However, some are used in rings, necklaces, and bracelets. They make a good gift for a wife or girl friend.

Chapter XI.
The Coming of the Americans

During the winter of 1938, Mr. Charles M. Robinson, known as "Skipper" from Maryland, U.S.A., Mr. Theodore R. Zickes, or Uncle Ted, and his nephew, Laurence J. Ptak or Larry, both of Cleveland, Ohio, found their way to Man-O-War Cay.

How did they get here? These three yachtsmen, fleeing the chill of the cold north, learned about Man-O-War and our boat-building from some of our local crawfish exporters in Miami and West Palm Beach.

The American trio came across the Gulf stream in a boat named *Windstark*. They got as far as Allan's Cay, a Crawfish Station, and enquired from Captain Leland Albury of the boat Alburys and if he could recommend a good pilot to guide them on their way through the rest of the Abaco Cays. There was no "Yachtsmen's Guide To The Bahamas" such as we have today. Uncle Norman was recommended. He and his son, Vernon, were at Allan's Cay crawfishing in his sloop the *V. M. R.*, named for Vernon, Marcell, and Ritchie.

Now the big question arose! What would it cost? Uncle Norman offered to take the responsibility for $10.00. This meant, at least, ten to fourteen days. Sounds like a small sum, but this would be double or triple what Uncle Norman and Vernon would make at selling a limited amount of crawfish at two cents a pound!

The trip was arranged. Uncle Norman got aboard the *Windstark*. Vernon started on his way home in the *V. M. R.* Some Guana Cay fishermen came along with him. All went well until they got near Whale Cay Channel. There was a "rage" on. Vernon made it through, but Uncle Norman thought it best to turn around and put into Green Turtle Cay for the night. Skipper, Uncle Ted and Larry thought this a good idea, as the battery was dead and the motor would not start. Fortunately, they were able, through the kindness of the wireless operator, Mr. Neville Key, to get the battery charged—"good and hot" as he described it!

The next day the *Windstark* left Green Turtle Cay, and with Uncle Norman at the wheel made it safely through Whale Cay Channel. On his arrival he was glad to learn that Vernon and the others had made it all right. There were no telephones in those days!

After arriving at Man-O-War, Skipper, Uncle Ted, and Larry met Uncle Will, Uncle Dick, Papa, and other men who were here at that time. The trio were given a tour of the settlement including the boat-yards. In those days visitors were given fresh fruit, vegetables, and 'chicken' eggs. Emphasis should lie on the 'chicken' as there were 'bird' and 'turtle' eggs as well. When they got to Uncle Will's house, he ran out in his back-yard, and came bringing some special grapefruit. Uncle Ted thought he would try one right away. So he cut it open; and as the juice ran down his chin, he said, "I'm getting a bath as well as a drink!"

Just before our visitors left, one of them said, "I'd like to be a little bird after we leave and hear what you people say about those 'crazy Americans'!" This saying stuck and often after, Uncle Will would call them "crazy Americans" or they would refer to themselves as such!

They left Man-O-War and Uncle Norman guided them on their way, showing them the main places of interest. They stopped at White Land, met Uncle Earnest, and enjoyed some fresh coconut water or milk as it is sometimes called. Uncle Norman then saw them safely out over Little Harbour Bar where he received his pay! The trio went on their way, and Uncle Norman returned home in the boat which had come along for that purpose.

As a result of this visit, many Americans have come to know and love this place and our people. An immediate result of the visit, Uncle Will was commissioned to build a 30-foot Auxiliary Sloop, *Sweet-heart* by Uncle Ted.

The *Sweet-heart* was left here, and each year until World War II ended Uncle Ted, accompanied by Skipper or other friends, came down for a week or two. Uncle Will would have the boat spick and span for their arrival, and usually met the mail, freight, and passenger boat from Nassau at the East Side of Marsh Harbour or at Hope Town. These were stops before Man-O-War, and Uncle Ted was anxious to get on board his *Sweet-heart*. Generally, Uncle Ted and his friends cruised the Abaco Cays. Vernon was hired as cook and pilot. He became a favourite of Uncle Ted, and was highly praised for his tasty meals by all who were fortunate enough to get to the *Sweet-heart*'s table. A common expression Vernon would hear as he worked in the galley, "How long will it be?" Of course, this came from those in the cabin who sniffed the odour of the food on the stove! Uncle Will, Uncle Dick, Mr. Maurice, and others were sometimes invited and went along with Uncle Ted. I had the privilege to go on one cruise. Here is a copy of the log kept by Skipper on that trip:

LOG OF THE CRUISE OF THE SWEETHEART   February 1944.

Left Man-O-War Cay Saturday, February 12th, 1944 with five aboard.

T. R. Zickes	Owner
C. M. Robinson	"Skipper"
Wm. Albury	Builder
Vernon Albury	Cook and general Advisor
Haziel Albury	Secretary

Bound for Green Turtle Cay. A most beautiful day. 12 noon, have made 15 miles under sail. Lunch served on deck. Clouding and wind going N.W. (ahead) 3 p.m., beating still 2½ miles out. Steady and beautiful sailing so far. Aground entering Green Turtle Cay harbour. Anchored and all ashore except Vernon. Town unchanged. Back aboard for supper after which William, Haziel, and

Vernon went ashore to see "COUSINS" and friends. Ted and Skipper to bed. (The rough sailing had stirred drinking water badly and that had to be taken care of.) The boys back aboard very late!

Sunday, February 13th. Corn-cakes for breakfast "YUM YUM". Weighed anchor at 9:45 a.m. bound for Spanish Cay. Wind fresh N.E. Fair for us. So far—so good. 12:31 up to dock at Spanish Cay. Children soon reported arrival of "Boat." Mrs. Bootle came to greet us. Soon Mr. Bootle, giving us a cordial invitation to come up to the house. So we planned our lunch and then a visit. Bootle is the caretaker, and it is interesting to note that the owner has not been on the island for eight years. Later we found things a bit neglected, since our previous visit some four years ago. Knowing the reason for this would be interesting. The palm trees in front of the house have become a beautiful grove, but also are beginning to break the most beautiful view of the Sea. After going into the man-made hurricane cellar (this is cut right out of the solid rock), we returned to the "Sweetheart" at 2:53 p.m. and cast off for Allan's Cay. Sailing still beautiful. Wind steady N.E. and clear. Arrived in harbor at Allan's Cay at 5 p.m. Anchored in a very quiet spot and were visited by the Crawfish Inspector. Wind still N.E. strong at 8:10 p.m. Captain and entire crew full of mackerel and ready for bed. In bed all discussing "World Topics." All saying the N.E. wind will last three days.

Monday, February 14th. 7:30. All up and corn-cakes for breakfast. Wind still fresh easterly so cannot fish outside. Long discussion which ended in a question of ages, and this suggested the old song, "I'm going to live anyhow until I die." Dinner at 1 p.m. and in spite of boisterous wind weighed anchor at 2 p.m. Trolling near Umbrella Cay. Result two mutton and two rock-fish, totaling 45 pounds. Trolling one hour which spells good fishing. On way back to harbour we presented the crew of the Bahamas Sea-Food Company's barge with the larger rock fish, and the other rock fish to a woman ashore, hoping to make some trade for sweet potatoes or pumpkin, but this idea failed. One of the mutton-fish was presented to the Crawfish Inspector. The remaining mutton-fish is now being prepared with potatoes, tomatoes, onions, and does it smell good! Result a very delicious stew and there must be a pause here. Still blowing fresh and William has decided to put out two anchors which indicates that something real might happen tonight. We all hope he is wrong. There is much evidence that Capt. Zickes is really becoming interested in an island. In fact he has today suggested to Skipper that they go 50-50 and buy one. That started some argument which will take some time to settle. However, the problem of which island will take time to solve, so no decision can be made. The second problem is proper transportation from the U. S. Many happy hours will pass before these two weighty things can be untangled.

Tuesday, February 15. All awake at 7:20 a.m. and bound for Umbrella Cay for "Whelks." To the reader a sort of enlarged snail. They cling to the rocks and are exposed at low tide. They make a delicious stew. On our way we caught two mackerel about 5 pounds also one hog-fish too large for our scales. We started to motor from Moraine's Cay to Fish Cays but Isabella (the motor) refused to move! Bill jumped her and worked all day under the very numerous suggestions from Capt. Ted to no avail. Haziel succeeded in getting us inside Fish Cays with sail, where the rest of the day was spent wrestling with Isabella. Looks like we will spend the night here with Isabella still rebelling. Haziel and Vernon fished all afternoon and Ted and William worked all afternoon while Skipper took his usual sun bath and nap. The fishermen brought a good supply of whelks, crawfish, hog-fish and margots. We certainly won't starve. The problem now is how we are going to use up all the food stuff we brought from Nassau. Weather dead calm, clear and promises of more of the same. At present we are waiting for the cook to say how long it will be before the hog-fish will be ready. He says about 45 minutes. Hog-fish for supper and we all decided it was better than any fish served in the U. S. A. Then we started in a shark expedition, and did things happen! Capt. Ted had provided a shark fish hook. This started an argument as to how long a chain should be on a shark hook. The first shark hooked decided for us at once that a two foot chain was not long enough. This was done by his swallowing bait, hook and chain and then bit the line off after considerable tugging by three of us at once. Thereupon we rigged up some smaller hooks on which we caught several sharks and a moray, no less! When this was discovered the crew almost left the boat. But Vernon, with his handy club (bilge pump handle) immediately went to work and quieted things down even the moray. After hopping down about a half dozen times, Skipper decided to turn in for good, whereupon the crew decided to move the boat and it seemed as if all work was done on deck directly above his berth. All in bed and quiet at 10 p.m. Weather promises clear and quiet.

Wednesday, February 16th. Day breaks beautiful and clear. Light easterly wind. William and Haziel went ashore to operate on about one hundred fine whelks and also to get some fire-wood. Incidently, on their way they caught a fine turbot. They went ashore without a knife which is a lazy man's way of passing the buck. So the job fell on our good cook who performed it gracefully, resulting in about a peck of beautiful whelks. Weighed anchor at 9 a.m. bound for Carters' Cay. Vernon and Haziel went off in dinghy at Fish Cay Rocks and caught some crawfish, while Capt. Ted, William and Skipper went slowly on their way with very little wind. This lasted all the way to Carters Cay where we anchored at 5:15 p.m.

The sight that greeted us ashore was most primitive. The folk were peaceable, but not inclined to note us or to greet us in any way. Squatting around the thatched huts near open fires on which their evening meals were being prepared, they paid not the least attention to us when we were looking and those whose meals were ready were busy indeed chatting and eating. A few late-comers returning from their day's fishing were selling their catch to the Crawfish Inspector. Strange to say, the Government Inspector was also their only buyer. Their shouting from boat to shore and back made a weird lot of noises which meant not the least thing to us but was obviously well understood by all of them. Ashore we found what they called a store from which we were able to procure a few food supplies, mainly cane syrup. To our surprise we found that the storekeeper was the same Inspector and he preferred to receive our order, prepare it and deliver to the *Sweetheart* later. We decided that this was done in order to make sure of an invitation to board the ship. He did this later stating that our bill was 13 shillings and 9 pence. Finding that Isabella had refused to perform he graciously offered to take it to pieces. Very much to our surprise, because of the many detailed instructions offered by our beloved Capt. Ted, he was given the opportunity. His services did not suit the engine though Ted had given him full privilege to go the limit. So that now we wonder if the good ship *Sweetheart* can rightfully be called an auxiliary sloop, for on the quiet we really suspect that the Crawfish Inspector wanted to find out just how *Isabella* looks on the inside. Now it is 9:30 p.m. and Capt. Ted is in his bunk looking very much disturbed by the recording of this log. So that after stating that the weather is still beautiful and clear, light easterly, we will softly climb in bed and hope for another such perfect day. GOOD NIGHT.

Thursday, February 17th. Gentle S.E. wind. We were up at 6:30. Haziel and Vernon took the dinghy and headed for Joe's Rick, two miles away, for much needed water. Borrowed two galvanized wash tubs from store. Capt. Ted and William again on their knees before Isabella but still rebellious she refused to move. The boys returned at noon with every vessel full of fine clear water, then began to prepare lunch. They had brought home a good mutton fish which Vernon prepared for supper. Meals still fine. A couple of puffs from Isabella pleased William and Ted so much they immediately covered her up for the night. The atmosphere in the engine-room suggested the old song, "I've got nerves that jingle, jangle, jingle." However, all went well and we spent a pleasant peaceful evening on the after deck in the starlight. The harbour was alive with what the natives call "Sea Fire" which is a brilliant form of phosphorescence. Natives ashore all quiet so we all went to bed at 9 p.m. The sunset had promised another fine day.

Friday, February 18th. Up at 6 a.m. and every one expected to get an early start but while Skipper and the boys were ashore getting fire wood and a Lignum Vitae stick for a cane, William and Ted unfortunately attempted to start the engine. Better make no further comments for she refused to start. So we did not get started until after 11 a.m. Light S.E. breeze clear and beautiful. We started under sail alone and soon caught an eighteen-pound yellow jack, but having had such fine luck with better eating fish, its life was saved by returning it to the sea. We also caught an almaco. I don't know that fish. After studying it carefully it was returned to the sea in time. Wind is steadily getting lighter so at noon we are in a dead calm during which there was much singing of the old song, "Show me the way to go home." At sunset a light easterly breeze has sprung up, and we have sailed gently towards Allan's Cay where we hope to spend the night. At supper Ted and Skipper induced the cook to introduce the two natives to a large dish of sauerkraut. There is still some question as to what they think of it. It is interesting to note that there is a goodly supply of lignum vitae on Carter's Cay. Wind very light and after passing Umbrella Cay we finally entered the harbor of Allan's Cay shortly after midnight. Soon all was quiet aboard.

Man-O-War: My Island Home

Saturday, February 19th. Left harbour at 9 a.m. Light S.E. wind and sky overcast and we are promised a long beat to Green Turtle Cay. In an attempt to help the sailing, Haziel got the sail up on the dinghy and sailed her leaving the tow line intact. He amused himself by sailing with his left hand and holding a troll line with his right. First he landed a four-pound mackerel and then a thirteen-pound mutton fish. One tack brought us to the N.E. end of Spanish Cay where we anchored for dinner, the meat course being the fresh caught mackerel. William took Skipper and Ted in the dinghy to explore the harbour of Spanish Cay. Like most harbours in these parts there is plenty of water in the harbour but a shoal bar over the entrance. After a complete inspection William left Skipper in the dinghy while he crossed the land to the sea side to gather a bucket of whelks. While he was gathering them the first shower of the trip appeared finding Skipper and Ted well covered with the sail. Looked for a time as though they were in for a real drenching, but like most such squalls here it was soon over and we got to the *Sweetheart* in good condition. Weighing anchor we started again on the long beat to Green Turtle Cay. A spell of about an hour of dead calm and then a light westerly breeze until about 10 p.m. when a stronger breeze pushed us nicely into the harbour at 12:45 a.m. Good Night.

Sunday, February 20th. After breakfast at 6:30 William and Haziel went ashore to say good-bye to the "Cousins." Light S.E. wind. Weighed anchor at 8:30, bound for Man-O-War Cay. About 11 a.m. we were in another dead calm between Dont Rock and the Mainland of Abaco. About six o'clock a nice breeze came and we decided to spend the night at Great Guana Cay. As soon as we dropped anchor we were boarded by one William Christie Albury who gave us the first war news of the week. Then the boys put on lots of *Irresistible* (a favourite hair tonic in these parts) and went ashore. Christie took them around the village and after spending an hour in front of the Church they met their girl friends. They told us nothing of what happened after that till they reached the ship about 10 p.m. Weather promises another beautiful day.

Monday, February 21st. All awake at 7:15. William and Haziel went ashore to buy eggs and returned with the town's entire supply - seven. This suggested corn cakes for breakfast and they were good. They also brought a goodly supply of fine tomatoes. William dropped one of them but Skipper had it before it hit the deck consuming it at once. Of all things, the wind is fair, so light, however, that William had to help turn the boat with an oar so we could lay our course for Man-O-War Cay. After travelling about a mile we were overtaken by a dinghy boat which was being sculled by a young man, who seemed surprisingly happy. The answer seems to be that he was moving his MOTHER-IN-LAW to another island. As this is being written, he is about a mile ahead of us which confirms our idea of the reason for the young man's willingness. These natives think nothing of sculling for miles when the winds fail them. This young man has a trip of about five miles to make mostly by scull. Now abreast Job's Cay which has little interest. Went ashore at Cotland Cay (called Scotland Cay) and inspected one of the best harbours found so far.

The Coming of the Americans

It is between Cotland and Cain's Cay, which, by the way, interests Skipper no little. Ask him about it later. Entrance for about one hundred feet would have to be cleaned but the strong tide would keep it open by constant scrubbing. Perfect quiet water inside. Good soil. Flat calm afterwards on our way and we enjoyed studying the bottom, which was perfectly clear and about two fathoms deep. The undersea life under such conditions is very interesting. Spotted a large stingray and the boys went after it with a lily iron. Got it into him and they were towed at a merry pace for about an hour. Too large to boat so after reclaiming the iron, by a sort of butchering process, they returned to the boat. This was an interesting sight for all. Arriving off the western end of Man-O-War Cay, William took Skipper ashore to inspect a cave which is on some of his property. It was large enough to make a good hurricane cellar. William suggests this property for winter cottage, and it has real possibilities. We climbed to the top of the hill and had one of the finest views of the sea. Beautiful blue water with white breakers over the reef about a mile off shore. Oh, for the day when this war will be over and definite plans can be made. Back aboard and then William and Haziel walked to the village with the week's laundry. This was done because we only expected to stay there a day and they wanted to get it started. Vernon took Skipper across the land to the ocean-side after crawfish, and Skipper took a much-needed bath in the ocean on a beautiful beach. All returned to the boat, and then we sailed to Sandy Cay, another prospect in William's mind, but the only appeal found was the numerous coconut palms. Much coconut water and jelly was consumed, but it was decided that the island was not up to others already inspected. Then we sailed to Man-O-War in a fine balmy breeze. We are all glad the engine won't work, for the sailing has been wonderful. After supper, all the natives ashore, Ted and Skipper talked about the trip so far 'til 9:30. Then to bed. Another fine quiet night. The end of Haziel's trip on the *Sweetheart*. On Tuesday, February 22, she took off for the final leg of the trip, with Uncle Dick aboard instead of Haziel. On February 26th Skipper and Uncle Ted stepped from the *Sweetheart* to the *Richard Campbell* our mailboat at Little Harbour Bar to return to Nassau and then to their home in the U. S. A.

In 1944, Uncle Ted and Skipper considered buying an island 50-50 while cruising in Abaco aboard the *Sweetheart*. No decision was made because transportation from the U.S.A. was still a problem.

When no agreement could be made regarding the buying of an island, Uncle Ted thought he should have some property on Man-O-War Cay. As mentioned in Skipper's Log, when I got off, near the end of the cruise, Uncle Dick joined the lively crew. On the way out of our harbour Uncle Ted expressed his desire for land here. Just at that time they were passing near the South-east entrance of our harbour. Uncle Dick, who owned the land on the left going out, offered to sell the lot there.

"What do you want for the land, Uncle Dick?" asked Uncle Ted.

"Well," replied Uncle Dick, "I think I should get as much as $7.00!"

Man-O-War: My Island Home

Uncle Ted told Uncle Dick that he would give him $10.00; but when he took out his wallet, he had only $9.00. Skipper willingly paid the extra dollar; and even though Uncle Ted, on several occasions, tried to repay him, he refused saying, "I'll always have an interest in that property!"

Uncle Ted had a house built on this property and he and his dear wife, Mrs. Zickes, Aunt Lily, spent many happy seasons there, It was my privilege to enjoy many delicious meals with them. After the death of Uncle Ted and Aunt Lily, this property was sold to Mr. and Mrs. Hobart Ford (Uncle Hoby and Aunt Betty) of Rowayton, Connecticut.

In 1945, Skipper seriously considered buying Matt. Low's Cay for $600.00, but persuaded by the Man-O-War people, that at his age he should be near a settlement, he finally decided on the Cave Hill property which he leased from Uncle Will. Skipper had three small buildings built during the summer of that same year and he and his son-in-law, Dick Hartge, came out in November to see the lay-out. He returned to the States in time for Christmas, finding that the 36' power boat was too small and uncomfortable for the gulf stream. Skipper found a 45' Matthews Hull on the 29th January 1946 and returned to Man-O-War Cay in February with his daughter, Alice, her husband, Bill Lee, and their two boys, Tod and Lance.

In the meantime Uncle Will was building a sloop for Skipper. It was launched on the 10th February 1946. The boat was named *Wynne*. I painted the name on the stern, *Wynne* on one side of the rudder and *Man-O-War Cay* on the other. Skipper said *Wynne* was the name of the place where he found his wife and Man-O-War was the place he found to get away from his wife! Of course, he said this jokingly. Later, Mrs. Robinson (Miss Tup) would come here with Skipper; and after he died, she continued to come until she was not able to travel.

On the 20th February 1946, Bill Lee arranged to buy land at the "Head-of-the-Harbour" from Uncle Willie Sweeting. Later he bought other land and built a home here. Bill Lee's brother, Derek, and also their mother, Mary Davis Lee (Mother Lee), and Mr. and Mrs. Neil C. McMath (Uncle Neil and Aunt Peg) were among the earlier Americans to build homes here.

Bill Lee and Alice used their 57' motor sailer which was built by Uncle Will April 1947 to March 1948 to bring several of their friends to Man-O-War. The result was that they bought land and built here. Mr. and Mrs. Carleton S. Francis, Jr. bought property from Papa. This place is known as "Treasure Hill" and is now owned by Mr. and Mrs. Francis III.

To date, there are two Canadian, one French, and over seventy American homes here. Some live here year-round, some spend the winter months here, some come down for Thanksgiving, Christmas, and Easter, and some for a month or two holiday. More and more are finding the summer months very enjoyable, especially, those who have small children. Some visitors come every year and live aboard their boat, either tied up at the Marina or at a mooring in the harbour. Word-of-mouth is our main source of advertisement!

Because this island is unique and enjoyed by people who want to be quiet and away from the so-called "rat race," there has been a steady increase in the number of American homes. This gives more employment opportunities to all who are not engaged in the boat-building industry.

Furnished homes are available for rent. Several of our property owners rented at first and finding out what life is like on this small island came to stay.

Over the years a very unusual, interesting and mutually profitable arrangement has developed between the local residents and Americans who have bought property and built vacation homes on Man-O-War Cay, which, for lack of a better name is called the "Care-taker System."

This does not mean that the caretaking is limited to caring for the house during the owner's absence; it involves far more than that. In many cases, the builder of the house continues as caretaker for a modest fee, or it might be a Man-O-Warian, nicknamed "Sojer" who sold the property. Whoever it may be, the "Sojer" and his family feel responsible for the visitor and his family and as sponsor go to great lengths to make sure the visitor's stay is as pleasant as possible.

The service includes seeing that the house is aired and cleaned before an expected visit. The visitor may be met in Marsh Harbour, and certainly at the local dock. The dinghy is available and running. There may be flowers, fresh fruit, fresh home-made bread, and even the first meal in the house. During the visit the caretaker or sponsor and his family are always available for advice on fishing, or to help in obtaining supplies, doing the laundry, or helping with any problem that may arise.

Once begun this relationship seems to become very personal, like being members of the same family and already in some cases involves the third generation. This is just one of the many reasons that all visitors feel Man-O-War is a very special place. "Caretaker" in the U.S. implies watching out for vandalism of vacant homes; but on this island that is hardly necessary since breaking and entering, burglary, or even "borrowing" for practical purposes are completely unknown. This same kind of personal relationship carries over in a somewhat lesser way, between the rental agent and the visitor who comes for a shorter time.

Chapter XII.
Some Personal Experiences

Drowning and Rescues

One afternoon in the year 1896 Uncle Dick and his nine-year-old nephew, Richard, "Little Ritchie," left to go out for a short fishing trip. Uncle Dick told the people at home that he was going out to the "musk-melon patch"—a name given to one of the well-known fishing-drops on the back of Dickey's Cay, or the Abaco Sea side of Dickey's Cay. I've fished there many times.

That fishing drop proved to be a failure, so they went to another place some distance away called the "Inner Deep-water," near "Fish-hawk Cay" or the "Upper Cay" as we call it.

After enough fish had been caught, Uncle Dick told Little Ritchie to pull up the anchor and hoist the sail. Just as they were about to get under way, a whirl-wind struck and to use a common expression "Down she went!"

To add to the trouble, Uncle Dick found his feet tied up in the fishing lines which he had not 'made up' or coiled before starting out. (This reminds me that Papa taught us to be sure that all lines were out of the way before hoisting the sail. He had a good reason, or this is an excellent rule!)

When the dinghy sank, Uncle Dick heard Little Ritchie say, "Catch the coca, Uncle Richard!" It, with other things, began to float away. No doubt, his first thought was to save this valuable item, a cup made from a gourd, which was used for bailing out the boat. There were no pumps then. When Uncle Dick got himself freed from the fishing lines, Little Ritchie was nowhere to be seen!

The tide was ebbing, the current going towards the ocean. Uncle Dick was taken out with the current for a while. Then he managed to swim across the running stream and into the upper cay where he crawled up to safe ground!

When the outcry was made that the couple was overdue, Grandpapa Bill and Uncle Edgar went to search for them. By the time they got to the upper cay, it was beginning to get dark. They called and called. Just as they were about to give up hope, Uncle Edgar said to Grandpapa Bill, "I see a person moving to the shore, and if that's your Richard, my Richard is gone!" (Uncle Edgar and Aunt Sarah had unofficially adopted Little Ritchie.) Uncle Dick was rescued, but sure enough and sad to say, "Little Ritchie was gone!"

Man-O-War: My Island Home

One cold wintry day about the year 1916, the schooner *Try-on* was returning from one of those famous sponging trips. She was within about eight miles of Man-O-War when a strong "Norther" came down. An unusual gust of wind struck and turned the *Try-on* over, resulting in the sinking of the vessel!

Among the crew was Mr. Basil Sands of Man-O-War Cay, an uncle of our now-famous boat-builder, Basil Sands. Some of the people made it safely to the shore in a small boat. A woman had one dry match. After preparing kindling wood, Dr. Robert Stratton, who was also on the vessel, prayed that they might be successful, with one match, to get the necessary fire so that the people could sit around and warm themselves! God heard the prayer and the answer was "Yes!" The tiny flame spread to the kindling giving a good fire for that cold night.

Efforts were made to get Mr. Basil and others from the submerged vessel, but the storm was too great. When help finally arrived, Mr. Basil and a man from Marsh Harbour were both drowned. When the news reached Man-O-War, everyone was filled with sorrow. Mr. Basil was loved by all. Before leaving on a trip, he often went to every home to bid relatives and friends "Farewell." He was engaged to Glynton, the eldest daughter of Mr. Neulon and Mrs. Patience.

Mr. Blatchley Sands, an uncle of Captain Lambert Sands, was drowned in the fall of 1939. He was always friendly, particularly to children. His wife, Vernell, died at a young age, and he never remarried. He often spent some time with relatives or friends at Hope Town, doing odd jobs and going "hauling" or fishing with a net.

The afternoon of the 15th of November, Cyril and I had rushed home from school and gone out on the back of "Dickey's Cay" to try to get enough fish for supper. This we did in good time, and when we returned, we noticed that it seemed the whole of the population of Man-O-War were on the foreshore. When we arrived at our dock, someone came and told us that the *Atalanta* with a flag half-mast was going down on the back of Dickey's Cay. Incidentally, this was before the dredging of the South-east entrance of our harbour and the larger boats had to go to the western entrance at low tide. Everyone knew this was a signal of death, but who? Some suggested that it might be Uncle Earnest who was away on a few days' trip, but it was not! It was Mr. Blatchley who had been out on a hauling trip in Hope Town. The boat had sunk not far from land, but still our good friend was drowned. This sad news soon reached his father, Mr. Talbot, who mourned for his son with tears. Shortly after he posted a note of gratitude on the Notice Board thanking all for their help during his bereavement.

When some of the people had thought it might be Uncle Earnest, one said to him, "I thought that was you they were bringing in the coffin that day!"

Uncle Earnest smiled and said: "So I've heard; they thought it was me!" Little did he realize that he would be going a similar way within a couple of months.

On Thursday, the 18th of January, 1940, Uncle Earnest left to go to his field at "Hall's Point," leaving word with his wife, Mrs. Mainer, that he would be back that evening. When he did not return, she thought perhaps he had gone to another field some distance away at a place called the "White Land." He often did this and might stay for several days! However, Mrs. Mainer sent Mr. Robbie Sands to Hall's Point that evening; and in the darkness he searched and called, but no answer. His boat was not seen, so they all took for granted that he had actually gone to the other field.

Friday and Saturday passed and during that time we had a "North-wester." By Saturday night everyone began to wonder what had happened. Early Sunday morning Mr. Carl Russell, who was living at the North-west end of the local settlement, came and reported that they saw something like a boat bottom-up near the shore by our property at "Old Scopley's" which is near the place where Johnnie Bell now has his dock. Mr. Carl wanted help to go and investigate. Sure enough, it was Uncle Earnest's sunken dinghy! A search for his body was made, but without success.

Uncle Earnest was a kind and gentle person with a smile for everyone. I often think of the happy times I had with the other boys when he would come from the "White Land" with a dinghy load of coconuts. We helped to take them up to his yard. He always gave us a coconut or two. What a treat! Also I often helped him to sort his tomatoes and limes before he sent them to the market in Nassau. I was given some of the non-sale tomatoes, and smacked my lips as I ate some of them dipped in the seawater for salt.

Uncle Earnest was one of the few men who had met the first Americans, Skipper Robinson and Uncle Ted Zickes. He had shown them how to open a coconut, and also told some of his stories about the sea.

One of the most exciting experiences during my years of teaching was the saving of a life from drowning! In February 1968, Mr. Gordon P. St. Clair of Rockford, Illinois, made a tour of the Bahamas, stopping at most of the settlements, teaching and demonstrating with "Annie," a dummy which was a replica of a twelve-year-old Norwegian girl, the mouth-to-mouth method of artificial respiration.

At our Headteachers' Conference, the summer of that year, we were fortunate enough to have Mr. St. Clair there for more lectures and demonstrations. Each headteacher was requested, there at the Conference, to practice with "Annie" this very important life-saving act. The Royal Police Department and the Ministry of Education worked together in this effort. After the Conference, "Annie" was sent and loaned to all the schools so that pupils and teachers who were not at the Conference could learn more about this. The headteachers at Abaco were requested to be at the Marsh Harbour International Airport at a certain time when the Police plane would arrive there with a Police Officer to demonstrate with "Annie." When the plane arrived, one of the Police recognized me, for we had met at the Conference in Nassau. He placed "Annie" in my charge and said: "Here, you take over and we can return to Nassau!"

Of course, I obeyed the Police Officer; and there at the airport, we the teachers went through the procedure again. "Annie" then went from school to school here at Abaco.

The following winter, one morning at nine o'clock, Aunt Mady came by the school and said, "Where's Mary? They want her to come to Edwin's Boat-yard. They think Alma's boy is drowned!" As already mentioned, even though Mary had

Man-O-War: My Island Home

only one year in Nurses' Training, she was often called upon in times of accidents and illness.

In a flash I was off on my bicycle, feeling confident that I could render the help needed. Mary followed. When I arrived at the scene, there was a crowd of workmen, as well as all who had heard the news. The men had the boy lying in the road. They had tried the old method of rolling him over a barrel to get the water out of him. I motioned for the people to stand aside, taking off my jacket at the same time. Seeing what I was about to do, one man said: "It's no use; the boy is dead!"

Realizing there was no time to be lost, I immediately went to work: tilted his head backwards until his chin came in an upright position, pinched his nose and blew gently into his mouth, at the same time watching the rise of his chest. After repeating a few times, one of the men who had been feeling for a pulse-beat said excitedly: "Mr. Albury, do that again! I felt a beat!" The boy soon started breathing on his own, and became conscious about three hours later. He was examined by Dr. Gottlieb to see if there was any damage to his ribs, as this is possible in babies and small children when mouth-to-mouth resuscitation has been administered.

Rodday, who was about three years of age at that time is alive today. Whenever I see him, instead of calling him by name, I call him "My boy." Truly, I see the Hand of God in this—the timing of Mr. St. Clair's visit, my lessons at the Headteacher's Conference, and my responsibility given by the Police Officer followed by the incident itself!

Hurricanes

The settlement of Man-O-War, although on a small cay, is considered one of the safest places in times of hurricanes and storms. Because of its high ground and the fact it has two entrances to the main harbour which prevent the high rise of water, the inhabitants have weathered out hurricanes and storms with little damage to homes, except for the severe one in 1932. Fortunately, there have been no casualties.

One of the first severe hurricanes experienced by the people of Man-O-War was in 1866, and has always been referred to as the "Sixty-six hurricane." It lasted for three days. It is told that when the wind became strong and gusty, Uncle Ben, wearing his long flannel shirt—for that was the only protection he had from the wind—went up to his brother, my great-grandpapa Bill and said, "Billy, it's time to get Lydia and the children down to my house!" It seemed that he thought his house would be stronger or safer, or maybe he wanted them to be together. Some of the other relatives also went to Uncle Ben's house. The storm was severe; but, when it was over, there was only damage to the crops and some of the separate kitchen buildings. There were other hurricanes with wind velocity 150 to 180 m.p.h. Some of the outstanding ones occurred in 1898, 1926, 1932, 1947, and 1965. I was just seven years and ten months in the severe 1932 hurricane. We had no radios in those days, but a few homes had good barometers.

Some Personal Experiences

On the Monday morning of the 5th of September, these barometers began to fall and the winds increased with every puff harder and harder. The vessels in the harbour were all put to their moorings and the dinghies hauled across the sea-road to high ground, the men and boys all helping one another. The houses did not have glass windows. The shutters were let down or closed and a wooden batten put across. There was a door left unbattened on two sides of the house just in case we had the centre or eye of the hurricane, which would mean a calm spell and then the wind would come from the opposite direction!

No one before or since experienced such high winds. When the preparations were made, everyone went inside their homes not knowing what they were about to experience was something very different from an ordinary storm or hurricane. The wind continued to increase and those who had barometers saw them go down to the minimum.

Before the height of the winds, we watched the coconuts blow from the palm-trees and then to our surprise some of the trees blew down on the ground. Our dining-room and kitchen which were separate buildings blew to pieces. By that time our house was shaking badly. Most of the shingles on the roof blew off, and Papa seemed to breathe a sigh of relief when the house slid off the ground-pins on to the ground, thus making the building firmer. The house trembled or shook less. We were all wet, but Papa managed to keep our full sack of flour dry.

Papa decided we should try to find a better shelter. He and my brother Victor helped us crawl against the wind and rain, and among flying debris, to Uncle Wesley's store. This also had gone off the ground-pins, but the roof was still all right; hence it was a much dryer place than our house. By that time other people had found shelter there.

Late that afternoon someone came and told us that Mr. Nelson's house was not damaged at all, and that there was room for us there. This was good news because Uncle Wesley's shop was partly hanging over the road, and Papa did not think this very safe. We again braved the storm, not very bravely for us children, and went to Mr. Nelson's house, just a few hundred feet away.

We had not eaten since early Monday morning, so we were all very hungry! Fortunately, there was a galley or wooden box off one of the spongers found in Mr. Nelson's yard. Some of the men put this inside the house while others got soil to put in it so as to be able to have a fire without burning the box. The wood for the fire was taken from under the house. This was left over from the Sunday supply. With the winds well above hurricane force, Papa struggled to our house and came back bringing some of our flour which was still dry. Uncle Dick went to work making dough-boys or dumplings. They were very tasty! He made batch after batch until all had a share. Afterwards everyone agreed that they were the best dough-boys they had ever eaten. That experience is a bright spot in my memories of the 1932 hurricane.

The winds began to abate during Tuesday night. However, it was still quite stormy for a few days. There was much damage but all were thankful there was no loss of life here.

We moved from Mr. Nelson's house to my brother, Lewis' new house which had withstood the hurricane. Lewis was not married then. We lived there until Papa and my brothers got our house rebuilt.

As soon as the weather permitted, the *M.V. Cordeaux* with Government Officials was sent up from Nassau to investigate damages. Among them were Dr. Quackenbush and a nurse to render medical aid. The doctor and the nurse stayed in this area for some time. Some food and building materials were supplied by the Government and Red Cross. This was a tremendous help in the repairing of homes and boats.

All the fruits were on the ground, and we knew with the trees damaged and some up by the roots, it would be a long time before we could expect more. We buried the citrus fruit in the sand to preserve them. Refrigerators were unknown here at that time. It was fun afterwards digging for these fruit. We never knew when we had them all.

The 1947 hurricane did very little damage to homes. Needless to say, some trees and crops were destroyed. Uncle Will had five boats, including the Motor-sailer, *Lucayo*, for Bill and Alice Lee, under construction in his yard at that time. Uncle Will spent most of the high winds in or near his yard trying to do what he could to avoid damage. As I stated earlier, we do not have much rise in water and that is what does so much damage in low lands. When the wind was over, the *Lucayo* had blown down on its side. With a little man-power she was in position again.

Mr. Dalbert had the large schooner *Tepee* under construction over on Dickey's Cay at that time. The owners, Mr. and Mrs. Crandall were here living in a little thatched hut also on Dickey's Cay. Friends invited them to come across to a safer home, but they wished to stay there. Apparently, they did not know much about hurricanes. When the winds dropped suddenly and there was a calm, they began to tidy up the place to pretend to visitors that their house was not bad after all. They were surprised greatly when they heard and then felt the gusts of wind coming from the opposite direction. The puffs of wind seemed higher during the latter half of the 1947 hurricane.

I was married in 1946, and this was my first experience as the head of a home in a hurricane. My youngest brother, Eddie, came by our house before the winds were very strong. He went home and told my parents that I had a worried look on my face! He learned later after he got married what the responsibility was like. A storm or hurricane usually meant fun for young people and children—no school, plenty of free fresh fruit to eat as well as sugar-canes to suck.

I did not have a barometer in 1947; but one of my many good friends, Mr. Kenneth, had one and he kept me well informed especially when it began to rise. He came to our house in that strong rain and wind to let us know that the worst would soon be over.

The 1965 hurricane "Betsy" gave us all a surprise. We had listened to the reports and traced her path for some days. On Saturday night the 4th of September, she had turned her back on us and was moving away from the Bahamas. During the local news that evening the news reporter on our Bahamian Radio Station ZNS said there would be no further news about Betsy as she was no longer a threat to us.

Some Personal Experiences

On Sunday afternoon the reporters said that the hurricane had slowed down and then come to a stand-still. Our barometers were falling, and the winds became stronger and stronger. By late afternoon we were told there would be a special bulletin on 'Betsy' at 11:00 p.m.

We had our usual church services on Sunday. It was our eldest daughter, Minerva's birthday, so we invited the young people to our home for refreshments after the evening Gospel Service. By that time the wind was so strong and gusty, I began to make preparations. I took advantage of the young men who had come to our home by having them help me, although they did it without my asking and pulled my eighteen-foot power boat to safe ground. Then I went to the school house and other government buildings to fasten the shutters and doors.

I could not wait until 11 o'clock. I turned on the radio at 10:30 just in time to hear the reporter say: "Hurricane Betsy has changed her course, picked up speed and is now heading for the Northern Bahama Islands. All precautions against high winds and rough seas should now be taken!" It did not take long for this news to spread in our Settlement. The caretakers of the American homes set out to batten these houses first as most of them were out of the local settlement. The sound of hammers could be heard above the noise of the wind which by that time was up to gale force. We worked most of the night until preparations were made. When it became dangerous to be out-doors, we went to our homes.

The electricity was shut off so no one would get hurt from falling wires. We got out our flash lights and old kerosene lamps. By means of battery walkie-talkies we were able to keep in touch with some of the other people here. Our new home on Madeira Avenue stood firm as a rock. Unlike most hurricanes, Betsy's eye moved around us somewhat like a semi-circle, so we took her force for about thirty-six hours. Then she headed for Florida.

Monday evening, in the height of the unpleasant visitor, we gathered around the table for our supper. I told the children of my experience in the '32 hurricane. What a difference! We all gave thanks to God and had a good meal.

After that I threw myself across the bed, not intending to go to sleep, because I wanted to continue to keep in touch with my brother Eddie who lived near my parents. He had been reporting to me off and on of their condition. Having been awake the night before, I fell asleep and slept soundly until Tuesday morning. When I turned on the walkie-talkie, Eddie told me that Papa and Mamma were quite upset because they had not heard from us during the night. He also said they felt badly as their little old kitchen, a separate building, was destroyed.

Betsy was still pushing winds of hurricane force. When I heard that my parents were upset, I prepared to go to their home to see them. My daughters, as I had no sons, said, "No Daddy, you can't go out; it is still blowing too hard!"

I replied, "I'll go through fire for them." Mary said she would go with me. The girls seemed more contented. On the way we held on to each other, climbing over and then under trees or branches that had fallen in the road. My parents were relieved to know that we were all right. One of the grocery stores was open so we got some food for them as well as for ourselves. Then we returned home.

After Betsy's departure the people of our community went to work to clean up our roads, yards, houses, and boats. There is a saying "Plenty of hands make light work." How true! In a short time Man-O-War was in shape again minus a few trees. Fortunately, we had lots of rain and the trees budded like spring. When our Senior Commissioner, D. H. J. Jones, came to visit us, he found the whole community working together in the clean-up effort. He often commended the Man-O-War people for what they had done. We did get some help from Government — materials for the school house and other small buildings that had been damaged or destroyed.

Here is a funny little story with an interesting twist. When John Cameron and his wife came here and bought property and then had a house built, one of his friends at home said to him: "Aren't you afraid to have a house down there in the Bahamas where they have so many hurricanes?"

John said, "No!"

John also had a boat built here and sailed it up to Connecticut a few years later. That same year a hurricane by-passed us and went up that way. When it was over, John's boat was some miles inland together with parts of buildings, refrigerators, stoves, and other damaged boats. When John wrote to tell us about this, he said he told his friend: "I wonder who's kidding whom about the hurricane zone!"

For many years the hurricanes have been given the names of girls. One of my daughters heard a radio reporter say he wondered why they did not name some of them after men. She immediately wrote to the reporter and told him the reason in the form of a question: "Have you ever heard of a 'himmicane'?"

When I Was a Boy

When I was a boy, some of our people had fields on property in the Eastern or South-eastern Harbour, usually referred to as the Head-of-the-Harbour and sometimes "up in t'ead." Aunt Sarah went with Vernon and Marcell; for Uncle Norman would be home making sails for the sponging vessels. Uncle Wesley had a field on his property. Our field nearby was on the land now known as "Treasure Hill." There was a period when we did not have even a sail for our dinghy. We sculled and poled all the way to the field. On the return trip when the wind was favourable and it generally was, as the summer trade winds came from the east, we cut a large bush or the branch of a tree with lots of leaves, put it upright in the bow of the boat, and this served as our driving power. We steered the boat with the sculling oar. In the melon season, we all enjoyed a feast of one of these that had been put out under a cool tree or in the sea. If it was in winter during the vegetable season, tomatoes, dipped in the sea-water, were eaten as we returned slowly to our dock or landing place on the seashore. Sugar-canes were also pealt, or stripped and cut into small pieces and sucked. The feasts also took place after we had sails; and the lighter the wind, the more we ate. This eating time was something to look forward to during the work in the field.

I was taught to scull and sail during these trips. In learning to scull, I sat on the stern bench, the seat right across the after part of the dinghy. I placed my hand on the oar just above the sculling hole and let it go with the movement made by the sculler who was standing on the stern-sheets, the platform in the aft or stern part of the dinghy. By doing this I got the idea and the feel of oar and in due time I was able to propel the boat with an oar all by myself. This served me in good stead for the years to come. After we had sails, on "flat calm" days, we found it necessary to scull to the field, to get fire-wood, and also to the fishing grounds. Even the five-mile trip to Hope Town and Marsh Harbour, the seven-mile trip to Guana Cay, and the twenty-mile trip to Green Turtle Cay might be done by sculling, especially if a girl friend or "Sweet-heart," as they were called in those days, were involved.

Over thirty years ago, when I began working for the Government, I often visited the Commissioner, who was stationed at Hope Town then, in Papa's sailing dinghy. If it was calm, there was no way of movement except by sculling. It was not generally calm all the way. Now and then we would get a break when a "cat-paw," or "cat-skin," the name given to a light puff of wind coming towards you, came and pushed us on.

During the summer of 1949 I built my boat named *Minerva*. It was about fifteen feet overall and was powered by a two and a half horse-power air-cooled Wisconsin motor! I must confess, I was proud of this boat. It made the going so much easier, and was used mainly for my visits to the Commissioner, and as a tender to serve Bahamas Airways' planes which landed in our harbour, sometimes twice a day. Of course, I did some fishing in the *Minerva* also.

One of the highlights of my boyhood days was to go down to the seashore when the fishermen came in from hauling. I enjoyed watching them divide the fish which they had caught and then cast lots for each share, but the most exciting moment came when they finished sharing and someone cried out "Scrabbling." That meant the unshared fish, usually small ones, were free for all to take. We all tried to get a portion, but little hands can only hold so many and especially slippery fish! If the catch was a good one, there was a better quality of fish left for the scramblers!

Fish-hooks, which are plentiful today, were once a scarce item. As a boy, I made fish-hooks out of straight pins. I could get a card of pins of sixteen for one cent. Did I value them! These were good only for little fish around the seashore. We always managed to get enough hooks for the larger fish. We usually bought about three to six at a time, sometimes only one, the size for groupers and mutton snappers. I remember one of the first real fishing lines I owned. Papa bought it for me from Mr. Joseph H. Bethel at Hope Town. I used this mainly for catching porgies and grunts. The same hook was on the line for a long time. When a hook was rusty, we did not throw it away, but scraped it and used it as long as possible. That fishing line was one of my treasures; and after a fishing trip, it was properly coiled. Papa taught me how to do this. It was then hung up on a nail in the wall of our dining-room. Each member of the family at that time generally had their own line.

Conch pearls were sold in order to earn a little money. We saved used paper bags and took them to the store-keeper. We made washing or scrub boards for cleaning clothes. I used to save the straight-grain short pieces of lumber at Uncle Will's boat-yard and make them using a sharp chisel. If the lumber was thick enough, I'd put grooves on both sides, one side coarser than the other for thick and thin material.

Another job was to put handles on cans and making bread-pans. I remember when Mr. Isaac used to do it. There was a saying: "If 'ifs' and 'ands' were cans and pans, Mr. Isaac would be out of a job!"

One day Papa, Cyril, and I went down to the "Low Place" or "Rocky Crossing." Papa and Cyril went down on the "back" to look for fire-wood, bleeding-teeth shells, or drift. I stayed by the Low Place to keep an eye on the dinghy as it was blowing a strong breeze. I found amusement by standing face to the wind with my hat, instead of on my head, on my chest trying to have the wind keep it there. This was fun for me, but suddenly the hat blew away, into the sea and was carried out by the waves. In my great distress, I ran until I could see Papa and Cyril. I shouted and signaled with my hands and arms for them to come! Judge, to their surprise, when they found out what had happened! The hat was quickly recovered. For some reason, Papa took this kind of funny, and he often teased me about the hat story.

A Friend In Need

In the beginning of April of 1957, my first wife, Ena, noticed there was a lump on her right side, just under her ribs. Some of the local doctors thought it could be caused by wearing tight clothes. However, we continued to try different or other doctors. Finally, Dr. Rassin of Nassau, after an examination, said to me, "Get your wife to a good doctor or hospital in the United States as soon as possible!"

Our good friend, Mr. Harold Johnson, one of our representatives in the House of Assembly at that time, had given much of his valuable time taking us to the doctors. Our relatives and other friends in Nassau had shown us so much kindness. In fact, when we walked out of Dr. Rassin's hospital, Mr. Jack I. Albury of Bahamas Telecommunications, met us; and when he learned our problem, he immediately offered help.

We had no passports, so we went to work and by the help of kind relatives and friends, these were obtained in a very short time. But we had not traveled abroad before. How were an island boy and girl going to manage this trip? Well, God provided the help as you shall see.

When we called home from Nassau with the sad news, we were told that Dr. and Mrs. Howes with their family were leaving Man-O-War shortly to return to their home in South Yarmouth, Cape Cod, Massachusetts. Dr. and Mrs. Howes were some of the first Americans to start visiting here regularly. Even though we were flying to Miami, and the Howes to West Palm Beach, Hermon and Betsy kindly offered to meet us in Miami and take us all the way to the Cape and then to the Massachusetts Memorial Hospital in Boston, where Dr. Reginald H. Smithwick was standing by with all his qualified staff to give some of the best service in the world!

With very little money in my pocket, we started out on this journey. The three or four days' trip with Hermon and Betsy and their children in their station wagon did not cost us a penny. Hermon paid our motel and restaurant bills all the way; and then when we arrived at their home, we had the best of everything. The first evening after we arrived, Mrs. Smithwick, dear Elio, and others called to offer help and good wishes. Then came a call from Mr. Robert B. M. Barton, President of Parker Games. He said, "Haziel, I just want you to know that this trip is not going

Some Personal Experiences

to cost you a penny! We, your American friends, want to show our appreciation for what you have done for us since we started to visit Man-O-War!"

Ena was admitted to the hospital and went through thorough tests. Finally the operation took place. It proved unsuccessful. She never regained consciousness.

During the day of the operation, Patricia, my sister-in-law, who was visiting in that area with her husband, Vernon, at that time and also Elio and Janey Lukens were with me at the hospital. About mid-afternoon, when Dr. Smithwick called me up to his office to give me the sad news of my wife's death, he had arranged to have a nurse on either side of me to render help in case of an emergency. Dr. Smithwick spoke words of comfort to me and showed his deep sorrow.

Earlier we had met Peter and Jean Bruce. Peter is the famous blacksmith on Cape Cod, and he and Jean have visited Man-O-War almost every year since that time. They arranged for me to go to a meeting or Church Service one night in Boston during Ena's tests in the hospital. It was the Mount Auburn Gospel Centre Assembly of Brethren. Of course, I felt at home there. Mr. and Mrs. Barnes of that meeting kindly invited me for dinner that night as well as board for the night and breakfast the next morning before taking me to the hospital.

After we had received the sad news, Janey Lukens took Patricia and myself in her car and drove us all the way to Dr. Howes' home in South Yarmouth. Naturally, I wanted to get home to my children and other loved ones as soon as possible, even though love and sympathy were showered upon me by friends there. I can't mention them all, but I remember the tender loving kiss of Alice Lee Pearse. Betsy was outstanding in her kindness and care; Hermon, Derek Lee, and others spent much of the night making reservations for me to get home. Patricia was a great comfort to me through it all.

Before dawn the next morning, Hermon drove me to Hyannis Airport to board a plane to New York. When I arrived in New York Airport, there were two more of my good friends, Mr. and Mrs. Hobart Ford, to meet me and see that I got on a plane. I was shivering with cold when I landed. Uncle Hoby took off his top coat and put it around me. He and Aunt Betty gave me breakfast while we waited for the plane to depart for Miami. And that's not all — Aunt Betty put some money in my hand saying, "You might need this on your way."

When the plane arrived in Miami, I had no idea that I would have any help there. But to my great relief, Greetie Wick was there to greet me. She and her husband Phil were also among the early visitors to our island. Their home was in Darien, Connecticut. They happened to be in Florida; and when they heard the news, Greetie was very kind and came to my rescue. There was some time to pass away before my plane to Nassau, so Greetie took me to a nearby store to try to occupy my mind during the waiting period. She asked if there was anything I'd like to buy. Then I remembered I had promised to bring Minerva and Denise a camera. These were purchased plus a rag doll for Winnie, and Greetie paid the bill. Bless her heart.

The flight to Nassau was short. Again I was met by relatives and friends. It was now late Saturday evening. Uncle Walter, or Shorty, and Aunt Winnie took good care of me in their home that night. Mr. and Mrs. Chester Bethel were among the many who poured in love and words of comfort. I flew home by charter plane early

Sunday morning. I was greeted at the dock by almost the whole community. During the following week, while waiting for the body to arrive from Boston, during the funeral service, and for some months after, I was overwhelmed at the help I received from so many who really cared!

Evangelist Bernard Fell conducted the funeral service—one of the largest at Man-O-War. Mr. Fell stayed here for the services during the following week. His text on Sunday Morning was "Weeping may endure for a night, but joy cometh in the morning" Psalm 30:5. These precious words have meant much to me since that time.

Well, just as my good friend Mr. Barton said, the bills were all paid by the generous donations—enough and to spare. After taking care of the hospital bill and other expenses, Dr. Smithwick, my dear Reg, did not charge a penny for his services. The balance was used to buy a small refrigerator and a mattress for our little clinic here at Man-O-War. May I take this opportunity to thank all of my readers who helped in so many ways to relieve the burden of that experience. Truly, a "friend in need, is a friend indeed!"

On 11th October 1956, I married Mary Albury, and we have found much happiness together.

Experiences With Royalty

When Her Royal Highness, the Princess Margaret Rose, visited Nassau in 1955, I had the honour and privilege of meeting her at Government House gardens in Nassau. She was escorted through the gardens and met fortunate ones of Nassau and also from the Out Islands.

After the reception, my good friend and lawyer, the late honourable Donald B. McKinney, came over to me and said, "Haziel, the Princess spent more time talking to you than anyone else. What did you have to talk about?"

I told Donald that when I was introduced as from *Man-O-War* Cay, she seemed to want to know something about our island. I told Her Royal Highness that it was the largest "Man-O-War" Great Britain owned! Then jokingly, I told him, maybe it was because my height and hers were about the same. That we had in common.

Later, the 24th April 1959, His Royal Highness, the Prince Philip, the Duke of Edinburgh, visited Nassau. I had the privilege of meeting him, and enjoyed a chat with him. Sometime after I had a dream that I met Her Majesty, Queen Elizabeth II. I said to her, "I've talked to your sister, and also your husband. Now I've met you and I want to kiss your hand!"

On the 27th February 1966, when Her Majesty visited Nassau, Mary and I went there for the occasion. The Royal Yacht *Britannia* docked at Prince George Wharf that early Sunday morning. Her Majesty, dressed in Yellow, walked from the *Britannia* through Rawson Square to the dais, while shouts went up from the crowd: "Isn't she beautiful? Isn't she lovely? Welcome, Your Majesty!"

Booths, called "Bahamarama," had been built and each major island of the Bahamas was represented by people and products. Just before Her Majesty arrived at our booth, Captain Leonard Thompson, Member of the House of Assembly, came to me with a hand-written scroll—a very brief history of Abaco, and said, "Here, Haziel, you're a good one to present this to the Queen!" Naturally, I accepted the offer!

Some of the outstanding things in Abaco's booth were two half models of boats built by Uncle Will, and a dinghy partly built so as to show the construction by Mr. Maurice. The dinghy was framed with those natural-crook Abaco timbers, and had on the top streak of plank.

After presenting Her Majesty with the scroll, she asked me about the boat-building at Man-O-War. She said she had heard about it and was pleased to hear of the good work being done here. Shame on me, I forgot all about my dream and did not ask to kiss her hand! I shan't forget it the next time!

On the afternoon of the 10th of June that same year, Minerva, who was operating the radio telephone at the time, sent a messenger for me to come to the station for a telephone call from His Excellency, the Governor. My first thought was that H. E. wanted a boat built for himself or for a friend. By the time I arrived at the radio telephone station, Minerva had been informed that it was not a call but a telegram. She began to take it, and got so excited that she said, "Daddy, I knew you would get it!"

The following is a copy of the telegram:

> Government Mr. Haziel Albury, J. P., Man-O-War Cay, Abaco. In the name of Her Majesty Queen Elizabeth II and in the recognition of your valuable services to the people of the Bahama Islands particularly in Abaco in the public services and as a Justice of the Peace and community leader I have been pleased to award to you the Queen's Certificate and Badge of Honour.
>
> Ralph Grey, Governor.

It is difficult for me to express my feelings as I read this telegram. Suffice it to say that there were tears streaming down my cheeks! I wondered if I was worthy of such an honour, and then I thought of what it will mean to hear the "Well Done!" by the King of Kings in that great Day! I realize all I am and have and hope to be comes from Him.

The latter part of December 1966, I was invited to Government House in Nassau to receive the Certificate and Badge from H. E. Sir Ralph Grey, who presented it on behalf of Her Majesty, the Queen. Mary and our two youngest daughters, Winnie and Martha, went with me. It was a memorable occasion. I was pleased to see others there who were honoured by Her Majesty.

Story of The Son of a Loyalist

Man-O-War, although small and very insignificant, especially at that time, had the privilege of knowing that one young man was representing us during World War II. That young man was my cousin, Thomas, who volunteered for the Royal Navy. The following is his story and used by his kind permission.

Son of a Loyalist

The Sweetings were among the Empire Loyalists that settled in the Abaco Cays, one of a group of islands in the Bahamas. My father was born at Sweeting's Village on the Mainland of Abaco; but when farming gave way to sea-faring, the family moved to Man-O-War Cay, a small island with a good harbour and better channels.

Life had a tragic beginning as I lost my mother two weeks after my birth. However, having been adopted by my aunt and uncle, a captain of a three-mast sailing ship, I enjoyed the love of two families. I recall one native sponge boat captain saying to my adopted father: "Cap'n Sweeting, how come he has a daddy and a papa?" At the age of fifteen my real father was lost at sea.

Childhood was spent at Man-O-War Cay, the place I still call home. Except for occasional visits to Nassau to see relatives, the island was my world, a world full of adventures any boy would envy. I recall seeing my first whale at the age of four from the deck of the local mailboat (our only contact with the outside world). As a small boy my first gift was not a tricycle but a skiff, later a dinghy, not a bike, then a sailing-dinghy instead of a motorbike. For fun, we sometimes caught small sharks off the dock in front of our house. When I was eight, Abaco suffered a severe hurricane which lasted for four days and caused great devastation. Although accustomed to such onslaughts of nature, this one was the "Granddaddy of them all" and is still referred to locally as the '32 Hurricane. Life on the islands was never dull.

In my teens, we moved to Nassau and then in 1942 while working for a department store I decided (along with eleven others) to volunteer for the Royal Navy. Allegiance to King and Country was strong in the Bahamas and natives of Abaco took a back seat to no one in this respect.

Royal Send-off

H. R. H. the Duke of Windsor was then the Governor of the Bahamas, and the day before our departure for England we were invited to Government House where H. R. H. wished us good luck. We also had a group photo taken with him; he later sent an autographed copy to our parents (which I now have). So, shortly after my 18th birthday we left for England via Miami, New York, Montreal, and Halifax, finally embarking on a troop ship for England.

Safe Arrival

After a safe journey we arrived in Scotland and were soon bound for London, where we arrived in the middle of a pea soup fog. I had never seen a fog before, let alone a London Fog. It seemed I'd arrived in some alien world. However, we had a week's leave and then reported to Portsmouth where we formally joined the Navy and started training.

High Adventure

I joined my first seagoing ship at Londonderry, Northern Ireland—H. M. S. *Swale* (a Corvette) and at dawn on Christmas Day 1942 left for my first trip of convoy duty on the North Atlantic. We soon encountered a howling gale where friend and foe alike had to fight the fury of nature gone wild to survive. Lookout duty from the crow's nest of a Corvette under such conditions was indeed high adventure.

Contact

The Battle of the Atlantic was at its height at this time, and contact with the enemy was frequent and losses heavy on both sides. I saw my first snow off Newfoundland on that first trip. I never knew this world could be so cold where ships listed and guard rails bent with the weight of frozen salt water.

Contrast

Atlantic... Africa... Artic... India. It seems the navy liked to do everything the hard way—at least in my case. After convoy duty in the North Atlantic we were sent for some months to West Africa, right on the equator, where it was extremely hot, even for me. On my next ship we were sent on a trip well inside the Arctic Circle before finally going to the Indian Ocean and eventually ending up in the Pacific. Who said variety is the spice of life?

A Royal Shipmate

After a period of time ashore for some special training, I joined a new destroyer *H. M. S. Whelp*. Our second in command was H. R. H. Prince Philip, now Duke of Edinburgh, and during the following eighteen months I came to respect him as a good officer, sailor and sportsman—having played water polo with him and against him on the ship's team. Little did I realize at the time that over 20 years later, while working for the Bay (Hudson Bay Company), I would meet him again on Remembrance Day at the Cenotaph in Toronto.

A Different War

Shortly after D-Day we made a trip to Spitzbergen; I shall never forget the majestic white cliffs that seemed to tower over us in this cold, silent, yet somehow beautiful world. Soon we were off again, this time to a different war. So after a trip through the Mediterranean, Suez and the Red Sea, we joined up with units in Ceylon.

A Special Welcome

After some air strikes around Sumatra we steamed full speed for Western Australia due to a critically ill seaman on board. We arrived in Freemantle twenty-four hours ahead of the main force, so becoming the first ship of the British Pacific Fleet to arrive, and what a royal welcome we received. Crates of eggs (normal ration was one a week), fruit, etc., and every man on board received a package, including his own Christmas pudding. This was Aussie Hospitality par excellence.

Combined Operations

After a journey across the Great Australian Bight, some of the roughest waters on earth, and a short stopover in Sydney, we left to join up with the

American strike force for the invasion of Okinawa and continued with diversionary attacks before and during this operation; this was indeed a different war from the North Atlantic. There danger was mainly from under the water. Here it came from the air, out of the sun, or the clouds. After damage from a typhoon, we headed for the Philippines and finally Australia for a refit.

A Special Birthday

Remember V. E. Day 1945? This was my 21st birthday, and we were near the Admiralty Islands on our way to Australia. The bursts of tracer bullets and star shells we fired that night in V formation were of special significance to me. Not often do enemies surrender the moment one reaches manhood.

Final Victory

I was in Sydney waiting for passage to go home on leave when Final Victory came. Sydney went wild with jubilation, and who could blame them? This war was close to home, and they had been more or less on the front line. Now plans would change. I never did get home on leave, but was sent the long way around back to England.

The Journey Back

The Troop Ship back to England stopped at Bombay to pick up a thousand or more ex-prisoners of war. These were men who had fought in Burma and paid a terrible price for this Victory, but spirits were high and it was a happy journey back.

Another Special Day

On arrival back in England, my fiancee and I made plans to be married. We had met on my arrival in Londonderry to join my first ship back in December 1942, but as we were both in the Royal Naval Service, we decided to wait until the war was over to be married. Finally, on April 2nd 1946, we were married in Londonderry and spent a short honeymoon in Dublin before going back to duty.

Homecoming

Some months after my marriage, I was released by the navy and our passage back to the Bahamas arranged. My wife and I went on the Liner Queen Mary to New York via Halifax, then by train to Miami, and finally by air to Nassau. After four years and three months, it was a great thrill seeing all my relatives again. Some had grown up and I no longer recognized them.

The Adjustment

Adjusting to civilian life was not easy; somewhere along the way I had lost over four years. For a while I went as mate for my brother on the *M. V. Tropical Trader*, a boat owned by a company with its own private island called Cat Cay about eighty miles across the gulf from Miami. The island had its own

Some Personal Experiences

private casino, even its own money, and visitors came by invitation only. Tuna and Marlin fishing tournaments were held there for the rich and famous.

Eventually we returned to Nassau, and I went back to manage the department store where I worked before going overseas. However, it became apparent that the warm climate was endangering my wife's health. So eight years and a son and daughter later, we decided on a doctor's advice, to move to Canada.

In 1954 I arrived in Toronto and was joined by my family ten months later. After working five and one half years for a company (that shall remain nameless) and another son later, I finally arrived at the Bay. It was a long way round, this journey to the Bay. So far, the visit has lasted fifteen years, but that's another story....

Chapter XIII.
Stories and Anecdotes

The Meat-Grinder Story

Sometime in the 1930's there was only one meat-grinder on Man-O-War and that belonged to Uncle Norman and his wife, of course. In those days it was customary to borrow and loan many things in order to make life easier. This meat-grinder was no exception and it found its way into many kitchens.

One afternoon Mamma Lina wanted to make conch fritters for supper. She had loaned the meat-grinder to my sister-in-law Mizpah, so she told Uncle Norman to go down to Mizpah and get it for her. Mizpah had loaned it to Mrs. Emma. Uncle Norman went up the hill to find out that Mrs. Emma had loaned it to Mrs. Eureka Thompson. Continuing his search he discovered that Mrs. Charity had borrowed it from Mrs. Eureka. To Uncle Norman's surprise he learned from Mrs. Charity that Mrs. Therese, Uncle Will's sister-in-law, had sent up to her just a while before to borrow it. Finally, after a trip all over the settlement of Man-O-War the meat-grinder was found to be almost across the road from Uncle Norman's house.

If there had been as many visitors on our roads at that time as there are today, there would have been no conch fritters for the Norman clan that night. He likes to entertain our visitors with his many stories including this one about the meat-grinder and some of the others in this book.

The Tale of the Shirt

For some years it has been our great privilege to entertain visiting preachers. One of the things that Mary did to help out was to take care of their laundry. Frank Perry, one of our famous Evangelists, often kidded Mary or me for taking his clothes. I think one time he was a sock short or it might have been handkerchief. However, he really got one on me; and I am going to tell you how it all happened.

In February 1969 Colonel and Mrs. Eugene Muller rented a cottage from me. They arranged to have their friends, John and Barbara Eisenhower, come to visit them. The Eisenhowers flew to Nassau on a scheduled Eastern Flight, but we had arranged a charter in my name for them to come to Man-O-War. It was at this time that John was appointed the American Ambassador to Belgium, and his book, *The Bitter Woods*, had just gone on the book shelves. While the Eisenhowers were here, they were hidden from all the news men and women. After they left here, I let the pig out of the bag by calling a certain newspaper and told them the secret. The party at the other end of the line said, "So that's where he's been. We have been trying to locate him for days!"

Now to get back to the shirt tale. While the Eisenhowers were here, Mary did their laundry. I don't know why, but one day I came home to change my clothes; something I seldom do. I went to the clothes-line and instead of getting my T-shirt, I got John's.

When Mary went to take the Eisenhowers' clothes from the line, she missed one T-shirt. I had been wearing it, thinking it was mine. When Frank heard of this, he sat down and composed the following:

The teacher went off to school one day
Feeling so fine and pert,
But soon discovered to his dismay,
He had stolen Mr. Eisenhower's T-shirt.

At first he said, "This cannot be!"
And would not the truth believe.
So he hurried home to undress and see
Whether he did deceive.

Imagine the look on Haziel's face
Who now appeared baggy as a barge.
How come this shirt was thus misplaced,
Which read extra large?

This certainly proves a serious point,
Not easy to define.
If this matter devised by joint,
Now I know what happened to mine.

In fairness this I must confess:
The shirt he did return,
To avoid no doubt a quick arrest
Or at the stake to burn.

All my friends I now alert
As we go from door to door;
Begging please just one li'l shirt,
To send this boy so poor.

I'm happy to say we did succeed
In getting his little shirt,
In hope this desire would now recede
As they seek to remove the dirt.

This tale disclosed, I hope no offense,
Yet the horrible thought occurred to me:
Suppose it had been the dear man's pants
What an awful sight we then would see!!!

Stories and Anecdotes

Lost Suitcase

The story is told of a little boy who told his teacher that "memory is the thing you forget with."

Uncle Norman is a well-known story-teller as all who live or have visited our island know. Besides the old stories, he often picks up new ones, especially on his visits to Nassau. Here is one of them.

Uncle Norman went to Nassau by plane. When he claimed his baggage, he did not notice his claim check number. He picked up a suitcase which looked like his and away he went into town. When he arrived at a friend's home where he was going to stay, he opened the suitcase. To his surprise, he saw lady's clothes! Realizing what had happened, he called the Nassau Airport, and finally made the exchange. Uncle Norman thought that this was a funny story on himself; and when he returned home, most of us heard it several times.

Some months later, Evangelist Frank Perry came here, and Uncle Norman began to tell him about the incident. He went on and on, telling how other people had lost their baggage, but in so doing he got away from his story on to other topics. After about twenty minutes, he paused and said to Frank, "Why did I tell you all this? What did we start talking about?"

Frank replied, "Uncle Norman, you've got me. I don't know." After thinking a while, Uncle Norman said, "Oh, I know; it was about my suitcase." By this time, Frank, who had heard enough to digest at one time, said, "Never mind, Uncle Norman, you can tell me the rest later!"

Hidden Treasure

It is believed that treasure was hidden on Man-O-War during the days of the pirates. According to the records or rumours, the treasure-laden vessel landed on the North-east side of our cay or island near a cove or small cave, went south across the island and buried the treasure under the brow of a hill. Papa owned that lot of land for many years. Papa, Uncle Will, and others found the spot—a hole hewn in or out of the rock. After digging out the loose stones and soil, unfortunately, the valuable stuff was not there. When Papa sold this land to Mr. and Mrs. Carleton Francis, Jr., some of the first Americans to build a vacation home here, it was with the written agreement that if ever the treasure is found the seller or his heirs and the buyers or their heirs would go 50-50 in dividing it. When Carleton Francis III, who is now the owner of the place known as "Treasure Hill" was a boy, he became so excited about the treasure that he thought he would use up some of his energy and dig and sift the soil in that area. He dug all the way to solid rock, but was not successful. Later he decided to try again. In the meantime, his parents bought some gold-coloured chocolate coins and put them in the hole. Judge the surprise on Carlie's face when he first saw these! Well, true to their agreement Carlie's parents, my good friends, Carlie and Denise, brought Papa half of the candy coins! It is believed that the treasure was or had been hidden there, but was either collected by the owners or some other pirate. Who knows? It could have been the famous English Seadog, Sir Francis Drake, or Black Beard! Over the years several treasure-hunters have searched the reefs and waters around Man-O-War. It has not been revealed how much has been recovered. When I was a boy, there was a common expression "So and so has gone to Cuba to learn how to make sugar." It was said that these people have dug gold!

The Recovery of Our Cannon

Among the many things of interest along the water-front of our main harbour, there is a mounted gun at the foot of our public dock.

Is it for defense? No, it does not even work! How did it get there?

One beautiful day, the date to be exact, was the 29th of January 1949, the motor-sailer *Lucayo* skippered by the owner Bill Lee with Uncle Will, Uncle Ted, Skipper Robinson, Vernon, Cyril, Hilland, and others went out to our reef where this gun with others had been for eighty-seven years. During these years other valuable things had been removed, and no doubt, attempts had been made to take up one of the guns, but without success.

This crew of brave Man-O-War men went with one thought in mind and that was to bring one of the guns to our shore. Vernon was the diver. In those days it was considered a venture to dive anywhere in our reefs and channels. Now it is done without any thought of danger both commercially and for pleasure. Vernon took a cable down and fastened it to the gun. After some doing they managed to break the coral that had grown around it. They found the gun so heavy that the best they could do was to drag it to deeper water. Now that it was off the bottom, the *Lucayo* moved slowly in the deeper water along the reef and in our North-west Channel.

Anchored in this Channel, off the north-west end of Man-O-War was the large Yacht *Janene* which had come to tow a boat. It had been built by Uncle Will for Sir Oliver Simmons of Nassau.

The *Lucayo* went over to the *Janene* and Bill Lee asked the Captain if he could help in the lifting of the gun. The captain and officers thought Bill Lee and his crew wanted the gun on the deck of the *Lucayo*. When they understood that it was only wanted to the surface of the water, one of them replied, "Yes, we'll do that little thing for you!" With the winches on the *Janene* and the *Lucayo*, they managed to get the gun to the surface! Then with the high tide, it was brought in our harbour and along side the dock and finally with quite a bit of man power it was dragged ashore and mounted in its present location.

After the gun was recovered, it was suggested that some research be done, so my dear friend, Mr. Neil C. McMath, who came to be affectionately called Uncle Neil, took up the challenge and wrote to the U.S. Naval Academy in Annapolis, Maryland, requesting information on this gun and the wrecked vessel which we had always known as the *Adirondack*. They were very much interested in our recovery and kindly supplied valuable information which I have summarized and which should be of interest to my readers.

The U.S. Screw Steam Sloop *Adirondack* was built by the U. S. Government in 1862. Cost: $209,242.70. Length: 207 feet. Beam 38 feet. Draft: 10 feet. Tonnage: 1240.

Stories and Anecdotes

Shortly after the outbreak of the Civil War, or War between the States, in 1861, the North blockaded the Southern ports to prevent the shipping of cotton to England and the bringing in of supplies and munitions to the South. Although Queen Victoria had issued a proclamation of neutrality, the sympathy of the English and colonials was naturally with the South, since that was the source of the cotton for the booming English Mills. This sympathy was especially strong in Bermuda and Nassau since these islands quickly began to prosper by being convenient places to transfer all sorts of goods from the bigger vessels to smaller and faster blockade-runners. By the summer of 1862 this had become big business for Nassau and many Bahamians. Since officially Nassau was a neutral port, ships of the North, the South, and England were permitted entrance.

First trip of the *Adirondack* to Nassau:

On the 11th July 1862 Commander Gansevoort of the U.S. Screw Steam Sloop *Adirondack* received in New York orders to go to sea as soon as the ship was ready. The ship left New York and after opening the sealed orders found that they were to proceed to Nassau, investigate the situation, and report back as soon as possible. Especially Captain Gansevoort was to investigate a rumour that a fast-sailing steamer of professedly British Registry, was in Nassau being fitted out for war purposes and to be used against the North. It had also been reported that a Southern Captain of a Confederate ship, which had been sunk, had arrived in Nassau with a good many of his crew. Putting two and two together it seemed this rumour was worth checking up on.

The *Adirondack* arrived in Nassau on the 25th of July after an eight days' passage from New York. On the way, 120 miles North of Hole-in-the-Wall, the southern end of the island of Abaco, they captured the schooner *Emma* of Nassau. They also fired on another vessel, which was faster, and escaped to Nassau, where, because of the neutrality proclamation they were safe. Three days after arriving in Nassau, Commander Gansevoort made his first report. He described how, because of the bad weather on the trip, he needed coal and supplies as well as time for repairs, and was granted permission to anchor by Governor Bayley.

He reported that "nearly the whole population is in open and notorious sympathy with the rebels." Steamers in large numbers were arriving from England with all sorts of goods, the warehouses and even some houses, were full, awaiting shipment to the South. Guns and munitions of war marked C. S. A. (Confederate States of America) were openly hauled through the streets, loaded on steamers well known to be blockade runners, without any attempt at concealment of their intentions. All harbour regulations were nullified for the rebels, and not only enforced for the Northern ships but all sorts of delays and evasions were encountered.

The report also included the status of the *Oreto* which was openly being fitted out as a war vessel with sixteen ports not large enough for heavy guns, and the purpose was known to everyone. Almost every vessel arriving from Charleston brought out men to form her crew. The vessel had ostensibly been seized by the British naval authorities, but the Southern crew and officers were free to roam the streets of Nassau.

Man-O-War: My Island Home

After gathering as much information as possible, the *Adirondack* returned to Hampton Roads, Virginia, and on the 4th of August 1862 a more complete report was made. As a result the *Adirondack* received new orders to proceed to the vicinity of Nassau to spread the word to other Northern ships and to intercept and capture the rebel steamer *Oreto* but not to violate neutral rights by doing anything within a full marine length of neutral territory.

Under their new orders the *Adirondack* left Port Royal, South Carolina, headed for Nassau with crew and officers to a total of 216. Everything went well until Saturday the 23rd of August when at about five minutes before four in the morning the ship struck a reef about a mile north of Man-O-War Cay. On the very first thump, the engine was disabled. An anchor was carried out astern but did no good. The ship was lightened as much as possible to no avail. A large force of wreckers went out to their assistance, presumably from Man-O-War, Great Guana, and Green Turtle Cays. Since the *Adirondack* had no boat which could carry out a big bow anchor, the captain tried to hire a wrecking schooner for that purpose, but could come to no agreement with any of the owners. Finally, at about two o'clock in the afternoon, he succeeded in getting the anchor out, but only by purchasing one of the wrecker's boats at what he reported to be an exorbitant price. During the morning the eleven-inch guns had been put overboard, coal had been thrown overboard, and provisions and other articles had been transferred to the wrecking fleet. All efforts to save her were to no avail and at about six p.m. both cables parted, the ship bilged, and her back broken and keel forced up under engine-room floor nearly to a right angle. Except for the Captain and a small crew, the rest of the officers and men were sent to the wrecking fleet for safety. The grounding was on Saturday, and the Captain reported he stayed on board until Tuesday the 26th trying to save as much Government property as he could.

Very soon after the ship struck, a boat was dispatched to Nassau to let the U.S. Consul there know of the wreck. The message was "Send us a steamer immediately; we are ashore. Don't delay. Charter her at once. The sea is smooth and we hope to escape." Head winds prevented the boat from going any further than Hole-in-the-Wall so that message did not reach Nassau until Tuesday morning of the 26th.

On Monday the 25th of August a U.S. Navy Ship, the *Magnolia*, happened to come by and spot the wreck. They had received word that the *Oreto* had left or escaped from Nassau. This caused the Captain to decide to spike and otherwise mutilate all the guns remaining on board to prevent their being taken and used against the North. Two vessels were hired to hold the salvaged goods and provisions. The agreement with the owner of the vessel which had been purchased to carry out the anchor at a cost of $2,500.00 was canceled, and $625.00 was paid for the vessel's use.

The Consul in Nassau did not receive word of the wreck until Tuesday the 26th as mentioned earlier; and when he tried to charter a boat to come to their assistance, he met with no success; no one having any sympathy for a Northern warship. The Consul did come in a small boat but too late to do anything, except make arrangements for the Government property which had been saved, all but arms, munitions, powder, etc., being sent to Nassau.

Stories and Anecdotes

The Consul reported that stores and materials had been removed into the harbour and that the crew were "comfortably bestowed on shore under spacious tents, and were under the best discipline, and in good health." Although not mentioned by name, it could be assumed he meant Man-O-War Cay, since it is the closest.

After returning to Port Royal on the 5th of September Captain Gansevoort in his report attributed the loss of the ship to a mistake in calculating the position made by his navigator, Lt. Parker, and to a westerly current, but at the same time praised him highly as an excellent officer and able navigator.

The Consul in Nassau also praised the Captain and Navigator reporting "The most consummate seamanship and the most perfect navigation are often at fault among the treacherous currents of the Bahama reefs."

The Navigator's statement was that he had a good morning sight at 7:30 a.m. on Friday the 22nd which would place the vessel about forty-five miles due north of Moraine Cay, and while the report does not say so, they seem to have been on a course, which would have run them to Nunjack Cay. Carrying this same course backwards will take you straight to Port Royal, their departure point. There was some difference in the two sights taken at 4:40 in the afternoon, but the Navigator made a dead reckoning of position at 8 p.m. and went to the Captain. This reckoning placed them about fifteen miles due North of Powell Cay and definitely on a 1630 course towards the reef. At 8:30 the course was changed to S.E. by E. or 123 degrees. This course was to be run for forty miles at which time it was to be changed to S. by E. or 968 degrees and then run until daylight. This course should have taken them about seven miles east of Elbow Cay.

The report states with no explanation that the log shows that at midnight the course was changed to S.E. by S. or 146 degrees which should still have taken them by Elbow Cay with at least three or four miles to spare. It could be that someone decided to take the short side of the triangle and save five or six miles. On paper this would still have been a safe course.

The Navigator's report is also interesting in giving the location of the wreck as latitude 26 38' N. Longitude 76 54' W., which according to present charts places the wreck six or seven miles almost due east of its actual location, in about six hundred feet of water.

Whether or not the wreck of the *Adirondack* was due to navigator's error, five miles off after a run of three hundred and fifty to four hundred miles is not too bad; and they had been five miles west of where they thought they were for some time, or whether the set of the current was more than expected is debatable. It is interesting that the stated position of the wreck is almost about five miles east of its actual location, which might indicate that the navigator's dead reckoning position of the night before was off by five miles.

Two things are certain. First, the local legend that the *Adirondack* was being chased by an enemy vessel when going aground is without any basis. Second, there are still numerous cannons close to the reef only a mile or so off the northern end of Man-O-War Cay. They are easily visible from small boats on a windless day if there is no rage or surge. Such a calm perfect day on Man-O-War is now referred to as a "Cannon Day."

Stories of Three-Pences

One Sunday afternoon Thomas, Marcell, and I were taking our usual walk. It seemed that at the same time the three of us sighted a bright shining coin right before us in the road. Quickly we picked it up. It was one of those tiny coins—a threepence! We hurried to get this changed into three of those large English pennies so we could share it. We felt at that time we had found a small gold mine.

One day Mamma gave me a three pence and sent me to get a hat from Mrs. Charity, Mr. Kenneth's mother. She sewed the hand-plaited hats for our people for threepence. When I arrived at Mrs. Charity's, the threepence had disappeared, or at least, I could not find it! Then a search began—from Mrs. Charity's home to our home and back again. Night was coming on and there was no time to be lost. After spending some time looking for this valuable piece of money, it was found! Where? In a pleat or crevice in my pocket.

Mama Nellie

Mammy Nellie seemed to be respected by her family and she made a good leader in the settlement. As a boy, I wondered why we always heard so much about Mammy Nellie and not Pappy Ben. I think the answer is: she owned the land which was given to her by her father, Pappy Ben Archer. "This kinda made her the boss!"

She was what we call today a strict lady. When she saw any of her grandchildren misbehaving, she broke a switch or small branch from a bush, gave them a switching, and then tied the switch and the hands of the child behind him or her. Without any question, when the child returned home, there was another whipping as all parents respected Mammy Nellie.

"Sparits" and Dreams

It was said by some of the early settlers that they heard "sparits" on certain occasions. One day some of the Sawyers left their home which was situated near the spot now known as "Angel's Landing" owned by Ruth Rodriguez, and went to their field on "Jack's Hill." The women and girls were busy at their chores, when they heard the call, "Bring the taletons (a kind of medication, and old rags) Par's cut!" Quickly, they took these things and ran up the dirt path to find, to their pleasant surprise, the men and boys all at work! Before they really saw that all was well, they called out, "How bad is the cut? How did he get it?"

Par and the boys questioned them, and then said: "Nothing's happened; we did not call you!" This incident sort of confirmed the "sparit" belief.

Since that time, and even today, you might hear the saying: "Bring the taletons and old rags, Uncle Sam or Uncle John has a bad cut!"

Uncle Norman's mother, Aunt Sarah, who used to work in the fields with her grandchildren on the property in the Head-of-the Harbour, often dreamt of houses on the various hills on the land in the Eastern Harbour. Of course, those were the days before the Americans came, and no one thought there would ever be such a colony as it is today. Her dream "came true." There's a house on every hill-top that she dreamed about.

Aunt Sarah's brother, Uncle Dick, at one period kept a field on the land just to the South-east of the cemetery. He often came from his field with the report that he had heard voices, he thought children's voices, coming from the South-east where the American homes are now. Uncle Will, son of Uncle Dick, sometimes questioned him about this, but Uncle Dick assured him that he heard voices!

A Sailor's Unthankfulness

Man-O-War people have always been known to be hospitable. About the 1840's a ship was wrecked on our barrier reef. The Captain and his crew all managed to get ashore safely on our island. Grand-papa Bill and Grand-mamma Lydia tried to help them and fed them with such food as they had, and also gave them lodging, pending the arrival of a boat to take them to their home.

One morning it was about nine o'clock when Grand-mamma Lydia got around to serving the last of the crew. One of them complained by saying, "This is sometime of a morning for a young man to get his breakfast!" Grand-mamma Lydia accepted this and said nothing, but one of the sailors told the Captain about it. He soon ordered all of his crew to assemble in the yard, and then told Grand-mamma Lydia to point out the one who had complained. Reluctantly, she pointed him out. The Captain scolded him in the presence of them all by saying, "These people have showed us every kindness and are giving us the best they have, and you can be so ungrateful!" The Captain gave the sailor a good flogging. He behaved himself from that time until he and the others left our shores.

The Rooster That Had Warts

There is plenty of food nowadays, so young men having a cookout on Christmas and New Year's Eve, as well as any other time, generally buy their own food. This was not the case years ago. It was customary to steal the chickens from the coops or from their roosts in the trees, clean, fry and eat them. If anyone had a special hen, she might be kept in the home for the night.

One time about thirty-five years ago, the young men or boys, in the darkness of the night, stole an old tough sickly rooster. The next day the owners said they didn't mind losing him, as he was covered with warts, and they never would have eaten him anyway. A poem was made up about this incident. The author regrets that he does not remember all of it, but here's one line: "He had no sign of warts, but fat as he could be!" There is no certainty if it referred to the rooster or the boy.

Chapter XIV.
In Conclusion

I, the writer, have tried to share with you, the reader, the story of my beloved Man-O-War. All of my life has been lived here in the Settlement. The longest time I have spent away from my island is three weeks and that was only within the last ten years. In 1968 Mary and I went to England to visit the land from which my people came over two centuries ago. It was also the country to which my first loyalty was given and it too is an island.

How many people have written, sung, and talked about getting away from the hustle and bustle of life in the city. To find a quiet spot in the country or an island in the sea is part of all of our dreams. To me it has been a reality. I used to sing about it as a student in our Man-O-War school, and we still do.

> If I had a hundred golden pounds
> I would leave the great City's roar
> And I'd buy a little country house
> With a shining stream at my door
> In the country-side I would settle down
> Far from all the din of the busy town
> And a happy life I'd lead there
> And a happy life I'd lead.

The life of our first islanders was a hard one. The daily tasks done or left undone meant survival or starvation. Fish were caught to eat at the next meal and the left-overs if there were any were salted to preserve them for our future needs. The beaches were combed for planks, sperm, ambergris, rope, and rubber.

Coral hillsides were cleared for farming. Trees were cut down and sawed into planks for boats and boards for our homes. Palm fronds were cut for roof thatching. Fresh water only came as rain; so pits were dug into the coral rock bed for cisterns and in our cemetery on the northeastern shore for our loved ones' graves.

Now many come to our island for relaxation, for a short change from the usual routine of life at home on the mainlands, and a few have come to stay with us.

I watch our visitors walk along the Sea Road and The Queen's Highway stopping to see the ship builders, sail-makers, craw fishermen, carpenters, shell crafters, shop keepers and the boat skippers at their work. I think they stop and look because of the craftmanship. It isn't how many nails we put in an hour, but how well they are put in.

Papa had a saying, one which I'm sure is a familiar one: "Whatever is worth doing is worth doing well." I remember it very well. As a boy I was doing one task but anxious to get to the next exciting adventure, and I was putting putty over the sunken nail heads in a dinghy with little care, hoping to be off and away. But Papa came by, saw my sloppy job, and started me over by saying the statement above.

Industry and craftsmanship have been part of our island heritage, one of which we are very proud. It could be seen in the early years in the lines of a dinghy, a sculler's oar, the carved handle of a kitchen pot, or a rocking chair for the parlour. Craftsmanship is still a by-word today as we build our homes and houses for the Americans and others who come to rent or to stay with us. The skill of our shipyard managers and workers is evidenced in the boats which come to us for hauling and repairs, the Albury ferries built here in our ship ways, the dinghys, and our renowned racing boat, *Rough Waters*.

Our visitors from afar and even our neighbors on the other islands have brought us many things, maybe too many. We now have and enjoy a better standard of living. We do feel that there are certain things we have cherished over the years we may lose. As a teacher, when I see sleepy-eyed children at 9:00 a.m. in my school room, I am sure they watched a late T.V. show the night before.

When Uncle Norman looked for the meat grinder as a boy his only obstacles were natural ones. Today with golf carts, motor bikes, big and little bicycles, trucks, and jeeps, one has to be alert so as not to be hit by a wheeled vehicle. We have no policeman to direct traffic or to represent higher authority on our island. We have always been able to settle our disputes internally. I hope we can continue to do so.

We want tourists to visit us. I would be foolish if I was not appreciative of the benefits our island economy has had from tourism. We want them to feel part of our life and at home on our island. But I and my family, immediate and island wide, have a love for Man-O-War ingrained in us and I guess we are protective of its shores, trees, homes, churches, harbours, school and way of life.

My great, great, great, great, great grandfather and grandmother welcomed people to a shallow but protected harbour and a few thatched roof homes. Those early visitors were ship-wrecked sailors, spongers or fishermen. The fare was simple: fish cooked over an open fire, bread baked in an outdoor oven, soldier crabs, salt beef and maybe turtles' eggs.

Uncle Will welcomed the first Americans, Skipper Robinson and Ted Zickes, to Man-O-War over forty years ago and he continued to welcome many more over the years. Uncle Will's spirit of helpfulness, his sense of fair play and unselfish service pervaded every part of our way of life through the middle of this century. Naturally countless other islanders, men, women, and children contributed to make Man-O-War the island we know and love today. I was excited when I first began to write this book. Perhaps in some way I could catch the spirit of my island home, and my family's island and their family's so that others might learn of it.

In Conclusion

This book is a written history but most of its source material was oral. It is as Mamma Nellie told her children, who told their children, and so on down. Over the past few years as I have been writing about our island I have learned so much from Mama and Uncle Norman.

I hope too I have conveyed to you my appreciation of my heritage and maybe you will wish to tell your children so that they can tell their children about this island just to the northeast of Abaco in the Bahamas.

Appendix
A Genealogy

Births and deaths have always been recorded. In the early days in Family Bibles. Then the information was sent to the Registry of Records in Nassau. For many years in order for a person to get a Birth Certificate, it meant a trip to Nassau or asking a relative or friend to do the favour.

In 1966 a new method was introduced: so since that time it is much easier. The information is recorded here on the island on triplicate forms; the original is given to the relatives; one is sent to the Registry of Records in Nassau, and the other is kept in my files.

The family tree which follows was prepared with the help of Malvern and Pat Morse, two of our American residents.

NOTES:
1. A raised number by a name means the generation beginning with Mammy Nellie and Pappa Ben.
2. One line under the name refers to those who married and remained on the island.
3. A name in italics refers to single adults or children who have remained on the island.

Eleanor Archer[1] (Mammy Nellie) married Benjamin Albury of Harbour Island. They had thirteen children: Betsy, Henry, Benjamin, Jr., William, Samuel, John, Mary, *Celestia, Charlotte, Amelia, Joseph, Margaret,* and *Cecilia*.

Betsy[2] married Richard Sawyer. They had four children: John, Samuel, Nathanial and William.

John[3] married Eleanor. They had six children: John, Jr., Robert, Sarah Ann, *Sabrina, Eleanor* and *Richard*.

John Jr.[4] married Rachel Thompson. They had three children: Alice, *Nellie,* and *Teresa*.

Alice[5] married Wesley Albury. They had two children: Lillian and Maurice.

Lillian[6] married Isaac Roberts. They had two children: Bunyan and Hannah.

Maurice[6] married Miriam Weatherford. They had fourteen children: *Belle,* Edwin, *Walter,* Freddy, *Willard,* Alma, Benny, Paul, Sally, Blake, *Elaine, Effie (died)* Effie and Warren.

Man-O-War: My Island Home

Maurice's[6] second wife was Minnie Adams. They had three children: *June, Evelena* and *Wesley.*

Belle[7] married Edison Albury. They had three children: Neville, Karen and Melonie.

Neville[8] married Karen Albury. They had one child: *Brent.*

Karen[8] married Gurney Roberts.

Melonie[8] married Jimmy Albury. They had one child: *Tommy.*

Edwin[7] married Elsie Thompson. They had two children: Lee (died) and *Jannette.*

Freddy[7] married Cecile Roberts. They had three children: Rhonda, *Troy* and Myrid (died infant).

Willard[7] married Dollie Albury. They had three children: *Don, Donna* and *Jamie.*

Benny[7] married Jennie Albury. They had three children: *Glenn*, Doug (died as an infant) and *Lisa.*

Paul[7] married Jackie Key. They had two children: *Carmon* and *Vanice.*

Sally[7] married Arthur Elden. They had four children: *Jill, Pamela, Wendy* and *David.*

Blake[7] married Agnes Albury. They had one child: *Chad.*

Effie[7] married Elliott Roberts. They had one child: *Lee.*

Warren[7] married Sherry Roberts. They had one child: *Doug.*

Sarah Ann[4] married Thomas Albury. They had five children: Ada Ann, Estward, Richard Edgar (Eddie), Celia and Dawson.

Ada Ann[5] married William Sweeting. They had six children: Miriam, Howard, Daisy, Milton, Venie and Mary.

Milton[6] married Doris Weatherford. They had three children: Gloria, Kenneth and Willie.

Gloria[7] married Emanuel Albury. They had one child: *Ada Ann.*

Eddie[5] married Fleetie Saunders. They had nine children: Lewis, Victor, Marie, Alice, Florrie, Cyril, Haziel, Richard Edgar, Jr. (died infant) and William Edward (Eddie).

Lewis[6] married Mizpah Weatherford. They had nine children: Betty, Albert (died as an infant), Hartley, Roland, Myrtle (died as an infant), Joseph, David and Samuel (twins), and Jeffrey.

Joseph[7] married Gerrie Gouchnour.

David[7] married Sharon Roberts. They had one child: *David,* Jr.

Samuel[7] married Arlene Key. They had four children: *Melissa, Leonora, Samantha* and *Mary Lou.*

Jeffrey[7] married Phyllis Roberts. They had two children: *Valerie* and *Sacha.*

Victor[6] married Lorrinda Weatherford. They had three children: Johanna, *Marilyn* and Lorraine.

Johanna[7] married Gladstone Newbold. They had two children: *Lance* and *Cliff.*

Marie[6] married Arthur Weatherford. They had seven children: Everett, *Nellie,* Scott, Ella, Willis, Molly and *Ray.*

Appendix

Scott[7] married Kay Laury. They had two children: *Laura Lynn* and *William*.
Alice[6] married Robbie Weatherford. They had four children: *Tuppy, Sarah Ann, Edith* and Robin.
Robin[7] married Myrna Collins.
Florrie[6] married Emerson Albury. They had nine children: Una, Dollie, Jennie, Lily, Ben, Karen, Agnes, Andy and *Bernard*.
Una[7] married Antonio Albury. They had one child: *Deanna*.
Dollie[7], Jennie[7], Karen[7] and Agnes[7] and their children previously mentioned.
Lily[7] married Keith Albury. They had twin boys: *Timothy* and *Gregory*.
Ben[7] married Barbara Albury. They had one child: *Mamie*.
Andy[7] married Marina Sands. They had one child: *Sonya*.
Cyril[6] married Lois Albury. They had two children: Annie and Jimmy.
Annie[7] married Richard Albury. They had two children: *Randy* and *Caroline*.
Jimmy[7] previously mentioned.
Haziel[6] married Ena Albury. They had three children: Minerva, Denise and Winnie.
Haziel's[6] second wife was Mary Albury. They had one child: Martha.
Minerva[7] married Billy Lowe. They had two children: *Dianna* and *Patti Ann*.
Denise[7] married Wallace McDonald. They had three children: *Charmaine, Mady,* and *Haziel*.
Winnie[7] married Walter Sweeting.
Martha[7] married Richard Roberts.
Eddie[6] married Sarah Thompson. They had six children: *Daisy, Bill,* Jerry (died as an infant), *Bessie, Jane* and *Fannie*.
Celia[5] married Ernest Sweeting. They had four children: Austin, Dorothy, Percival and Thomas.
Percival[6] married Venie Sweeting. They had twelve children: Redith, Robert, Earnest (died as an infant), Charlie, Celia, Walter, *Peter*, Linda, Earnest, *Jerry, Brenda* and *Reggie*.
Redith[7] married Elaine Pinder. They had three children: *Debra*, (Baby boy who died as an infant), and *Kevin*.
Robert[7] married Maggie Russell. They had two children: *Robbie* and *Jessie*.
Charlie[7] married Heather Duff. They had two children: *Tommy* and *John*.
Walter[7] previously mentioned.
Linda[7] married Eugene Weatherford. They had one child: *Amos*.
Henry[2] married Matthia Key. They had seven children: Katherine, Matthia, Jane, Edgar, Nathan, Phoebe, and Sarah.
Matthia[3] married Benjamin Roberts. They had one child: Mary Ann.
Mary Ann[4] married Henry Augustus Fisher, Sr. They had four children: Susan, Rebecca, Annie and Henry, Jr.
Edgar[3] married Sarah Albury. They had one child: Norman.
Norman[4] married Selina Weatherford. They had six children: Vernon, Marcell, Ritchie, Lois, Mary and Hilland.
Vernon[5] married Patricia Albury. They had three children: Stan, *Sandra* and *Gayle*.

Man-O-War: My Island Home

Marcell[5] married Christine Sands. They had two children: *Ralph* and *Matthew*.

Ritchie[5] married Sylvia Russell. They had three children: <u>Barbara</u>, *Michael* and *Ruth*.

Barbara[6], Lois[5], Mary[5], and their children previously mentioned.

Nathan[3] married Priscilla Albury.

Benjamin[2] married Eliza Weatherford. They had eight children: Benjamin Jr., Livingstone, <u>George</u>, Charlotte, <u>Evelina</u>, Nattis, Catherine and Ella.

George[3] married Reca Sands. They had four children: Horace, <u>Emerson</u>, <u>Emanuel</u> and <u>Iva</u>.

Emerson[4] married Florrie[6] Albury. They had nine children and twelve grandchildren all previously mentioned.

Emanuel[4] married Gloria[7] Sweeting as mentioned earlier.

Iva[4] married Marton Weatherford. They had two children: <u>George</u> and <u>Eugene</u>.

George[5] married Clara Albury. They had three children: *Deric*, *Hank* and *Renee*.

Eugene[5] previously mentioned.

Evelina[3] married John Russell. They had two children: <u>Eliza</u> and Hezekiah.

Eliza[4] married Harrison Sands. They had one child: <u>Christine</u>.

Christine[5] and her family already mentioned.

William[2] married Lydia Thompson. They had ten children: <u>Sarah</u>, <u>Thomas</u>, Winer, Annie, <u>Joseph</u> and <u>Richard</u> (twins), <u>Edwin</u>, <u>Minnie</u>, <u>Jeremiah</u> and <u>Wesley</u>.

Sarah[3] married Edgar[3] Albury. They had one child, six grandchildren, thirteen great grandchildren and five great, great grandchildren, all previously mentioned.

Thomas[3] married Sarah Ann[4] Sawyer. Their five children, the grandchildren, great grandchildren and great, great grandchildren who live on Man-O-War have been previously mentioned.

Joseph[3] married Susan Fisher. They had one child: <u>Dalbert</u>.

Dalbert[4] married Blanche Roberts. They had two children: <u>Edison</u> and Norma.

Edison[5] married Belle Albury and their family has been previously mentioned.

Richard[3] married Ida Albury. They had seven children: <u>William</u>, <u>Nelson</u>, <u>Emma</u>, Romelda, <u>Elizabeth</u>, <u>Delaney</u> and <u>Rosa</u>.

William[4] married Madeline Saunders.

Nelson[4] married Therese Cash. They had two children: John and <u>Iva</u>.

Iva[5] married Estelle Thompson. They had two children: *Amy* and *Therese*.

Emma[4] married Newton Sands. They had four children: <u>Lambert</u>, <u>Ruby</u>, <u>Naomi</u> and Morrill.

Lambert[5] married Enid Sawyer. They had one child: Carroll.

Ruby[5] married Carl Russell. They had five children: Shirley, Myrtle, <u>Roy</u>, Carleton, and Philip.

Roy[6] married Ivamae Sands. They had one child: *Artie*.

Naomi[5] married Isaac Roberts. (Naomi was Isaac's second wife.)

Morrill[5] married Virginia McDonald. They had one child: <u>Cannis</u>.

Cannis[6] married Hughena Bethel.

Elizabeth[4] (Lizzie) married Alfred Weatherford. They had three children: Robbie, Marton and Doris. These and their families have been previously mentioned.

Appendix

Delaney[4] married Wilton Albury. They had one child: Redith.
Rosa[4] was the second wife of Wilton Albury. They had four children: Ida, Arelia, Audrey and <u>Richard</u>.
Richard[5] married Annie Albury as previously mentioned.
Edwin[3] married Amanda.
Minnie[3] married Roger Sweeting. They had five children: Issie, Venie, <u>Redith</u>, <u>Tweedie</u> and Louise.
Redith[4] married Laura Albury. They had one child: Venie.
Venie[5] married Percival Sweeting and their families are previously mentioned.
Tweedie[4] married Louise Sands. They had five children: Issie, Minnie, Pat, <u>Roger</u> and *Tweedie, Jr.*
Roger[5] married Margaret Sands. They had six children: <u>Ricky</u>, *Terry, Steve, Wendy, Penny* and *Angel.*
Ricky[6] married Betty Sands.
Jeremiah[3] married Rebecca Fisher. They had one child: Winer.
Wesley[3] married Alice Sawyer. They had two children. Maurice, Lillian and their families who live on Man-O-War have been previously mentioned.
Wesley's[3] second wife was Lizzie Sands and his third wife was Susan Saunders.
Samuel[2] married Susan Weatherford. They had five children: Samuel Jr., Talmage, Thomas, John, <u>Neulon</u>.
Neulon[3] married Patience Albury. They had eight children: Glynton, <u>Gladys</u>, Leslie, <u>Walter</u>, Issie, Basil, Leola, Sammie.
Gladys[4] married Harold Albury. They had six children: Una (died young), Serveia, <u>Ena</u>, <u>Patricia</u>, <u>Vashti</u> and Neulon.
Ena[5] and Patricia[5] and their families have already been mentioned.
Vashti[5] married Harcourt Thompson. They had one child: *Ena*.
Leslie[4] married Mabel Bethel. They had two children: *Keith* and *Antonio*.
Antonio[5] married Una Albury as previously mentioned.
Walter[4] married Winnie Albury. They had three children: Kathryn, Janet and Tommy.
John[2] married Laura Weatherford. They had four children: Adeline, <u>Berdina</u>, <u>Charles</u> and Jeremiah.
Berdina[3] married Johnny Roberts.
Charles[3] married Mottie Saunders. They had four children: <u>Wilton</u>, <u>Laura</u>, <u>Dalphone</u> and Matrid.
Wilton's[4] and Laura's[4] families have already been mentioned.
Dalphone[4] married Irene Weatherford. They had ten children: Floyed, Broward, Inglis, Jerlene, Edna (died as an infant), Edna, Kathy, Allen, Tommy and Johnnie.
Mary[2] married William Thompson (Billy Bo). They had thirteen children: Margaret, William Jr., Elizabeth, <u>Napoleon</u>, Calvin, <u>Emanuel</u>, <u>Evangeline</u>, Donya, Julia, <u>Rachel</u>, Richard, Christiana and Bennett.
Napoleon[3] married Martha Sands. They had five children: <u>Benjamin</u>, <u>Napoleon Jr.</u>, <u>Percy</u>, <u>Laura</u> and Richard.
Benjamin[4] married Charity Sands. They had three children: <u>Kenneth</u>, Hattie and Beauman.

153

Kenneth[5] married Lilias Russell. They had three children: Sarah, Harcourt and Patsy.
Sarah[6] married Eddie Albury and their children are previously mentioned.
Harcourt[6] married Vashti Albury as already mentioned.
Napoleon[4] married Eureka Malone. They had five children: Leonard, Louise, Rowena, Percy and Elsie.
Rowena[5] married Basil Sands. They had seven children: Wayne, Darwin, Gaylene, Steve (died as an infant), *Sherry*, Andrea, and *Ronnie*.
Darwin[6] married Joanne Roberts.
Andrea[6] married Lincoln Albury. They had one child: *Chantelle*.
Elsie[5] married Edwin Albury and their children have already been mentioned.
Percy[4] married Sarah Fisher.
Laura[4] married Willard Sweeting.
Richard[4] married Romelda Albury.
Emanuel[3] married Eleanor Jane Sawyer.
Evangeline[3] married John Sands. They had five children: Harry, Treason, Basil (drowned while a young man), Reca and Vernell.
Harry[4] married Eliza Russell and their family has already been mentioned.
Treason[4] married Millie Albury. They had nine children: Basil, Vera, Wilson, Eula, Charles, Levern, Lola, Vernell, and Margaret.
Basil[5] married Rowena Thompson and their families are previously mentioned.
Vera[5] married Burrall Roberts. They had eleven children: Gurney, Elliott, Sharon, *Larry*, *Buddy*, *Errington*, and *Gerald*. (Clarissa, Issiemae, Paranel and Mark died as infants.)
Gurney[6], Elliott[6], Sharon[6] and their families have already been mentioned.
Wilson[5] married Mabel Sands. They had three children: Elizabeth, Ivamae and Earl.
Ivamae[6] married Roy Russell as already mentioned.
Levern[5] married Sally Roberts. They had four children: *Philip*, Marina, *Lorraine* and *Rowan*.
Marina[6] married Andy Albury as already mentioned.
Lola[5] married Martin Sawyer. They had two children: Marty (died as an infant) and *Gary*.
Margaret[5] married Roger Sweeting and their family is previously mentioned.
Reca[4] married George Albury. Their children and families are previously mentioned.
Vernell[4] married Blatchley Sands.
Rachel[3] married John Sawyer and their families are previously mentioned.
Families on the island who are not directly related to Mammy Nellie and Pappy Ben are listed below:
Robbie Sands (brother of Charity Sands who married Benjamin[4] Thompson) married Vestelle Fisher (sister of Rebecca Fisher, wife of Jeremiah[3] Albury). They had five children: Deweese, Mabel, Winer, Jezreel and Stuart.
Mabel married Wilson[5] Sands and their family is previously mentioned.

Appendix

Donald Russell (half-brother of Maggie Russell who married Robert[7] Sweeting) married Corene Sweeting (half-sister of Percival[6] Sweeting). They had five children: Donnie, Ann, Tony, Jack and Joan.

Perley Roberts (another half-brother of Maggie Russell who married Robert[7] Sweeting) married Sheila Sawyer, from Green Turtle Cay. Sheila is a cousin of the author. They had four children: <u>Richard</u>, Janice, <u>Sherry</u> and *Mark*.

Richard married Martha[7] Albury and Sherry married Warren[7] Albury and are previously mentioned.

B Colorful Expressions

Down through — to the centre of the settlement.

Over back — from the harbour toward the ocean.

Out — from ocean or beach to settlement or harbour.

Down the Cays — means a northwesterly direction. It is believed this saying is used because of the prevailing southeast winds.

Rage — ground swell or rough seas.

Measuring a fish — showing length on arm or larger fish up the leg, rather than distance between hands.

Gully — seagull.

Killer-ka-dick — naming a bird by its call.

Winter birds — any small migrating birds.

Trying to make it — feeling only pretty good.

Pear — avacado.

A Sour — a lemon or lime.

Fishing out in the blue — the deep water beyond the reef.

Seabathing — swimming in the ocean as opposed to swimming in the harbour.

Chilly bin — insulated cooler.

Have a cut-up — salad, generally between meals.

Plane boat — a ferry.

They sent it to me — all useful items and valuable things which float in on the beaches.

Give him down the country or give him a piece of my mind — a scolding.

He gave me a blessing — a scolding.

I could have died — I was so embarrassed.

She's gone away wonderful — some sick person who has been sick and lost weight.

Swallowed the grunt — when someone has not been speaking to another, and then starts to be friendly.

I lotted to go — I intended to go or I expected to go.

If we could only get some rain out of it — Uncle Will used to like to tell the story about his daddy, Uncle Dick. One time during a drought there was a hurricane approaching. As usual, the men were discussing and predicting its course. Uncle Dick said, "If we could only get some rain out of it!" It seemed from his tone of voice that he'd be glad to get the hurricane but would settle for the rain only!

Fowled of ironing — ironing clothes, or getting started ironing.

A couple — Ask a fisherman, "How's the fish?" or "How many fish did you get?" The answer could be "A couple." But when you go and look at the catch, it might be five, six, eight, or more!

C Customs New to Americans

Baking bread in outdoor ovens.

Women were singing in their homes while they worked at their sewing machines, plaiting or preparing meals. Nearly all the men wore blue denim trousers and blue chambray shirts made by their wives or relatives, as were all the clothes for the family.

Mid-morning coffee brought to the men by their wives or the eldest children who were not yet in school.

Men went to work very early, returning for their breakfast about 7:30 a.m. Nearly all the work at the boat-yards was done by hand. Boys just out of school were first taught to saw the timbers brought from the forests into boards.

Children left school on their fourteenth birthday, not the end of the school-year.

When the mail came in from the *Richard Campbell*, all work stopped, school let out, and everybody gathered under the trees as the name on each letter and package was called out by the Postmaster.

Some people started the day by beach combing where many valuable things were found, particularly bales of rubber which were shipped to Nassau and sold during World War II.

One kind of thatch was used for roofing. Another kind for making hats. The leaves were gathered from palm fronds, stripped, dried and plaited, then sewn. It took nine fathoms for the average hat.

Although most of the men were employed at Uncle Will's boat-yard, some could build dinghies at home, send them to Nassau and get two-thirds of the value in cloth, food, and other supplies.

Captain Sherwin's *Arena* was a freight boat with sail. On his stop at Man-O-War he walked from the western end to the eastern end of the town, where people would give him lists of things for him to buy in Nassau. The ladies wanted thread, household goods and even trusted him to buy them Easter hats, more elaborate than the ones they made. Also he would take care of their banking for them, rather than sending it by mail-boat. The *Arena* made round trips as often as possible, but due to weather might take over a month. Her decks were covered with bicycles, shingles, and crates of soda on her return from Nassau.

Lumber was shipped from Nassau with only initials and M.O.W. for identification such as W H A M O W or K T M O W. Many American houses still have these initials on inside ceilings or beams.

Man-O-War: My Island Home

Uncle Will's store carried very little stock. It was necessary to buy everything via Nassau, and all of it retail until many years later when freight boats were able to go to West Palm Beach from Abaco. Only a few eggs were obtainable. The chickens ran wild so eggs were found under bushes and houses with little idea of their freshness.

Almost all food was grown. The local people lived in the village, but did their gardening on inherited plots at each end of the island. These plots were later sold to our winter residents.

The only refrigerator in the area at that time was at Joseph H. (Doddy) Bethel's store at Hope Town. This was used mainly for sodas.

Cables came through Hope Town's Station and were sailed to Man-O-War via dinghy—weather permitting.

Uncle Will took care of emergency accidents. If very serious through the Commissioner and then our Justice of the Peace, a Government plane was sent to take the patient to Nassau. Babies were born with the help of mid-wives.

Rope was made with the Sea Road serving as a rope-walk. Boats were careened on the shore for painting.

Hair cutting was done at the back of the boat shade on Saturday afternoons by myself. Price three pence (about 5 cents). The man having his hair cut sat on a wooden saw horse.

Cisterns were small and families large, so in dry seasons most men sailed to Marsh Harbour or Hope Town after work with all types of containers, buckets, cans, and pots to get water. When there was little or no wind, often they sculled.

The King's or Queen's Highway was a road kept open by the native men from one end of the island to the other to the last property owned or used.

When transportation other than mail-boat was started, planes flew in from Nassau coming up in the morning as far as Green Turtle Cay and back in the afternoon. People came to Man-O-War for business or visits or luncheon for a three-hour stopover in one day. Uncle Will met all the planes in a dinghy.

Since there were no bees, pumpkins were pollinated by hand, called "marrying the pumpkins!"

Young boys, not yet through school, start building a house for the future and before marriage it is livable and ready to move into.

Life for the family and the community is built around the teachings and beliefs of the people's religion, a quiet, genuine, understanding and beautiful way of life.

Burning conch shells in a built-up crawl for lime.

D Island Recipes

Mamma's Old Fashioned Fried Fish

Number of fish depends on size of family. Small fish. One for each child and two or more for adults.

Scorch (score) fish that have been properly cleaned. Sprinkle lightly with salt and pepper. Drain in pan. Length of draining time depends on how late the boys get in from the fishing grounds.

Sprinkle lightly with flour just before placing into a hot iron frying pan with a little lard or shortening. It is delicious on a rainy evening under the kerosene lights.

Mary's Fried Crawfish

6 medium crawfish tails
2 eggs
¼ cup of milk
1 cup of cracker meal
cooking oil or margarine
salt and pepper
lime juice

Break open crawfish tails. Scorch (score) until pieces are flat. Sprinkle lightly with salt and pepper. Lime juice is optional. Dip crawfish in mixture and then roll in cracker meal. Place in heavy pan with hot oil or margarine and fry over medium heat until crawfish is brown and tender. Can also be fried in deep fat.

NOTE: Scale fish and conchs can be cooked this way. Conchs must be pounded first.

Minerva's Conch Chowder

2 small V-8 juice
1 tomato soup
3 cups of water
4 conchs (large)
1 large onion
1 stalk of celery

1 sweet pepper
2 potatoes
1 package of frozen mixed vegetables
lime juice, thyme, tabasco, salt and pepper

Pound and cube conch, then cook until tender. (About 3/4 of an hour).

Fry onion, celery, sweet pepper and thyme. Add juice, soup, and water. Bring to a boil. Add conch, potatoes and vegetables and simmer for about 1/2 hour. Add tabasco and lime juice to taste.

Man-O-War Conch Salad

3 large conchs cut into very small pieces
2 diced tomatoes
1 diced onion
1 diced green pepper
salt and pepper to taste
juice of two Man-O-War limes

NOTE: Hot pepper may be added instead of black pepper as is the custom of most Bahamians.

Martha's Cay Lime Pie

1 sweetened condensed milk
3 egg yokes
½ cup cay lime juice
a few drops of green colouring if desired
1 package of Dream Whip (whipped cream)
3 egg whites

Blend together first four ingredients. In another bowl mix whipped cream following instructions on package. Then add egg whites and whip until stiff peaks form. Now add to first mixture and blend thoroughly. Pour into baked pie crust and chill in refrigerator. Serve with whipped topping.

Mamma Lina's Coconut Pie

Crust:
    3 cups of flour
    2 cups of sugar
    ¼ lb. of butter
    1 cup of milk
    3 eggs
    2 teaspoons of baking powder
    2 teaspoons of vanilla
    ¼ teaspoon of salt

Appendix

Mix together flour, baking powder, and salt. Blend in sugar, butter, eggs and milk. Mix to dough consistency and roll out to put in pie pans. This should make four crusts or enough for two pies.

Filling:

Grate 2 coconuts (medium size). Add a little water and boil fifteen minutes. Add cups of sugar and continue boiling for 15 minutes. Pour into unbaked pie shell. Bake in oven at 350° for 30 minutes or until brown.

Poor Man's Cake or Sweet Bread

2 cups of flour
2 teaspoons of baking powder
1½ cups of sugar
¼ lb. of butter
1 egg
1 teaspoon of vanilla
milk
½ to ¾ cup of raisins

Mix together as you would bread and put in 350° oven to bake until brown.

Island Duff

Cream ½ cup of spry or butter, then add ½ cup of sugar. Add 2 eggs, one at a time and beat well. Combine 2 teaspoons of baking powder with 2 cups of flour. Add this to batter with 3/4 cup of milk and one teaspoon of vanilla.

Put batter in greased 5-lb. shortening tin and boil in a pot for 1½ to 2 hours.

NOTE: guavas, dates, or raisins may be added just before cooking.

Patricia's Pumpkin Bread

3 cups of sifted flour
½ teaspoon of baking powder
1 teaspoon of baking soda
1 teaspoon of nutmeg
1 teaspoon of ground cloves
1 teaspoon of ground cinnamon
½ teaspoon of salt
3 cups of sugar
1 cup of vegetable oil
3 eggs
16 ounces mashed cooked pumpkin
1 cup coarsely chopped raisins
1 cup chopped walnuts

Heat oven to 350°. Grease 2 loaf pans and dust lightly with flour. In a medium size bowl sift together flour, baking powder, baking soda, nutmeg, cloves, cinnamon and salt. In a large mixing bowl place sugar, oil, and eggs. Stir well. Stir pumpkin into egg mixture. Gradually add sifted dry ingredients to egg mixture stirring well after each addition. Fold raisins and nuts into batter. Pour batter into prepared pans and bake one hour and 15 minutes or until cake tester comes out clear. Remove bread from oven and cool on a wire rack for 10 minutes before removing from pan.

Florrie's Man-O-War Bread

8 cups of flour
½ cup of sugar
4 teaspoons of salt
½ cup of shortening
2 teaspoons of yeast
water

Put yeast in a cup of lukewarm water. Mix flour, salt, sugar, and shortening in a large pan. Stir yeast until dissolved and pour into flour mixture. Add enough water to make dough the right consistency for kneading. Knead out six times or about 10 minutes. Leave in a covered pan until dough is about three times its original size or in about 9½ hours. Cut into 4 even pieces, and shape into loaves. One loaf size piece will also make 1 dozen rolls. Put into loaf or roll pans and cover again until pan is full or in about 1½ hours. Bake in 350°–400° oven for 30 minutes or until brown.

Index

Abaco Food Supply 72
Abaco Lumber Company 55
Abaco Sea 4
Abbott, Mr. 69
Albury and Archer: For additional names see Appendix A Genealogy. Ada 78; Amelia 5; Ancil 90; Annie 64; Ben 78, 120; Benjamin 4, 5, 53, 56, 73, 142, 146; Benjamin Jr. 5; Benny 57; Betsy 5; Betty 44; Cecelia 5; Celestia 5; Charlotte 5; Cyril 10, 17, 23, 36, 118, 126, 138; Dawson 102; Denise 78, 127, 129; Dick 107, 108, 113, 114, 117, 143, 158; Dollie 56; Eddie 70, 81, 122, 123 (Papa) 23, 25, 27, 31, 41, 54, 62, 66, 68, 70, 78, 81, 93, 99, 102, 107, 114, 117, 121, 122, 123, 125, 126, 137, 142, 146, 147; Edgar 63, 69, 117; Edwin 51, 53, 54, 57, 69, 72; Eleanor 5; Elsie 51; Emerson 56, 72; Ena 126-127; Fleetie (Mamma) 21, 31, 77, 78, 81, 123; Florrie 77, 78; Garnet 90; Grandmamma Lydia 143; Grandpapa Bill 117, 143; Grandpapa Uriah 10; Great-Grandpapa Bill 95, 96; Henry 53; Horace 72; Hilland 138; Jack I 92, 126; Jeremiah 53; Joe 53, 63; John 5; Johnnie Sr. 63, 69; Johnnie Jr. 63; Joseph 5; Lee 51; Lela 22; Leland 56, 72, 89, 107; Leslie 1, 80; Lewis 31, 43, 44, 54, 57, 81; Lilian 90; Lily 44; Lloyd 90; Lois 64; Lydia 77; Mady 55, 119; Marcell 18, 72, 107, 124, 142; Margaret 5; Mary 5, 44, 64, 80, 104, 119, 123, 128, 129, 135, 136, 145; Maurice 57; Melonie 64; Mertland 72; Mizpah 135; Minerva 44, 80, 123, 129; Nellie (Mammy) Archer 4, 5, 35, 38, 42, 73, 142, 146; Norman 18, 41, 42, 54, 62, 63, 64, 69, 72, 78, 83, 96, 97, 107, 108, 124, 135, 137, 142, 146, 147; Patience 96; Patricia 64, 127, Rebecca 5; Ritchie 107; Sarah 77, 124, 142; Sarah Ann 19; Samuel 5; Scott 100; Sherman 90, 91; Thomas 17, 53, 102, 142; Vashti 44; Vernon 18, 64, 96, 107, 108, 109, 110, 111, 112, 113, 124, 127, 138; Victor 54, 97, 102, 121; Wesley 10, 53, 90, 121, 124; Will 4, 18, 19, 25, 32, 42, 54, 55, 56, 63, 78, 79, 81, 82, 97, 101, 103, 107, 108, 109, 110, 113, 122, 129, 137, 138, 143, 146, 158, 160; William Christie 112; Williard 57; Willie 4; Wilton G. 49; Winer 53; Winnie 127, 129.

Albury's Ferry Service 57
Alma 119, 120
Animals 17, 18
Archers .... See Albury

Bahamas Airways Limited (B.A.L.) . 91, 92
Bahamas Family Island Regatta ... 99-101
Bahamian Language 49
Bain, Mr. Rodney 44
Barnes, Mr. & Mrs. 127
Barton, Mr. Robert B.M. 126, 127, 128
Bayley, Governor 139
Belize 25
Bethel: Archie 90; Chester 96, 127; John 44; Joseph H. 124, 160; Victor 72
Birds 27, 30
Birth Records 149
Boats: *Abaco* 57, 62-63, 99-101; *Abaco II* 101; *Abaco Bahamas* 62-63; *Adirondack* 138; *Albertine* 81-89; *Alice* 65; *Arena* 90, 159; *Atalanta* 35, 118; *Britannia* 128; *Church Bay* 56; *Complete* 65; *Doctor Fly* 80; *Donald Roberts* 56; *Doris* 65, 99; *Edna M* 89; *Emerald* 65; *Emma* 139; *Eulah M* 65; *Evangel I* 79; *Evangel II* 79; *Faith* 53, 63; *Galvanic* 65, 99; *Good News* 100-101; *Green Cross* 79; *Janene* 138; *Joyce Roberts* 56; *Lena Grey* 57; *Lily S* 65; *Lone Star* 65; *Louise* 67; *Lucayo* 122, 138; *Magic* 65; *Magnolia* 140; *Malola* 57; *Miami* 62; *Minerva* 125; *M. V. Content* 90; *M. V. Cordeaux* 122; *M. V. Deborah K* 90; *M. V. Fendo* 99-100; *M. V. Lady Dundas* 90; *M. V. Richard Campbell* 90, 113, 159; *M. V. Stede Bonnett* 90; *M. V. Tropical Trader* 132; *M. V. Tropical Trader II* 90; *Olive* 65; *Oreto* 139; *Primrose* 63; *Priscilla* 89; *Regain* 65; *Remax* 70; *Resolve* 65; *Resource* 57, 65; *Rester* 57, 63; *Robert Fulton* 80; *Rough Waters* 146; *Sea Horse* 63; *Sea Lark* 100; *Sea Witch* 69; *Serence* 65; *Signet* 65; *Spray* 65; *Stella* 65, 69; *Stormy Weather* 100; *Sweet-Heart* 55, 98, 108; *Temperance* 53; *Tepee* 122; *The Lily S* 99; *Thunder Bird* 100; *Tidal Wave* 100; *Trot* 35; *Truant* 65; *Try-on* 118; *Useful* 54; *Valiant* 53; *V.M.R.* 107; *Whistler* 64; *Wild Boar* 53; *William H. Albury* 57; *Windfall* 64; *Windstark* 107; *Witness* 79; *Wynne* 114
Boat Building 53-65

Bootle, Mr. & Mrs. 109
Braynen, Mr. A. R. 51, 52
Brooks, Mr. 31
Bruce, Peter & Jean 127
Butler, Sir Milo & Lady 33

Cameron, John & Wife 124
Campbell: John 35; Hugh 35
Charity, Mrs. 135, 142
Chickens 18
Christie, Frank 91
Churches: 35, 36; Brethren 35; Church of England 35; Gospel Chapel 36; Gospel Hall 136; Methodist 35, 36
Collins: Harry 5; J. W. 5
Commonwealth Day 33
Communications 92-93
Conchs 15, 16, 26
Cottis, Mr. Hugh 51
Cottman, Dr. Evans 79-80
Cotton 21
Cove, Dr. Norman & Yvonne 82
Crandall, Mr. & Mrs. 122
Crawfishing 70-72
Cross, Commissioner Kinnear 31
Curry, Captain Cromwell 89

Dalbert: Mr. 65, 122; Uncle Joe 65
Dredging 1, 4
Drownings 117-120

Edwin's Boat Yard 57
Eisenhower, John & Barbara 135-136
Emma, Mrs. 135
Erie Canal 4

Farming a Field 73
Farrington, Mr. William H. 36
Feinberg, Mr. Max 97
Fell, Mr. & Mrs. Bernard 36, 128
Fisher, Mrs. Henry 42, 53, 63
Flowers 26
Ford, Mr. & Mrs. Hobart 114, 127
Francis: Carleton S. Jr. 114, 137; Carleton III 114, 137
Fraser, Mr. James 35
Fred, Captain 72
Fruits 18, 19
Funeral Services 38, 39

Gansevoort, Commander 139, 141
Genealogy 149-155
George, Mr. 54
Gladys, Mrs. 22
Gottlieb, Dr. & Mrs. Ejnar 80, 120
Greenman, Mr. B. C. 35
Grey, H. E. Sir Ralph 129
Griffin, Jean 78
Grocery Stores 19

Harbours: Creek 1; Dickeys Cay 1; Eastern 1; Illustration 3
Harold, Mr. 51, 72
History of Independence 33
Home Remedies 82-83
Hope Town 31
Horton, Mr. 36
Howes, Dr. & Mrs. Hermon .. 81, 126, 127
Hurricanes 120-124
Hutchinson, Mr. T. 44, 51

Isaac, Mr. 126

Jobs 48-49
Johnson Dr. Sam 78; Mr. 4, 44, 81, 126; Steward 82
Jones, D.H.J. 124
J.P. Sands Company of Nassau 62

Kendrick, Dr. & Mrs. Walter .. 35, 38, 78-79
Kenneth, Mr. 122
Key: Gerald 72; Lewis 99-100; Neville 107
Knapp, Mr. Christopher 35
Knowles, Mr. R. E. 92

Lambert: Emma 77; Morrill 72
Land Disputes 4
Laura, Mrs. 20
Law-Suits 31-32
Lee: Derek 114; Mary Davis 114; Bill & Alice 1, 45, 82, 114, 122, 138
Liskey, Paul 57
Lowe, Mr. Harold 72
Lubber's Quarters 26
Lukens, Janey 127

MacKenzie, Mr. & Mrs. Murdo 36
Mallet, Dr. 78
Malone: John 41, 42; Maitland 42
Man-O-War Cay: Birth Records 149-155; Channels 4; Customs 159-160; Description of Island 1, 25; Expressions 157-158; Families & Genealogy 149-155; Government 31-33; Homes 10-15; Land Division 5; Origins of Name 1; Property Names 4; Recipes 161-164
Marsh Harbour Shipping Co. Ltd. 99
Mary's Hideaway 72
Maurice, Mr. 97, 108, 129
McKinney, Donald B. 128
McNath, Mr. & Mrs. Neil 45, 114, 138
Medical Care 77-83
Morse, Malvern & Pat 25, 149
Mount Auburn Gospel Centre Assembly of Brethren 127
Muller, Colonel & Mrs. Eugene 135

Napoleon, Mr. 78
Neilly, Mr. T. B. 44

166

Nelson, Mr. 121
Neulon, Mr. & Mrs. 118
Neville, Sir Robert 33
Norton, Mr. Bill 64

Party Government: Progressive Liberal P.T.L. 32; United Bahamian U.B.P. 32
Patience, Mrs. 21
Pearse: Alice Lee 127; Hermon 81
Peet, Nurse 78
Perry, Frank 135, 136, 137
Pinder: Aline 51; Cracker 26; Lucene 32; Samuel Grey 50, 51
Pindling, Honourable L. O. 32, 33
Pope: Caroline Lee 45; G. D. 45
Post, Mr. 41, 97
Prince Philip 128, 131
Princess Margaret Rose 128
Ptak, Laurence J. 97, 107

Quackenbush, Dr. 122
Quarrying 72-73
Queen Elizabeth II 128-129

Rassin, Dr. 126
Recipes 161-164
Recreation 99-105
Rescues 117-120
Robbins, Brigadier & Mrs. Thomas 25
Roberts: Augustus 89; Benny 63, 69; Birdina 41; George 56; Hartley 36, 89; Isaac 96; Jenkins 57, 62, 63; J. W. Sr. 55, 56; Leland 90; Lloyd 4; Max 72; Osbourne 89; Oswald 72; Roland 36, 89, 90; Rupert 72; Skip 62
Robinson, Charles M. 97, 107-114, 119, 138, 146
Rodday 119-120
Rodriguez, Ruth 142
Roswell, Captain 72
Russell: Carl 80, 119; Edison 91; F. 52; Ivan 31, 32, 43, 44; John 41; Reca 36; Robert 35; Robley 90

Sail-Making 63-64
Sanders, Uriah 69
Sands: Basil 57, 118; Blatchley 118; Eliza 36, 41; Harry 41, 54; John 20, 35; Lambert 97, 118; Lanford 97; Mabel 90; Malvena 97; Richardson 41, 42; Robbie 38, 42, 43, 118; Talbot 118; Treason 54; Vernell 118
Sawin, Phil & Dottie 100
Sawyer: Calvin 90; Charles 72; Dick 4; Eddie 70; E. L. 54; Ernest 72; Fred 72; Lem 54; Roswell 72; Sammie 72; Sylvan 72; Viola 79

Sawyers 4, 142
School 41-45
Seafoods (See also Recipes) 16, 17, 26
Selina, Mrs. 42
Shell Collecting 26
Sherwin, Captain 159
Shipwreck 5
Simms, Mrs. Cecil 36
Sisal 69-70
Smith, Surveyor General 4
Smith's Tract 4
Smithwick, Dr. & Mrs. Reginald H. 81, 126, 127, 128
Sponge Exchange 67
Sponging 10, 65-68
Sports 99-105
Stalin, Mr. Tom 63
St. Clair, Mr. Gordon P. 119
Stebbins, Mr. 35
Stewart: A. H. 35; Sam 35
Storr, Commissioner Carroll 33
Stratton: Lucien 25, 81, 82; Dr. Robert 35, 36, 79, 118; Stewart 25
Sweeting: Ernest 57; Milton 26, 57; Thomas 129-133; Willie 72, 114; William H. 57
Sweetings 130
Sweeting's Shell Shop 5
Symonette: Basil 54; Sir Roland 32, 54
Symonette Shipyards 62, 90

The Abaco Company 57
Therese, Mrs. 135
Thompson: Benjamin 54; Emmanuel 35; Eureka 135; F.O. 97; Leonard 91, 128; Napoleon 54; T.H. 49, 50; William 53
Transportation 89-98
Trees 25
Turtles 16, 26
Tweedie, Mr. 71
Typical Week 19-22

Van Ryn, Mr. August 35, 36

Wall, George 54
Weatherford: Arthur 96; Stanley 90; Robbie 32; Robin 5
Weather Forecasts 23
Wedding Services 38
White, Mr. Porter 36
Wick, Greetie & Phil 127
William H. Albury Shipbuilders, Limited 56-57, 99

Zickes, Mr. & Mrs. Theodore 1, 55, 107, 108, 109, 110-114, 119, 138, 146

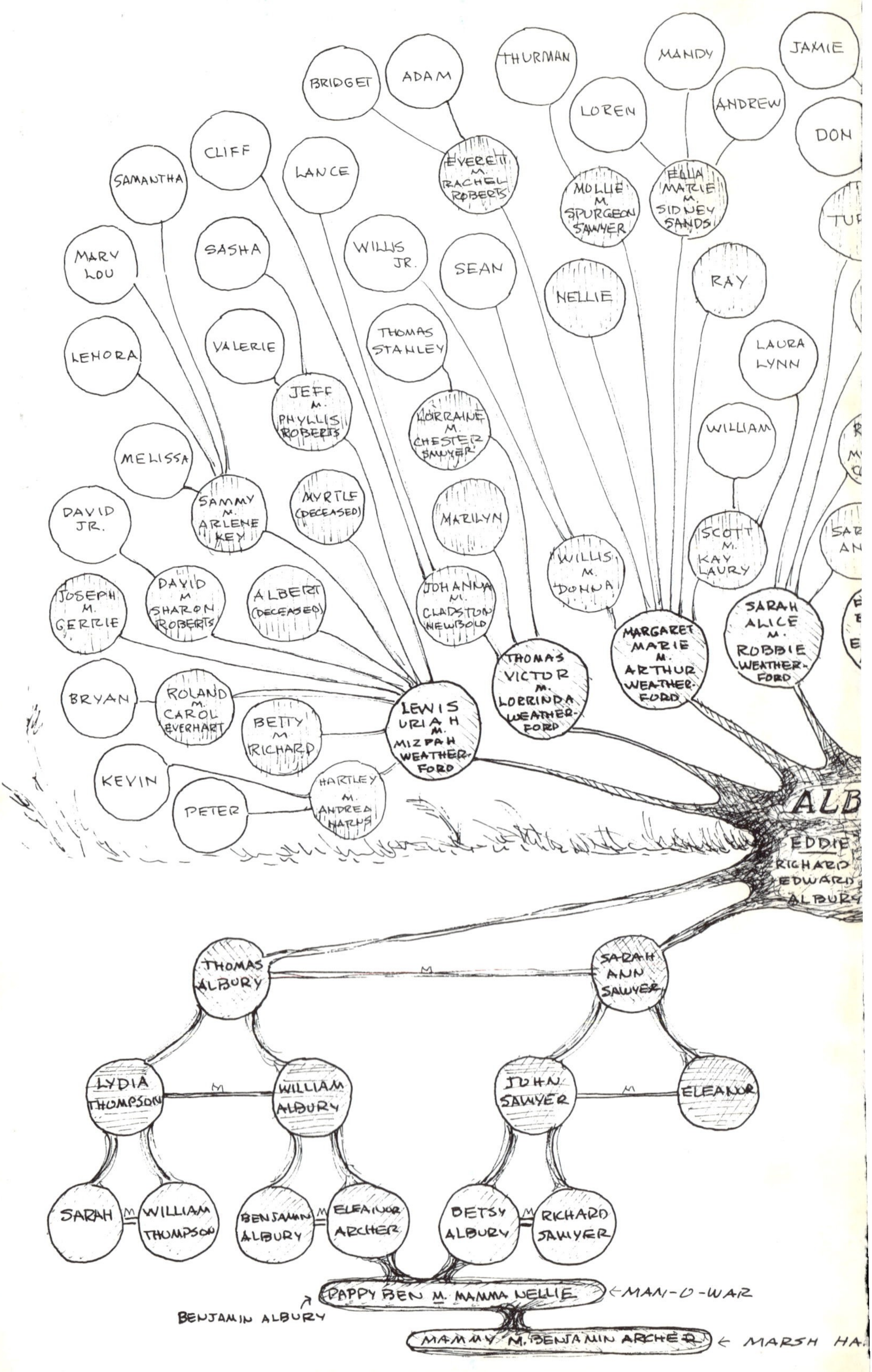

BRIDGET
ADAM
THURMAN
MANDY
JAMIE
LOREN
ANDREW
DON
CLIFF
SAMANTHA
LANCE
EVERETT M. RACHEL ROBERTS
MOLLIE M. SPURGEON SAWYER
ELLA MARIE M. SIDNEY SANDS
MARY LOU
SASHA
WILLIS JR.
SEAN
NELLIE
RAY
LENORA
VALERIE
THOMAS STANLEY
LAURA LYNN
JEFF M. PHYLLIS ROBERTS
LORRAINE M. CHESTER SAWYER
WILLIAM
MELISSA
SAMMY M. ARLENE KEY
MYRTLE (DECEASED)
DAVID JR.
MARILYN
SCOTT M. KAY LAURY
WILLIS M. DONNA
JOSEPH M. GERRIE
DAVID M SHARON ROBERTS
ALBERT (DECEASED)
JOHANNA M. GLADSTON NEWBOLD
MARGARET MARIE M. ARTHUR WEATHERFORD
SARAH ALICE M. ROBBIE WEATHERFORD
THOMAS VICTOR M. LORRINDA WEATHERFORD
BRYAN
ROLAND M. CAROL EVERHART
BETTY M RICHARD
LEWIS URIAH M. MIZPAH WEATHERFORD
KEVIN
PETER
HARTLEY M. ANDREA HARRIS
EDDIE
RICHARD EDWARD ALBURY
THOMAS ALBURY
M
SARAH ANN SAWYER
LYDIA THOMPSON
M
WILLIAM ALBURY
JOHN SAWYER
M
ELEANOR
SARAH
M
WILLIAM THOMPSON
BENJAMIN ALBURY
M
ELEANOR ARCHER
BETSY ALBURY
M
RICHARD SAWYER
PAPPY BEN M. MAMMA NELLIE
← MAN-O-WAR
BENJAMIN ALBURY
MAMMY M. BENJAMIN ARCHER
← MARSH HA